America's Historic Trails

with Tom Bodett

COMPANION TO THE PUBLIC TELEVISION SERIES

America's Historic Trails

with Tom Bodett

J. KINGSTON PIERCE

FOREWORD BY TOM BODETT

KQED BOOKS

SAN FRANCISCO

Publisher: James Connolly
Editorial Director: Pamela Byers
Editor & Project Manager: Rick Clogher
Research Associate: Ellen L. Boyer
Photo Research: Maureen Spuhler
Art Director: Jeffrey O'Rourke
Book & Cover Design: John Miller/Big Fish

Sources and credits for all photos will be found on page 254.

Educational and nonprofit groups wishing to order this book
at attractive quantity discounts may contact:
KQED Books & Video, 555 De Haro Street, Suite 220, San Francisco, CA 94107.

Library of Congress Cataloguing-in-Publication Data

Pierce, J. Kingston, 1957-
    America's historic trails with Tom Bodett : companion to the
public television series / J. Kingston Pierce : foreword by Tom
Bodett.
       p.   cm.
    Includes bibliographical references and index.
    ISBN 0-912333-00-6
    1. United States—Guidebooks. 2. Trails—United States—
Guidebooks. 3. United States—Description and travel. I. Bodett,
Tom. II. America's historic trails with Tom Bodett (Television
program) III. Title.
E158.P694 1997
917.304'929—dc21   97-7090
                                        CIP

ISBN 0-912333-00-6

Manufactured in Hong Kong
10 9 8 7 6 5 4 3 2 1

On the cover: Tom Bodett and Mission Santa Barbara by David Ris.
Flag image © 1997 PhotoDisc, Inc.

Distributed to the trade by Publishers Group West

Acknowledgments

BOOKS MAY BE BORN from a single writer's mind, but they are nurtured along with the helping hands of many other people. That has certainly been true in this case.

I should first thank my agent, Amy Rennert, and my former publisher at *San Francisco Focus*, Mark K. Powelson, for recommending me as the author of this work. Then I have to recognize Pamela Byers, the editorial director at KQED Books, who brought me into the project with such faith and enthusiasm and was blessedly liberal with her compliments as it progressed. A fond tip of the hat to four people at Small World Productions who gave me direction and lots of the background research they had collected for the *America's Historic Trails* television series: John Givens, Sandra Nisbet, Patricia Larson, and Patty Conroy. I'm also beholden to the innumerable museum officials, U.S. National Park Service folks, and independent researchers who happily answered even the most esoteric questions related to this book. Particularly helpful were James Holmberg, from the Filson Club in Louisville, Kentucky; Leslie Blythe, with the Natchez Trace Parkway; John Magill, from the Historic New Orleans Collection; Jenny Lund, with the Museum of Church History and Art in Salt Lake City, Utah; and Dr. Richard Tyler, at the Philadelphia Historical Commission.

I owe a vigorous round of applause to my editor at KQED Books, Rick Clogher, for helping me shape and refine my chapters, and for gently keeping me on pace. Thumbs up to designers John Miller and Eleanor Reagh, of Big Fish, who have presented my text in such a visually appealing volume. And, as usual, thanks also to my wife, Jodi, who is my best cheering section.

I owe a significant debt of gratitude to Ellen L. Boyer. As my research associate, she was resourceful in pursuit of information and adamant in double-checking facts and clearing up conflicting historical accounts. I think there are probably still librarians across the country smarting from Ellen's diligent but always well-intentioned grilling. Every writer should have someone like her backing them up.

Finally, I dedicate this book to my father, Alexander Bolton Pierce II. Although we may disagree on so many other things, we at least share a love of history and an appreciation for what it can teach us about the future.

—J. KINGSTON PIERCE
SEATTLE, WASHINGTON

AMERICA'S HISTORIC TRAILS

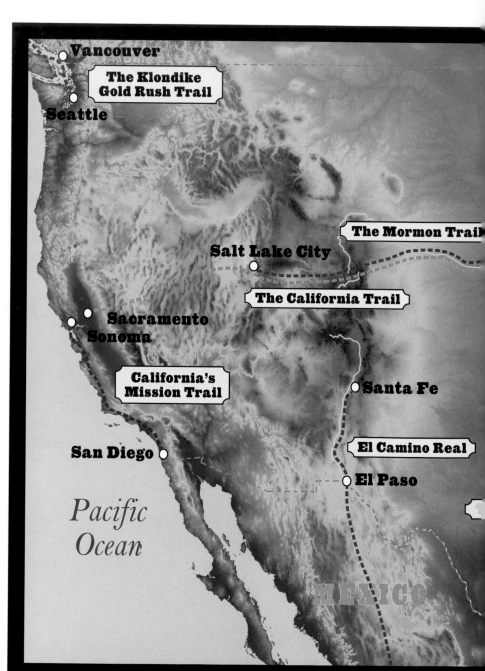

Vancouver

The Klondike
Gold Rush Trail

Seattle

The Mormon Trail

Salt Lake City

The California Trail

Sacramento
Sonoma

California's
Mission Trail

Santa Fe

San Diego

El Camino Real

El Paso

Pacific
Ocean

MEXICO

CANADA

Boston

The Boston Post Road

New York

Council Bluffs

Independence

The Wilderness
Trail

Philadelphia

Martinsburg

Louisville

Roanoke

Nashville

The Great Wagon Road

Natchez Trace

Augusta

Atlantic
Ocean

ver Road

Natchez

New Orleans

Gulf of
Mexico

N
E
S

Contents

6   **El Camino Real**

It was the first official trail blazed by Europeans in what is now the United States. Along its length Spanish settlers and Native Americans celebrated the truly first Thanksgiving; a small dog saved the lives of Juan de Oñate and his scouts; Pueblo Indians got a short-lived taste of freedom by rising up against Spanish authority; and the United States made its last military push for territorial expansion in the nineteenth century.

32   **The Boston Post Road**

Three hundred years ago, it was the first route for the organized delivery of mail in the British colonies. A hundred years later, the first president of our new nation followed it as he toured those former colonies. George Washington slept there; Benjamin Franklin marked it with milestones; and the first woman to serve in the American armed forces fought there. By the 1800s, the only sign of royalty on the Post Road was the "Stagecoach King."

56   **The Great Wagon Road**

Stark contrasts marked this route through the rolling fields and mountains of the mid-Atlantic region. In two centuries—and eight hundred miles—it stretched from a bastion of tolerance to the heart of Civil War South. Over its miles religious outcasts sought new homes, slaves found their way to freedom, and a failed New England businessman predicted a coming national tragedy.

Heroes and Fools

A YOUNG MAN STOOD ALONG the California Trail, faced into the rising sun and looking beyond the bleak terrain to the distance he'd put between himself and the secure Michigan home which sat flat in the middle of nothing he could make out from there. He was the first one he'd known in his short life to come this way—to come this far. It felt clear as the desert dawn to this dreamy young traveler that the Great Divide separates not just a continent, but whole lifetimes and fortunes and heroes and fools.

Westbound emigrants in the mid-1800s used the phrase "I've seen the elephant!" to put picture to their soaring sense of accomplishment. In nineteenth-century America, an elephant was an exotic, perhaps once-in-a-lifetime, spectacle. It represented something so new and extraordinary that a person could not be the same afterward.

This emigrant kicking alkali desert dust from his store-bought black boots outside of Elko, Nevada, had seen the elephant. He couldn't have known it, but since waking up that morning among the sage and prickers, there had been a sense that his adventure had become irreversible. Barely twenty years old himself, there was no way he could imagine where that many years again would find him. He raised his thumb to tempt the traffic whining by on Interstate 80 to provide him with some small leg of his journey: Winnemucca,

Reno, across the line to Truckee, and then the golden mythical shine of the Sacramento Valley and the heart of California.

That navel-gazing young hitchhiker, a refugee from an English Lit program stuck deep in the gut of the lower-Michigan factory culture, was, of course, yours truly. The journey wouldn't end in California; in fact it would barely pause. I hung a right at San Francisco and wandered north to Oregon. After a brief tenure working in the woods there—long enough to get myself burned to the bone on a high power line—I returned to Michigan for a few months to recover my strength. Then it was back down the way of the Mormons and every other determined pilgrim whose crooked path I followed to my own personal Zion—which lay nestled, I was certain, somewhere in the Cascade Mountains of southern Oregon. It wasn't.

After several dirty months work planting nursery-raised lodgepole pines in the barren earth of clear-cut mountainsides all around Crater Lake and Klamath Falls, and watching Shakespeare in the park on weekends in Ashland, I realized I had not reached the land where the West began after all. In fact, by my measure, it appeared to be the bitter end of the West as I'd always fancied it.

So, once again like those impatient souls who stomped off ahead of me, I moved onward and northward, and I didn't stop until I reached the end of the westernmost trail ever blazed on this continent that could now be negotiated by an automobile. That would be Homer, Alaska, the end of the road—quenching, at least for me, the thirsty wanderlust that has always pushed Americans to the next horizon.

As I write this, it's nearly twenty-two years since I stood in the desert dawn beside the old California Trail at Elko and wondered where I was going. I went a long way in the year right after that—and not very far since. Whatever I found at the end of the road continues to hold me here and continues to defy my explanation of it. I never remember deciding to stay. I only know I haven't left. Alaska is full of people like me.

I always suspected that California and Oregon were full of people like us a hundred years ago—and Kentucky a hundred years before that. Every new territory that ever presented itself to the grandiose eyes of ambitious explorers over the centuries was eventually tamed and settled not by the arrogant aims of Manifest Destiny but by the individual and curious natures of ordinary men and women looking for a better way to live. Or at least a better place to live their way.

The ancient and remarkable indigenous cultures that were lost underfoot as these simple folk clodded around the landscape will never be recovered. As this series was produced we found fragments of America's native heritage preserved all along our way, and we made it our business to learn about and film what we found. During our visits to native sites and museums along these routes, I never failed to feel voyeuristic and more than a little saddened. Why hadn't we European emigrants managed a few hundred years ago to foster this fascination with Indian culture and to honor the way they lived?

Even as I write I am aware these are the guilt-ridden feelings of a twentieth-century white man relieved to be placed in history far from the scene of the crime yet still on the receiving end of the plunder. There is no way I know to travel America's most historic trails without being reminded of who they follow.

Every route we covered—from the quaint, colonial Post Road winding out of New York to the treacherous Chilkoot Pass into the Klondike—was worn into the earth by moccasins that were no doubt following in the tracks of simple animals who only traced their way by instinct and their need to multiply and survive. Perhaps the motives of those creatures who originated these routes are not so far removed from those of all who came after.

One such pioneer, James Clyman, made this diary entry on his way west in 1846:

"It's remarkable how people sell out comfortable homes, pack up and start across an immense barren waste to settle in some place of which they have uncertain information. But that is the character of my countrymen."

Were these people heroes? Some of them, certainly. Fools? Probably. Adventurers? Opportunists? Yes, yes. All of these and more and all of these and less. They were simply Americans—they were us. And not so long ago.

If you had told me twenty-two years ago as I stood along I-80 that I would one day come back to that very place with a producer, camera crew, and fists full of notes trying to make some video sense of America's historic trails, you might have scared me right back to Michigan. I find looking into the eyes of large wild animals far more comforting than gazing at a camera lens, although traveling these old roads proved far more entertaining than encounters with wild beasts. And besides, television cameras very rarely eat your legs off.

I suppose if I could tell you in this simple introduction all that I found along the thousands of miles of historic routes we traveled, then we wouldn't have had to film a series about it. But we did and here's what I think we found: For better and worse we found the soul of our nation. From the moment Christopher Columbus laid eyes upon the wrong continent to the day the Pilgrims fell off Plymouth Rock, up to the day the last unwashed college kid with peanut butter on his breath and Jack London in his knapsack comes stumbling up the Alcan Highway—America will be about people looking for their dreams. And the American Dream is not about what we find at the end of the road, because it is almost never what we thought it would be. The American Dream has always been about making the most of a situation, whatever it might be.

The forty-niners found gold and Californians assembled themselves into a state. Brigham Young found a brackish lake in the middle of a desert and the Mormons also assembled themselves into a state. Success is obviously not built upon what we find so much as on what we bring with us.

I witnessed a scene somewhere beside U.S. Route 1 through Virginia, or maybe it was along Interstate 25 out of Albuquerque. The Natchez Trace south of Nashville? I-80 west of Omaha? Actually, I can't recall where I was. It could have been along any or all of these roads, but what I saw has stayed with me.

Pulled over at a rest area was a sun-faded Buick leaned back on its springs under the load of a U-Haul trailer. The trailer was tilted on a rusty jack while a man wrestled a flat tire to the pavement. Off to the side a young woman entertained a toddler in the shaded grass while looking warily over to her mate. A road-weariness emanated from the family. I could almost hear their mental calculations: How far will the spare take us? To the end of the journey or just the end of our money? Everything will be OK if we can make it to

Louisville, to Nashville . . . Socorro . . . Sacramento.

This very scene has played itself out a thousand times over the centuries along America's trail and road system. Whether it was a family in Juan de Oñate's 1598 expedition into New Mexico nursing a lamed mule beside the Rio Grande, or a member of the Donner Party watching the snow fall in 1846 as she counted out her family's rations—the courage of the human heart reigns supreme in these worried pilgrims.

I would like to think that the determined families of the 1790s scrabbling over the Cumberland Gap had no more sense of their place in history than did the family I saw stranded in the shadow of their U-Haul last spring. History is written by those who follow, and the history of America's historic trails lies in the hearts of the people we followed along them. Without their hopes and dreams these would be nothing more than empty routes to another place to eat.

But don't travel these roads just to see who came before you. Travel them to see who goes with you now: heroes, fools, adventurers, and opportunists. The trails are still open and these roads still change lives.

Twenty-two years ago they changed mine the first time. Doing this series has changed it again. The rest is the gravy. The rest is history.

—TOM BODETT
HOMER, ALASKA

El Camino Real

SAND CRUNCHED BETWEEN their teeth, driven there by winds that swept the desert with a maddening regularity. The sun appeared bent on blinding them or at least burning them raw. After only a day's progress through this unforgiving terrain, the small advance contingent of Spanish explorers were more than ready to reach the river they presumed must lie somewhere beyond the next horizon. Twenty-four hours more and they had come to despise this territory strewn with creosote bushes and spiny mesquite trees. But they seemed unable to escape it, their procession strung out disconsolately, horses straining just to carry them a dozen or so miles each day, and their supply of water running low, running out.

In the arid Southwest, the first European-made road in the United States linked two worlds and made Santa Fe, New Mexico, a bustling hub of international trade and travel.

Things didn't look good for Juan de Oñate and his men in May 1598 as they crossed what came to be called La Jornada del Muerto (the Journey of the Dead Man), a notorious patch of desert in south-central New Mexico. No, things didn't look good at all.

Their spirits had been much higher in late January, when Oñate led his expedition north from the central plains of New Spain (as Mexico was called during three centuries of Spanish domination). Scion of a prosperous silver mine owner in the town of Zacatecas,

Juan de Oñate led the first colonizing expedition across the Rio Grande into the Pueblo lands of New Mexico—and might have died in the desert but for the actions of a small dog.

Oñate had contracted with the Spanish Crown to colonize the Pueblo Indian lands of New Mexico—half a century after conquistador Francisco Vásquez de Coronado traveled those same areas in his fruitless quest for the legendary "Seven Cities of Gold," rumored to lie somewhere north of Mexico. To this end, Oñate assembled a huge emigrant train consisting of 83 wagons, carts, and carriages; 130 men (Franciscan friars, soldiers, and numerous others who were bringing along their wives and children); and some 7,000 head of livestock—horses, cattle, sheep, pigs, and more. Behind Oñate, this train stretched for almost three miles.

It was rough going across the storm-battered plains and around the jagged mountains north of Zacatecas. Oñate could push on only in fits and starts, preceded by scouts hunting for any even halfway reasonable routes through the *tierra incógnita*. Not until the end of April did the settlers complete the initial leg of their trip, reaching the Río Grande del Norte (known in many early journals as the Río del Norte) for the first time near present-day El Paso, Texas. On the river they encountered a friendly band of forty Mansos (eastern Pueblo) Indians. "They had Turkish bows, long hair cut to resemble little Milan caps, headgear made to hold down their hair and colored with blood or paint," Oñate recalled in his official journal. "Their first words were *manxo, manxo, micos, micos*, by which they meant 'peaceful ones' and 'friends.'" In exchange for presents, the Mansos assisted the pioneers and their livestock, particularly the bleating sheep, across the Rio Grande, a tremendously long (1,885 miles from the Rocky Mountains to the Gulf of Mexico) but surprisingly shallow waterway. Then the natives pointed Oñate's caravan toward wagon-wheel ruts left by an earlier Spanish party that had been in New Mexico.

Oñate's record is thin on observations about the country through which his people passed as they followed those ruts, Indian footpaths, and the east bank of the Rio Grande. He was far more conscious of their progress each day and the approximate coordinates of every new *paraje* (campsite).

Many of the names they gave their camps—Robledo, for example—are part of New Mexico's landscape to this day. On May 20, 1598, Oñate noted that he had halted his train about sixty miles

Braving the Desert

It's easy to forget that there was a time when crossing North America took both skill and courage. Gaspar Pérez de Villagrá, who traveled with a scouting party ahead of Juan de Oñate's emigrant train as it moved toward New Mexico in 1598, wrote years later about how his party had become lost for several days in Los Médanos de Samalayuca, a 770-square-mile region of sand dunes located south of El Paso, Texas:

We journeyed on until it seemed we would never find our way out of those unpeopled regions, traversing vast and solitary plains where the foot of a Christian had never trod before. Our provisions gave out, we were obliged to subsist on such edible weeds and roots as we found. But we went forward, sometimes through dense thickets which tore our clothes and left us ragged; at other times over rough stony passes where it was almost necessary to drag our tired mounts.

Our shoes were worn out, we suffered terribly from the burning sands, for our horses were scarcely able to drag their tired bodies along and pack our baggage, let alone carry us. The horses suffered most, poor dumb brutes; they were almost frantic with thirst, and their eyes nearly bulged from their sockets. After four days of travel they were well-nigh blind, and could scarcely see where they were going, stumbling against the rocks and trees along their path. . . .

On the morning of the fifth [day] we joyfully viewed in the distance the long-sought waters of the Río [Grande] del Norte. The gaunt horses approached the rolling stream and plunged headlong into it. Two of them drank so much that they burst their sides and died. Two others, blinded by their raving thirst, plunged so far into the stream they were caught in its swift current and drowned.

Our men, consumed by the burning thirst, their tongues swollen and their throats parched, threw themselves into the water and drank as though the entire river did not carry enough to quench their terrible thirst. (*The History of New Mexico*, 1610) north of El Paso, where the river bows broadly to the west. There, he wrote, "we buried Pedro Robledo," one of several Robledo kinsmen under his command. For the next three hundred years that surname designated a popular *paraje* along the trail, and it is still attached to a group of mountains northwest of Las Cruces.

But the Robledo *paraje* holds still greater significance in the Juan de Oñate story. For it was from there, on May 22, that Oñate and a select handful of his company split from the main caravan and headed due north into the ninety-mile-long hell that was La Jornada del Muerto, tucked between the Caballo and Fra Cristóbal Mountains to the west and the San Andres range to the east. Oñate figured this to be a shortcut, and that he and his men would find the Rio Grande again in a couple of days. He also hoped to procure additional provisions for the emigrant train and—no minor sec-

Dead Reckoning

How did La Jornada del Muerto, "the Journey of the Dead Man," get its name? It comes, apparently, from the story of Bernardo Gruber, a central New Mexico trader known as El Alemán (the German).

In a drunken stupor on Christmas Day, 1668, Gruber is supposed to have mouthed off to a group of acquaintances about how he had learned a magical spell. With Spain in the midst of its centuries-long Inquisition, this was a bad time to be talking witchcraft, and Gruber was arrested for his heresy. Certain of his fate should he come to trial, Gruber broke out of jail in 1670 and, with his Apache servant, Atanasio, sped south on the Camino Real toward Mexico. Partway across the Jornada, tired and thirsty, Gruber stopped and sent Atanasio on alone to find water. When the Apache returned, Gruber was gone, his horse with him.

A month later, travelers found Gruber's dead mount, secured to a tree. Nearby was a heap of chewed-over bones, a human skull, and some hair, all of which they carried to El Paso and buried under a cross. But, skeptics wondered, were they really laying El Alemán to rest—or had he faked his own death and made his escape after all?

ondary responsibility—reassure Native Americans of the region that the Spanish wagons and horsemen snaking over their land posed no threat to their pueblos. What Oñate did not expect was to come so close to death.

It's not unusual for temperatures in the Jornada del Muerto to soar above one hundred degrees Fahrenheit. And Oñate's men could not find so much as a hint of a fresh spring in their path. After two days of killing heat, what saved the band was, of all things, a dog. As the tale goes, the scouts were making another dry camp about twenty-four miles north of Robledo, when a mutt with muddy paws happened by. Quickly backtracking the dog's prints, the scouts found pools of precious water, which they christened Los Charcos del Perrillo (the Pools of the Little Dog), in honor of the errant canine. Subsequent travelers through the Jornada shortened the name to El Perrillo.

Thus refreshed, Oñate's team fled west from the Jornada and back to the Rio Grande valley. They picked their way north along the river, contacting Native Americans at adjacent pueblos, from whom they received corn, beans, and water. And they convinced the natives to provide similar supplements to the wagon train bringing up their rear.

By the end of June, the horsemen had arrived at the point where New Mexico's Galisteo Creek enters the Rio Grande, southwest of modern Santa Fe. Close by stood a pueblo, which Oñate dubbed Santo Domingo. What remained of Oñate's original caravan—sixty-one conveyances, the rest having been abandoned to save the lives of exhausted oxen—caught up with him there a month later, six months after they had departed central New Spain. Oñate then continued north to found New Mexico's first provincial capital, San Gabriel, not far from the San Juan Pueblo.

For several years, Oñate reconnoitered the territory, traveling as far east as central Kansas and as far west as the Gulf of California, and claimed for Madrid as much land as he could. At the same time, he searched for the precious metals that Spain's King Philip II and his successor, Philip III, were convinced lay in this newest extension of their domain. When he found no such riches, and with San Gabriel in decline, Oñate returned to New Spain, a failure in the eyes of his superiors. He died in 1624.

Chapel San Elizario, east of El Paso, Texas, lies near where Juan de Oñate's expedition crossed the Rio Grande and celebrated the first Thanksgiving with local Indians. San Juan Pueblo, north of Santa Fe, New Mexico, is where Oñate set up the first provincial capital.

Yet Oñate can hardly be thought a failure as a trailblazer. His settlement campaign'had established an important link in what was now a 1,450-mile Camino Real. The Spanish gave the name El Camino Real (the Royal Road) to the major route in most regions they held. And the one that now stretched from Mexico City—the conquered heart of the ancient Aztec Empire—to the heart of New Mexico was the longest in North America. Over the next three centuries, this wagon trace would host missionaries and merchants coming up from the south, as well as traders who crossed the West via the Santa Fe Trail and continued down El Camino Real to peddle calico, cooking utensils, and champagne in the cities of northern Mexico. The oldest European road in the United States, this thoroughfare brought to the West the first domesticated live-stock, the first gunpowder, and the first government.

In short, it brought the future.

RELIGION, REVOLT, AND RICHES

AT FIRST THAT FUTURE came clad in the gray robes of Franciscan friars, who sought to impose Catholicism and a traditional Spanish lifestyle on New Mexico's Native Americans. This was no easy task, since there were so many divisions of natives in the area, from those semi-nomadic Athabascan peoples grouped under the rubric *Apache* to the linguistically diverse, town-building Pueblo (descended from the Anasazi, who had created a sophisticated culture at Chaco Canyon). But the friars were adamant, driven by their faith and the fear of royal reprisals should they not succeed in integrating, and thereby pacifying, the natives. They dismissed centuries-old indigenous religions and behavior, raised adobe missions using Indian labor, insisted on Christian wedding ceremonies, and demanded that the native men don shirts and pants; the women, blouses and skirts.

Meanwhile, a very different sort of change agent was busy in northern New Mexico. In 1610—a full decade before the *Mayflower* landed at Plymouth Rock with its complement of persecuted Puritans—Pedro de Peralta, the new Spanish governor of the province, began developing a capital to replace San Gabriel. Peralta set his capital on a high valley in the loom of the Sangre de Cristo Mountains and called it La Villa Real de la Santa Fe de San Francisco de Asís. Thankfully, that was soon trimmed to Santa Fe (Holy Faith). And while at first barely more than a plaza around which huddled a barracks and jail, a military chapel, and an administration center (El Palacio de Los Gobernadores, "the Palace of the Governors"), Santa Fe became the upper terminus of New Mexico's Camino Real. It was to there that royal supply caravans journeyed from New Spain.

Initially, these trains supplied the Franciscans, who had prompted their service. As more people took up residence in New Mexico, however, they began catering to those other settlers, too. Each caravan is said to have featured thirty-two heavy-service wagons, able to transport a total of sixty-four tons. For the friars, they brought bronze church bells, statues of saints, incense, and sacramental wine. For government officials and private citizens, there might be woolen fabrics, doublets, buffalo hides, books, and cushions.

The supply trains were scheduled to leave Mexico City every three years, on a round-trip to Santa Fe that was to take a year and a half—allowing ample time for the sale of their loads. In fact, the trains went far less often, leaving New Mexicans for years at a stretch without the goods they so desired, and depriving Mexican markets of the wheat, raw wool, salt, and native slaves that were carried on return trips. (Indian ceremonial items from New Mexico were also much prized down south, but the more aggressively the missionaries tried to quash Pueblo religious practices, the less available those items became.)

Wagon masters could derive a handsome income from the supply trains, especially if—as was common—they did a little profiteering on the side. This made the risks of the trip somewhat more palatable. Risks such as Navajo ambush. Or heat stroke and dehydration. Or simple loss and destruction of property. So rugged was the journey along El Camino Real that wagon trains had to pack spare axles, extra spokes, and iron tires, along with repair tools. And spare draft animals: two teams of eight mules plus four extras for each wagon, in the event that some animals should perish in transit. Rare was the wagon that completed the trip without a major overhaul.

If not for heightened Indian violence, this commerce might have become well institutionalized, tying New Mexico still more firmly than it did to Old Mexico. But in 1680, Pueblo natives, pushed to their breaking point by decades of Spanish despotism and the Catholic Church's relentless efforts to expunge their culture, hit back hard at the oppressors. Aided by roving Apache and led by Popé, a remarkable "medicine doctor," or priest, from the San Juan Pueblo, the natives began a revolt on August 10, the Feast of San Lorenzo. The element of surprise was with them; their retribution, devastating. Four hundred Spaniards were killed, including 21 missionaries, and some 2,200 survivors were forced into a hasty retreat—mostly on foot—to El Paso, a distance of 330 miles. Santa Fe was surrendered, and trade along El Camino Real was cut off.

The Pueblo had their homeland back. Yet their victory was not as sweet as they had hoped. Success went to Popé's head, and by the

> "SEEN FROM A DISTANCE, Santa Fe reminded the Americans of a prairie dog town, a fleet of flatboats, or, more frequently, a huge brickyard."
>
> —MAX L. MOORHEAD,
> *New Mexico's Royal Road:*
> *Trade and Travel on the Chihuahua Trail*

time he passed away, a few years after the Pueblo Revolt, he had become a minor tyrant, willing to execute any Indians who dared oppose him. The victory brought other pitfalls, as well. As Alvin M. Josephy Jr. writes in *The Indian Heritage of America*, "Without the protection of Spanish soldiers, the Pueblos were unable to ward off Apache raiders, who made away with tribute, Pueblo women, and horses." Prior to the revolt, Spaniards had kept a tight rein on the availability of horses—animals they had introduced into the Southwest in the mid-sixteenth century. After the Spanish expulsion, horses were free to spread among the Shoshone, Ute, and other tribes, who soon learned to employ them in raids against Indians and whites.

Unfortunately for the Pueblo, their triumph was also short-lived. The Spanish, captained by Diego de Vargas, recaptured New

Mexico in 1693 (though some sporadic fighting continued in the province's hinterlands for another three years). But by then, it was impossible to restore the old ways. The Indians had forced Mexico City into making concessions. Henceforth, there would be no more wanton destruction of sacred Native American objects, and Indians who chose not to attend church would be spared punishment. This was the price—and a fair one—that New Mexico paid for the next century of harmony with the Pueblo.

Amid this peace, trade with New Spain resumed; it even improved, due largely to the rise of Chihuahua, a new silver-mining city, located about 550 miles (about forty days' travel by wagon) south of Santa Fe. As New Mexico was strictly forbidden to traffic with the westward-advancing United States, Chihuahua became Santa Fe's main source for trade. That northern Mexico city presently grew rich as the middleman for New Mexican goods being shipped south. People came to speak of the trail connecting it with Santa Fe as something separate, something more important than El Camino Real as a whole: the Chihuahua Trail. By the mid-1700s, ambitious, frequently unscrupulous, Chihuahua merchants didn't just contribute to New Mexico's economy, they controlled it.

Only Mexican independence and the organizing of a second great roadway to Santa Fe broke Chihuahua's economic monopoly.

A TIME OF TRANSITION

EARLY IN SEPTEMBER 1821, William Becknell, an Indian fighter, veteran of the War of 1812, and Saint Louis trader, set off west from the Missouri River. With him were twenty or thirty mounted companions, all of them interested in hunting and perhaps, if they were lucky, nabbing a few wild horses, which they could sell back home to supplement their incomes. In addition, these men had packed extra knives, axes, and bolts of cotton for use in bartering with the Comanche of the southern Great Plains.

Ten weeks later, after following the dips and curves of the Arkansas River, the company pushed deep into the Southwest—

Murals abound in the Southwest. Many, like this one from a Tigual Indian reservation, celebrate the close ties to Christian missionaries. The town of Socorro ("Help"), south of Albuquerque, was named in tribute to the help Juan de Oñate received from locals there.

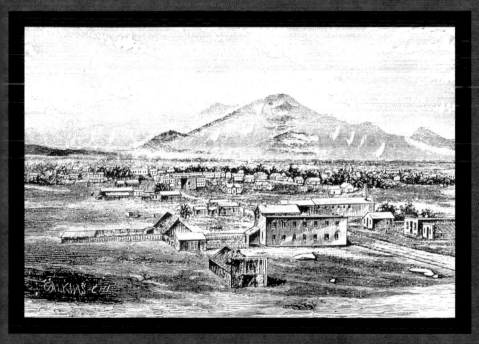

Spanish territory. Becknell knew this could be bad. He had heard stories about other Americans who'd been arrested, had any trade goods in their possession confiscated, and been imprisoned for trespassing on lands claimed by the Spanish. But Becknell wasn't ready to turn back. Not yet. Not when it seemed they could venture a little farther in relative safety.

They were roaming the area of Raton Pass in northern New Mexico when suddenly a squadron of Spanish troops appeared before them. The worst had happened. Or had it?

Neither the Missourians nor their captors were conversant in the other's language, yet the soldiers seemed unusually hospitable as they escorted Becknell and company back to Santa Fe. After reaching the town and recruiting a multilingual Frenchman as an interpreter, Becknell discovered the reason: While he and his party were hunting, Mexico had been granted its freedom from Spanish rule, and New Mexico had wasted no time in allying itself with the new government in Mexico City. The era of monopolistic trade along El Camino Real was finished. Not only were Becknell's men invited to sell what remained of their barter goods in Santa Fe, but the provincial governor himself asked them to carry word back to Missouri that New Mexico was now open for business with the United States.

Becknell was no dummy. He liked the jingle of Mexican pesos in his pocket. So in the spring of 1822, he headed back to Santa Fe, this time leading three wagons full of trade goods. Since his route along the Arkansas River and through Raton Pass was too precipitous for wagon travel, Becknell decided to open a new, shorter trail across the Cimarron desert, in what is today southwestern Kansas. Again, his inclination to take chances got him into trouble. His people were badgered by Comanche, and they ran so low on water that in order to suppress their thirsts, they had to cut off their mules' ears and drink the blood. Only the shooting of a buffalo, its stomach full of water, kept Becknell's party from being another casualty of western exploration.

Tales of the exorbitant prices Becknell exacted from his New Mexican customers that year inspired rivals for his business. In 1824, eighty merchants from Missouri decided to throw in together

on one well-defended caravan down Becknell's thousand-mile Santa
Fe Trail, taking with them $35,000 worth of goods. Despite rock
slides, washouts along the Cimarron Cut-off, and the threat of
Indian assault, the trip was far more than worthwhile. By one esti-
mate, the Missourians sold their goods for $190,000 in gold, silver,
and furs. Enough to instill in tenfold more merchants the idea of
wagoning the contents of their stores to the Southwest. By the mid-
1820s, writes Geoffrey C. Ward in *The West: An Illustrated History*,
Americans "carried home so many silver pesos that New Mexico
virtually ran out of coins."

Supply rapidly overcame demand. Sure, both the Camino Real
and the Santa Fe Trail were enlarging the population of New
Mexico. Scores of mountain men came to trap beaver and deer in
its northern extremes, and behind them were Americans itching to

Santa Fe or Bust

Like most of the pioneering or
trade roads across America in the
eighteenth and nineteenth centuries, the Santa Fe Trail was less a
single, well-defined road than a collection of tracks heading in one
general direction. It's convenient to
say that it began at Independence,
Missouri, but in truth its eastern
source was a score of towns dotting
the Missouri River. From those
towns, wagon trains drove west to
Council Grove, in present-day
Kansas, then rolled on to the banks
of the Arkansas River.

Traders, looking for the
most expeditious way west and
thus intending to follow William

Becknell's Cimarron Cut-off,
forded the Arkansas somewhere
between Pawnee Rock and
Dodge City, then headed southwest across Indian Territory
(Oklahoma) to Santa Fe. The
alternate route was similar to the
trail that Becknell and his fellow
hunters blazed in 1821. It took
travelers farther west along the
Arkansas River, then north into
Colorado to Bent's Fort. From
there it swung south into New
Mexico by way of Raton Pass.
Although this trail was a hundred
miles longer than the Cimarron
desert route, it offered greater
access to wood and water.

emigrate west long before the Oregon Trail, the Mormon Trail, and other transcontinental paths existed. Yet for all that, New Mexico still boasted only forty-three thousand inhabitants. And those folks didn't have the funds to buy all the necklaces and knives, muslin and mirrors, watches and wallpaper and window glass being shipped their way.

As a consequence, more and more American products were shipped through Santa Fe on their way to other destinations. Some went west to Los Angeles along the crooked pack-mule route known as the Old Spanish Trail. More, however, went south by way of El Camino Real. Wagonloads rolled over the Jornada del Muerto (mostly at night, when it was cooler), camped in circles under the stars, proceeded down through northern Mexico, and entered Chihuahua, Durango, or Zacatecas. This arrangement greatly upset the powers-that-be in Mexico City, who didn't like the fact that American goods were cheaper and of higher quality than their own. But enterprising Mexicans were anxious to take advantage of the reciprocal transport of their mustangs, sheep, and mules to U.S. markets.

THE SANTA FE BOOM

AN ENTIRE BOOK COULD be written about the vexatious customs procedures involved in the trade between the United States and Mexico. Suffice it to say that legislation won approval in both Washington and Mexico City that would grease the way for merchandisers wishing to carry goods north and south. Regional tensions periodically endangered this trade—the Texas rebellion of 1836, for instance, which freed Texas from Mexican control; or the periodic wars with the Apache on both sides of the border, ending in the barbarous extermination of those Indians. Neither these conflicts nor others, though, seriously undermined caravan traffic along the trail that linked Mexico and Missouri. American goods reaching Chihuahua in 1843 and 1844 were valued at an astounding $650,000. And just two years later, a new record was set when the first million-dollar cargo was carried west.

The town of Santa Fe—set conveniently at the junction of El Camino Real and the Santa Fe Trail—naturally benefited from the business that passed through its streets, if only in tariff charges. No wonder, as Max L. Moorhead depicts in his book *New Mexico's Royal Road: Trade and Travel on the Chihuahua Trail,* that every new caravan precipitated a flurry of excitement:

> It was the signal for long-awaited excitement and rejoicing, like the arrival of the annual fleet at Veracruz [Mexico] in colonial times. A shout went up on all sides heralding the arrival of *los americanos* and *los carros,* and crowds of women and boys flocked around to see what the bearded Missourians had brought in their great hooded wagons. Nor were the townspeople alone in their anticipation. Others from miles around were on hand to enjoy the bargains and general festivities. Even the American teamsters entered into the spirit. Before reaching town, they had scrubbed the dust of the road from their faces, slicked down their hair, and donned their Sunday best to parade before the first feminine eyes they had met in weeks.

For the overland trader, Santa Fe might have been, well, a less-than-enchanting sight, with its narrow, crooked thoroughfares and single-story adobe architecture, which made the skyline look as though it had been inflated straight out of the ground. "Seen from

Grave Humor

For many people, the hunger for profits to be made in trade outweighed the very real possibility of dying on the Santa Fe Trail and El Camino Real. Along the hundreds of miles, there were many deaths and many epitaphs left to intrigue—and occasionally entertain—subsequent travelers.

In *Wondrous Times on the Frontier,* historian Dee Brown tells of a U.S. cavalry troop that stopped at a Santa Fe Trail marker reading Here Lies Sandy McGregor, A Generous Father And A Pious Man.

"That's just like the Scots," Brown quotes an Irishman among the soldiers. "Three men in one grave."

a distance," Moorhead remarks, "Santa Fe reminded the Americans of a prairie dog town, a fleet of flatboats, or, more frequently, a huge brickyard." Yet this was also a place where trail bosses and young wagon hands could kick up their heels after hundreds of miles of lonely roadway. To welcome the travelers, raucous fandangos, or Spanish balls, might be held for several nights in a row. Gambling

The Spanish Ball

Several visitors to Santa Fe during the early 1800s, including famed explorer Zebulon Pike, mentioned in their journals that they had attended one of the town's fandangos, or Spanish dances. But it was American adventurer James Ohio Pattie who, having whooped it up in the town on New Year's Day, 1827, left behind the most vivid account of the revels in New Mexico's provincial capital:

The fandango room was about forty by eighteen or twenty feet, with a brick floor raised four or five feet above the earth. That part of the room in which the ladies sat, was carpetted and carpetted on the benches, for them to sit on. Simple benches were provided for the accommodation of the gentlemen. Four men sang to the music of a violin and guitar. All that chose to dance stood up on the floor, and at the striking up of a certain note of the music, they all commenced clapping their hands. The ladies then advanced, one by one, and stood facing their partners. The dance then changed to a waltz, each man taking his lady rather unceremoniously, and then began to whirl round, keeping true, however, to the music, and increasing the swiftness of their whirling. Many of the movements and figures seemed very easy, though we found they required practise, for we must certainly have made a most laughable appearance in their eyes, in attempting to practise them. Be that as it may, we cut capers with the nimblest, and what we could not say, we managed by squeezes of the hand, and little signs of that sort, and passed the time to a charm. . . . When the ball broke up, it seemed to be expected of us, that we should each escort a lady home, in whose company we passed the night, and we none of us brought charges of severity against our fair companions. (*The Personal Narrative of James O. Pattie*, 1831)

Albuquerque lies along El Camino Real in tho hoart of New Mexico's Pueblo country. Its original plaza sat to the west of where you'll find the Old Town Plaza now. Today, much of New Mexico's architecture maintains the adobe style.

Taos Pueblo, northeast of Santa Fe, has been continuously occupied for at least eight hundred years. Back in Santa Fe, the Palace of the Governors borders the city's main plaza and is the oldest public building in continuous use in the country.

halls offered hands of monte or rolls of the dice, and olive-skinned harlots awaited should a roll in the sheets be more enticing.

If never as wicked as San Francisco or as dangerous as Dodge City, Santa Fe nonetheless had a quirky character, the sum of its centuries-long isolation and its later crossroads role. Tourists, including former President Ulysses S. Grant, went there just to absorb the Mexican-American ambience. Gunslinger Henry McCarty—alias William H. Bonney, alias Billy the Kid—promised to stop over in Santa Fe, too, in the late 1870s, but nobody was much thrilled about that, least of all Territorial Governor Lew Wallace. Angered by the governor's campaign against range hostilities, the Kid had warned, "I mean to ride into the plaza at Santa Fe and put a bullet through Lew Wallace." Instead, it was Billy who was killed, in 1881, while Wallace, who had tried his hand at writing, saw his novel *Ben Hur* become a best-seller.

The End of the Road

DEVELOPED AS A SETTLEMENT route in 1598 and transformed into a commercial conduit, El Camino Real took on a third purpose in 1846. That year, President James K. Polk —unsuccessful in his attempts to purchase New Mexico and California from the Mexican government, and unwilling to forsake his expansionist dreams—sent troops down the Santa Fe Trail into the disputed Southwest.

Commanded by General Stephen Watts Kearny, the twenty-seven-hundred-member Army of the West closed on Santa Fe, anticipating combat with a volunteer force assembled by Manuel Armijo, governor of New Mexico. But Don Manuel, a tall, stout, peacockish gent (who had achieved his office only after renegade Pueblo natives killed his predecessor and severed the man's head to use as a football), was less valorous than pragmatic. And so, with a ninety-man bodyguard and a personal caravan containing $50,000 worth of American trade goods, he retreated to Mexico. Kearny strode into Santa Fe on August 19, 1846, without firing a shot. After sending a detail south along the Camino Real to capture El Paso and occupy Chihuahua, the general took another force west to press Polk's claims on California. By the end of the decade, Mexico had lost about half of its domain to the United States, including New Mexico, and the present-day states of Arizona, Texas, California, Nevada, and Utah. New Mexico became an American teritory in 1850 and won its statehood in 1912.

After nearly four hundred years of use, El Camino Real was finally superseded by the railroad in the 1880s, as tracks extended from Chicago to El Paso, where Mexican trains continued south. But the road had already served its purpose, helping to open the region for settlement and creating a legend of the West—a legend rich with Spanish horsemen and wagon trains and Native Amcrican resistance—that has not faded to this day.

El Camino Real Today

Travel conditions along El Camino Real are, thankfully, much more favorable today than they were in Juan de Oñate's era. The American section of this Royal Road begins in El Paso ("the Pass"), in the southwestern corner of Texas. Take Interstate 10 west out of the city and into New Mexico until you meet Interstate 25. Follow I-25 north, along the Rio Grande, to Santa Fe.

THE WAY NORTH

Before you head out from El Paso, stop at the **Chamizal National Memorial** (800 South San Marcial), which commemorates the 1963 settlement of a century-long boundary dispute between the United States and Mexico. Each spring, Chamizal presents a reenactment of "the First Thanksgiving," a feast that was prepared by area natives for Oñate's expedition in 1598 (more than two decades before that Plymouth scene). Not far away, the **El Paso Zoo** (4001 Paisano Drive, at U.S. 54) features animals that are descended from Oñate's extensive herd. El Paso's later history is remembered at the **Magoffin Homestead** (1120 Magoffin Avenue), an adobe-style hacienda built in 1875 by trader Joseph Magoffin; at **Concordia Cemetery** (Interstate 10 and U.S. 54), where the infamous gunfighter John Wesley Hardin is buried; and in bright murals painted around town by local artist José Cisneros.

Forty miles north along I-25, New Mexico's second-largest city, **Las Cruces** (The Crosses), stands as a poignant reminder of seventeenth-century history: The town began as a wayside graveyard for Spaniards defeated in battles with the Apache Indians—an all-too-common fate for early travelers up the Camino Real. **Fort Selden State Monument** (in nearby Radium Springs), erected at the site of a fortress once used as protection against native warriors, includes a museum that exhibits historic photographs of the area, along with vintage military uniforms. A weekly market in town features more displays of New Mexican history, as well as local art and home-grown cuisine. North of Fort Selden is where trekkers used to begin

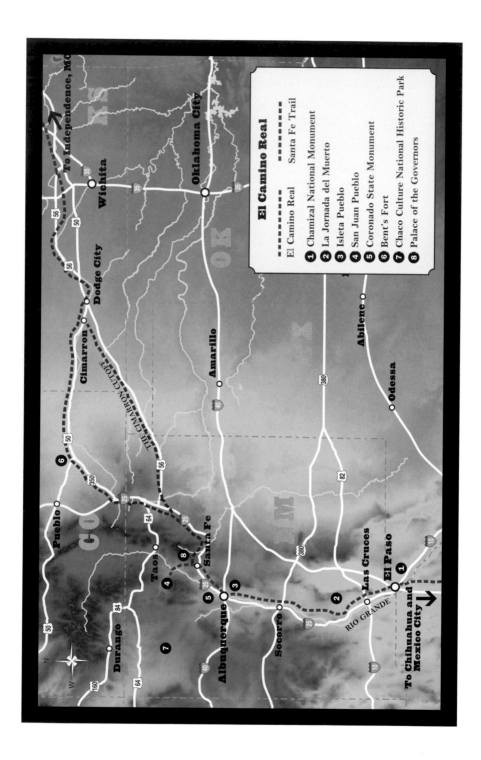

the dreaded desert passage known as La Jornada del Muerto. Today, it's even more inaccessible than in Oñate's time: It lies almost completely within the off-limits **White Sands Missile Range.**

Approximately 125 miles north of Las Cruces lies **Socorro** (Help), named by Oñate for the assistance he received there from local Indians. The town flourished in the late nineteenth century as a mining hub, and later, a farming community. You can examine the many rock specimens and artifacts at the **Mineral Museum** (at the New Mexico Institute of Mining and Technology, on College Street). Or take a long leap back in history at the **San Miguel Mission** (just north of Socorro's central plaza, at 403 El Camino Real). Built in 1598, this mission was abandoned and reconstructed in the 1620s, only to be razed during the Pueblo Rebellion of 1680. The present-day structure was completed in 1821.

Isleta Pueblo, about thirteen miles south of Albuquerque, is the largest pueblo of the Tiwa-speaking natives and home to one of the oldest missions in the United States—the massive **San Augustin,** founded in about 1613. The mission's church contains a chapel beautifully ornamented with paintings of saints. (It may also contain a ghost. Legend has it that Juan Padilla, a Spanish priest buried in the sanctuary, occasionally leaves his coffin and reveals himself to pueblo residents, many of whom regard him as a saint.) Pueblo artisans are recognized for the quality of their polychrome pottery.

ALBUQUERQUE

Using arts, crafts, and dance demonstrations, the **Indian Pueblo Cultural Center** (2401 Twelfth Street NW) gives visitors an appreciation for life on the state's nineteen native pueblos. Though Oñate and his men passed right by Abuquerque, it is still an important stop for history enthusiasts. The **Museum of Art, History, and Science** (2000 Mountain Road NW) details four hundred years of Rio Grande Valley history, while the **Spanish History Museum** (2211 Lead Avenue SE) charts Spain's influence over the American Southwest through photographs, drawings, and military memorabilia.

To understand more of this city's roots, go to the source: **Old Town,** site of the original 1706 settlement, now in Albuquerque's southwest corner. Though it has gone through periods of decline, Old Town is now nicely restored in the Pueblo Revival style and contains a wealth of galleries, shops, and restaurants. The **Plaza,** or old Spanish town square, dates back to 1780 and remains one of the best people-watching spots in the city. Wild West gunfights are still staged on nearby **Romero Street.**

To travel back in time even further, detour to the **Petroglyph National Monument** (4735 Unser Boulevard NW), which was declared by Congress in 1990 to be the country's first site for the preservation of prehistoric rock art.

About halfway between Albuquerque and Santa Fe, in the town of Bernalillo, is the **Coronado State Monument and Park** (New Mexico Route 44, off I-25), which honors Spanish explorer Francisco Vásquez de Coronado, who wintered here in 1540 during his search for the legendary Seven Cities of Cibola. Within the monument are found the partially restored remains of **Kuaua,** a Tiwa village that held as many as a thousand people before it was abandoned at the end of the seventeenth century. A *kiva* (underground ceremonial chamber) on site once served as a canvas for paintings of human and animal forms, now preserved in the monument's museum.

For a side trip off the Camino Real, continue on state Route 44 to Route 57 and you'll reach the **Chaco Culture National Historical Park,** which celebrates the mammoth Anasazi settlement that flourished in this area during the period A.D. 900-1300. An on-site museum preserves the ruins of thirteen pueblos and traces the culture of various local tribes through films and displays of pottery and other artifacts.

Santa Fe

Snug in the shadows of the Sangre de Cristo Mountains, fifty miles north of Albuquerque, sits the oldest capital in the United States. Its central **Plaza** once marked the end of the Santa Fe Trail, and it continues to play host to modern markets and fiestas. The adjacent **Palace of Governors,** built in 1610, is the nation's oldest public building in continuous use, and served as New Mexico's seat of government for three hundred years. These days, it's part of the

Museum of New Mexico, full of stagecoaches, pottery, and tools used by the ancient Anasazi. Native American vendors sell hand-crafted jewelry from blankets unrolled on the Palace's sidewalk. (More modern artworks can be had at the numerous galleries lining **Canyon Road,** immediately south of downtown.)

Just southeast of the Plaza lies the **San Miguel Mission** (401 Old Santa Fe Trail), erected by Spanish settlers in about 1625 and believed to be this country's oldest church. Inside, a crudely beautiful altar screen dates back more than two centuries. Northwest of downtown is the adobe **Santuario de Guadalupe** (100 Guadalupe Street), America's oldest shrine dedicated to Our Lady of Guadalupe and the blessed end to El Camino Real.

To find out more about sites along El Camino Real, contact El Paso's Chamizal National Memorial, 915-532-7273; Albuquerque's Indian Pueblo Cultural Center, 505-843-7270; and the Museum of New Mexico, in Santa Fe, 505-827-6451. —*Ellen L. Boyer*

The Boston
Post Road

BOSTON POST ROAD

W HEN THE BRITISH ROYAL governors of New York and Connecticut proposed in 1672 to establish the first mail-delivery route across New England, they could not have foreseen that the road would one day also help spread the seeds of rebellion throughout colonial America, or that it would become the haunt of characters as diverse as General George Washington and "General" Tom Thumb.

No, all that Francis Lovelace and John Winthrop had in mind was to execute an instruction from "His Sacred Majestie," King Charles II, to encourage a "close correspondency" among America's northern Atlantic settlements. Governor Lovelace really spearheaded the project. As he explained in a note to his Connecticut counterpart, the sending of mail between colonies could be "the most compendious means to beget a mutual understanding."

Originally used by colonial mail carriers, this link between Manhattan and Massachusetts inspired the growth of towns, taverns, and a more extensive New England road system.

Lovelace proposed that the mail be borne on horseback, in "divers baggs, according to the townes the letters are designed to" (the rider would have discretion in choosing where to deposit the mail for each town) and that the post rider leave Manhattan Island on the first Monday of every month "and return within the month from Boston to us againe." That rider, Lovelace stipulated, must be "active, stout, and inde-

Riders delivering mail on the Post Road started out from New York's Bowling Green. Up in Boston, Paul Revere delivered a different sort of message along the Post Road.

fatigable . . . [and] sworn as to his fidelity," and he should receive an annual salary which, together with money he would make from stated charges for letters and other packages, "may afford him a handsome livelyhood." In addition to his mail-carrying responsibilities, the rider was to double as a sort of itinerant guide, aiding any other journeyers along the post road who might need recommendations to nearby lodgings.

The selection of a specific course from New York to Boston was left up to Governor Winthrop, in consultation with "some of the most able woodsmen"; but Lovelace did mention Hartford, Connecticut, as "the first stage I have designed him to change his horse, where constantly I expect he should have a fresh one."

Although the identity of that first postal carrier dispatched from New York to Boston has been lost in the recesses of history, his woes in getting started have not. It seems that, due to the tardiness of a bag of letters arriving from Albany, New York, the initial rider's departure was delayed by three weeks. He didn't leave the southern tip of Manhattan until January 22, 1673, but he reached the shores of Massachusetts Bay about two weeks later—considered a fast trip in those days, when the 250 miles between the two cities were still predominantly wilderness.

Unfortunately, post riders had scant opportunity right away to improve on this record. In August 1673, the Dutch—who forty-seven years before had purchased Manhattan Island from the Manhatte Indians (reportedly in exchange for goods worth twenty-four dollars at the time), then lost it to Great Britain in 1664—returned with a naval squadron to recapture the settlement. They renamed it New Orange and terminated its fledgling mail connection to New England. By the time the Dutch gave the town back to the British in November 1674, Massachusetts, Connecticut, and Rhode Island were embroiled in "King Philip's War," a courageous but futile Native American campaign. Led by a Wampanoag Indian leader named Metacomet (known to colonists as King Philip), this was a last serious effort to rid New England of the white man.

Metacomet was killed in the summer of 1676, and the war soon died out. But it took another nine years before government officials were ready to divide their concentration between military matters and civil undertakings such as the creation of post offices in New York and Boston. In 1691, a formal postal service was finally developed in the colonies. Within a few years, mail was being carried to and from New England, as well as west to Philadelphia and north to Albany, and lawmakers in the Carolinas were agitating for service extensions. It would have been difficult—nay, impossible—in those pre–Revolutionary War times for anyone to predict just how profoundly the craving for letters and other correspondence from afar would affect the northeastern colonies.

ROAD WORK AHEAD

THE BOSTON POST ROAD. It's a name that evokes images of patriots in tricorn hats, steepled churches with loudly peeling bells, and John Hancock tromping through America's oldest public park, the Boston Common. Apparently even New Yorkers, who can usually be counted on to put their city before all others, called North America's first postal route by that name. Nonetheless, *Boston Post Road* is a rather misleading designation, because it implies that there was a single prominent pathway along which mail was transferred from New York to Boston. Such was not the case. There were actually *three* post roads that crossed New England. They covered the same ground between Manhattan Island and New Haven, Connecticut, but there they diverged.

What became known as the *Lower Road* proceeded east from New Haven along Long Island Sound, running through Guilford, Saybrook, New London, and Mystic, Connecticut, before it turned north to Newport and Pawtucket, Rhode Island, on its way to Boston Harbor. (Today, U.S. Route 1 follows most of this same course and is familiarly called the Boston Post Road.) An alternate path of the Lower Road swung northeast from New London and added Providence, Rhode Island, to its stops.

A *Middle Road* branched north from New Haven to Hartford. There it sliced northeast across Connecticut and Massachusetts, hitting Dedham on its last leg into Boston.

The *Upper Road* (which was the original route and is familiar to many as the *Old* Post Road) also headed north from New Haven but continued in an arc beyond Hartford, reaching Boston via the Massachusetts hamlets of Warren, Brookfield, and Worcester. It was the Upper Road that silversmith-turned-activist Paul Revere followed in the mid-1770s as messenger for the Massachusetts provincial assembly. In 1789, newly elected President George Washington used the same highway when he

Washington Slept Here . . . and There

Only six months after he had sworn to the oath of his new office at Federal Hall in New York City, President George Washington set off on a kind of victory lap around New England. It was October 1789, and the young nation's first chief executive would spend a month in travel, much of it on the Boston Post Road, observing the countryside, meeting local dignitaries, and availing himself of public facilities along the way. (Washington is said to have preferred taverns to staying in private homes when he traveled.) Fortunately for history, he kept a diary of this journey.

The presidential party left Manhattan Island on October 15 and that evening reached Rye, New York, where they stayed at the Square House, "a very neat and decent Inn," as Washington wrote, owned by the widow Tamar Haviland. (This building still stands and is now the Haviland Tavern Museum.) From there, the group moved north to Fairfield, Connecticut, and on to Stratford, New Haven, and Hartford, Connecticut, and Springfield, Massachusetts, where they lodged at Zena Parson's Tavern ("which is a good House," according to the First Travel Critic). As the president wound east through Massachusetts, his comments on road conditions and accommodations become fewer in relation to his notes about meeting military and civilian officials.

When he finally reached the streets of Boston on October 24, Washington remarked that he stayed at a Scollay Square lodging house owned by a Mrs. Joseph Ingersoll ("which is a very decent & good house"). But he was distracted from the pleasures set out from the then U.S. capital at New York to visit his constituents in New England. (On his return trip, Washington took the Middle Road.)

The length of the Upper Road was about 250 miles, compared with 225 miles for the Middle Road and 270 miles for the Lower Road. Early post riders, though, might have viewed these routes as equally challenging, for they all tended to be narrow (usually no wider than bridle paths), and there were occasional gaps where road

of touring by the insolence of John Hancock, former president of the Continental Congress and now governor of Massachusetts. Apparently still angry over the decision by Congress in 1775 to make Washington commander in chief of the Continental armed forces—a position that Hancock had coveted—the governor shunned the president during most of the visit. It was an unnecessary show of power, but one that vastly entertained Bostonians, already familiar with Hancock's pomposity.

Washington and his entourage continued north into New Hampshire before returning to Boston in early November. On their way back to New York, they decided to follow the Middle Road, stopping on the night of November 5 at a tavern in Uxbridge, Massachusetts, owned by Samuel Taft ("where, though the people were obliging, the entertainment was not very inviting"). Taverns seemed to decline in quality after that. Washington declared that Jacobs' Inn in Thompson, where he breakfasted, was "not a good House."

Of the states through which the Boston Post Road passed, only Rhode Island went ungraced by the president on his 1789 trip. That's because Rhode Island didn't ratify the Constitution until six months later, in May 1790. President Washington made a special visit to the state in August of that year, but wound up staying at a large inn in Providence (already renowned for having hosted the Marquis de Lafayette), rather than at taverns that might one day proclaim "Washington Slept Here."

builders from one town had failed to connect with the work of road builders from the next town along the line. It was difficult for riders to cover their requisite thirty to fifty miles a day in summer (fewer during the winter months) when they periodically had to blaze their own trails through the woods.

The Commonwealth of Connecticut is supposed to have been especially remiss in laying proper highways. "Topography was to blame," wrote Stewart H. Holbrook in *The Old Post Road: The Story of the Boston Post Road*. "The long ridges running from Massachusetts to Long Island Sound discouraged east and west roads. Except in the wide valleys of the Connecticut and perhaps two other rivers, the glacial remains of boulders, rocks, and outcropping ledges stood in the way. (Little wonder that today's tourists marvel at stone fences which mark Connecticut from border to border.)"

Sarah Kemble Knight, a remarkable Boston schoolmistress in her late thirties who went on horseback down the Lower Road to New Haven in 1704, left no doubt as to the need for improvements on Connecticut's shoreline. "The roads all along this way are very bad," she penned in her journal, "encumbered with rocks and mountainous passages, which were very disagreeable to my carcass . . . and once in going over a bridge, my horse stumbled and very narrowly 'scaped falling over into the water. . . . But through God's goodness I met with no harm."

Sarah Knight's safe passage may or may not have been attributable to divine intervention. But there were certainly post riders involved. Fulfilling their secondary duty as guides, they led her from township to remote township—and collected modest gratuities for their trouble.

Despite Governor Lovelace's promise to post riders of a "handsome livelyhood," the horsemen who toted packages and portmanteaus full of epistles down the post roads found themselves by the close of the eighteenth century increasingly in need of such tips to maintain their standard of living. To further raise their income, explained historian Holbrook, "many a rider acted as virtual agent in buying and selling bank notes and lottery tickets, a sort of customer's man for speculators. They performed shopping services in

From the seventeenth century until the present, commerce has
thrived in the port cities of New York and Boston, the endpoints of
the original Post Road.

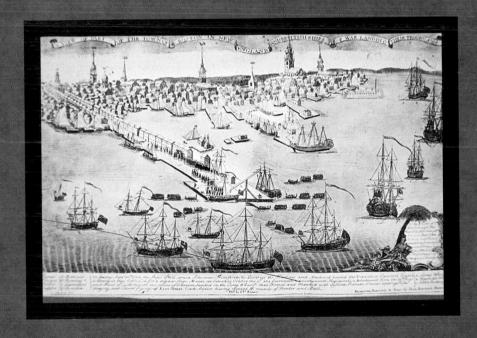

the cities for villagers, and collected commissions from both customers and merchants." One mail carrier was found consistently tardy with his deliveries because he tried to earn a few extra dollars by driving cattle between towns on his route. Some riders eventually decided they could make their purses fatter—and move the mails faster, to boot—by quitting colonial postal departments and starting independent express operations.

THE INN AT THE MILESTONE

HAD YOU BEEN A POST rider in the summer of 1753, you might have taken particular notice of a slow-moving, two-wheeled chaise along New England's post roads, one trailed by beefy men and carts laden with stone markers. Inside the carriage rode a short, portly gent who had spent many years as a printer and publisher in Philadelphia before indulging his desire to plumb the mysteries of science—especially electricity—and entering the world of politics. Most of the men who worked for him that summer knew little about their employer, save that the British had recently appointed him deputy postmaster general of the colonies—and that his name was Benjamin Franklin.

For Franklin to be given authority over post offices in the northern colonies (while his fellow deputy postmaster general, Colonel William Hunter of Virginia, managed offices in the south) demonstrates just how important mail was becoming to American colonists. After all, Franklin was even then recognized as something of a great thinker. He got promptly to work reforming the system he had inherited, for the first time charging for delivery of newspapers, opening Dead Letter Offices (to which were remanded unclaimed missives), and increasing the speed of deliveries. According to *The Old Boston Post Road*, by Stephen Jenkins, under Franklin "a letter could leave Philadelphia on Monday morning and be delivered in Boston on Saturday night."

As important as any of these other changes were the milestones that Franklin placed in 1753. Ten weeks he spent methodically cruising the post roads with an odometer strapped to one wheel of his chaise, registering every mile of travel. Each of those points then received a stone marker inscribed with the appropriate mileage number. Milestones would prove immensely useful in charging for mail deliveries, since the cost of postage in that era depended on how many miles an article was to go. They would make it easier, as well, for anyone who was trying to offer directions to travelers or record the location of events. An innkeeper might, for instance, instruct a lost patron to "head out past the 8th Milestone," or a military officer could report ominous troop movements "around the 15th Milestone."

One unintended result of Franklin's labors was the growth of taverns adjacent to his markers. But this made lots of sense: By what better means could taverns advertise their precise locations?

Alehouses had long been celebrated features of Yankee life. They served as convivial meeting places for friends, dispensaries for news of the outside world, and forums for political debate. (It was in Boston's old Green Dragon tavern that the colonial Sons of Liberty plotted the Boston Tea Party of 1773). And at least during the seventeenth and eighteenth centuries, pubs doubled as places of worship; it seems they were easier to keep heated than churches. As Holbrook observed in *The Old Post Road:*

The common room of the tavern was the town's business exchange until it outgrew the place and called for a building of its

Postal Codes

In the early years of mail delivery between New York City and Boston, according to *The Old Boston Post Road*, by Stephen Jenkins, there was "no security or protection for mails carried a long distance, as the post-riders opened and read all the letters; and there was no protection until the letters became too many to read. As a result, we find that many of our statesmen, [Aaron] Burr, [Thomas] Jefferson, [Edmund] Randolph, and others, were obliged to use cipher codes in communicating with their political friends or with other government officials. Burr had enough to answer for; but some of his detractors have used this fact of code letters to show the secretiveness of his character."

own. It was also the dance hall, theater, convention auditorium, the lecture and concert hall. In many a village it was the court-room, and a few taverns even had a strong room used as a jail. No few of the early insurance companies of Connecticut take pride in the fact that their first office was in a tavern.

Almost from the beginning, the post roads were bordered with taverns to save mail carriers from becoming dehydrated, and before post offices became commonplace, many of these drinking places were chosen as the obvious depositories for a community's letters. The number of taverns only increased after the Revolution, as more and more people roamed the post roads. Some of these establish-ments went by names familiar in Great Britain: thus, the King's Arms of Worcester, Massachusetts; Newport, Rhode Island's White Horse Tavern; and Crowell's Head in Boston. Others borrowed their appellations from heroes of the day—Franklin, George Washington, John Hancock—and came to offer not only plates of food and tankards of foamy ale, but lodgings. (There was usually at least one bedchamber of moderate appeal; other guests might have to stay in large dormitory-like rooms with beds—and some-times more than one occupant per bed. Lone women journeyers were, with good cause, contemptuous of these arrangements.)

KING OF THE ROAD

I F ANY SINGLE PERSON could be credited with boosting early traffic along New England's post roads, it would be Levi Pease. A native of Enfield, Connecticut, Pease had run delivery wagons through his home state and at one point may have been a post rider. He was blacksmithing when the Revolution broke out in 1775, yet he enlisted immediately in the Continental army and went on to distinguish himself in uniform. In *The Old Boston Post Road*, Jenkins commented that Pease "was so tactful, shrewd, and reliable," he was frequently asked to carry dispatches between officers. General Jeremiah Wadsworth entrusted him to buy horses and supplies for the army, and Pease

Revolutions on the Road: The Boston Massacre, outside the Old State House (Boston's first public building), helped spark the American Revolution. Slater's Mill in Pawtucket, Rhode Island, gave birth to America's Industrial Revolution.

went on to purchase horses for America's French allies, head-quartered in Newport.

After the war, Pease went to Boston with the idea of establishing a stagecoach line along the Upper Road, which he hoped would prove a convenient means of travel for folks who preferred mass transit to riding the entire way atop some bony steed. Lacking sufficient funds for the venture himself, he enlisted as a partner one Reuben Sykes (or Sikes), who had previously worked for Pease in Connecticut. They soon obtained a pair of wagons, and on October 20, 1783, Pease struck off west from Boston on his premier circuit to Hartford.

Passengers were slow to warm to this new service, and some of its initial runs went empty. Still, the partners weren't discouraged. They decided to start their westward runs from one of Boston's most popular taverns, the Red Lion Inn on Marlborough (now Washington) Street, and to operate an eastbound wagon from Hartford. The two coaches would exchange passengers at Spencer, Massachusetts, and then return to their starting points. The entire trip took four days and cost four pence a mile, or about ten dollars. Within a year, the Pease & Sykes stage line extended to New York, including a stop at the Roger Morris house in Harlem Heights (now the Morris-Jumel Mansion), which was converted into yet another tavern.

The vehicles of the times hardly fit our definition of *stagecoach*. They were rectangular wagons mounted on springs and fitted with four backless benches—enough to seat eleven passengers and a driver. There was a top over the wagon and curtains hanging from its sides to provide some measure of protection against wind and rain. Baggage was stowed under the benches and left unguarded when the stage stopped at meal breaks or for fresh horses. Not exactly luxury transportation. But then citizens of that age were more likely to forgive minor inconveniences than we are today.

Josiah Quincy, a passenger on the Pease & Sykes line in 1784, recalled his own experience:

> The carriages were old and shackling and much of the harness was made of ropes. One pair of horses carried the stage eighteen miles. We generally reached our resting place for the night, if no accident intervened, at ten o'clock and after a frugal supper went to

bed with a notice that we should be called at three the next morning, which generally proved to be half past two. Then, whether it snowed or rained, the traveller must rise and make ready by the help of a horn-lantern and a farthing candle, and proceed on his way over bad roads, sometimes with a driver showing no doubtful symptoms of drunkenness, which good-hearted passengers never fail to improve at every stopping place by urging upon him another glass of toddy.

As his operation caught on, Pease, the much-touted "Stagecoach King," was able to reduce his fares by one-fourth. And he installed conductors, who issued and collected tickets on the coaches—and kept stage drivers from pocketing the fares of riders they picked up and deposited between Boston and New York. When the new United States government issued its first mail contract in 1785, Pease & Sykes got it, saying that they could carry letters and packages on their coaches in greater quantity and almost as swiftly as post riders. So successful were they in that project that when the

Yankee Ingenuity

Seated on backless benches, and with the driver shouting at them periodically to lean right or left in order to prevent their vehicle from overturning in deep road ruts, passengers aboard early Post Road stages found travel challenging enough during summer months. But come winter, when dirt thoroughfares turned to mud and riders were asked to help loosen stuck wagons, conditions could get even worse. *The Old Post Road* tells of one group that finally decided to stand up for their rights:

"It was impossible for the horses to pull the coach out [of a mudhole], so the driver asked his passengers to alight; which they refused to do. They were astonished to see him sit down by the roadside and calmly light his pipe. They made anxious, and probably profane, remarks about his peculiar course of action, whereupon he replied: 'Since them hosses can't pull that kerrige out o' thet mudhole, an' ye wo'nt help, *I'm a-goin to wait till th' mudhole dries up!*' The passengers alighted at once and helped."

postmaster general sought to create the first U.S. government mail run by stage from Philadelphia to Baltimore, he naturally turned to Levi Pease for help.

By the time Pease died in 1824, at eighty-four, express companies had flowered all along the Atlantic seaboard. (Just two years later, fifty-eight stage lines operated from Boston alone, the majority based in raucous Scollay Square, now Government Center.) Most of them built upon Pease's model, starting out with one or more governmental postal contracts. Demand for faster, better roadways led to the construction of turnpikes (privately funded sections of roadway that were paid off through tolls on travelers) and plank roads (wood-paved highways that had the unfortunate habit of rotting within seven years). Wagons increased in size—some had double decks and could carry as many as thirty-two ticket holders. And mail deliveries from Boston to New York that once took six days could now be completed in just thirty-six hours.

The two cities that anchored the ends of the post roads thrived with the stagecoach trade. By the 1820s, New York, confined south of Wall Street in Revolutionary times, had expanded another ten or fifteen blocks to the north, near where City Hall now sits, and its population had climbed above 150,000. (By 1840, it would top 310,000, and cross the one-million mark by 1875.) In Boston, cattle were soon to be banned from grazing on Boston Common, downtown was a sea of commercial blocks, and the magnificent State House on Beacon Hill drew attention with its painted copper dome (the gilding it now features would be added in 1874).

It was a time of optimism and a window of peace during which Americans could begin to appreciate their homeland. The convenience and low cost of getting around led many Yankees to go exploring. "There is more travelling [in the United States] than in any part of the world," enthused the *American Traveler*, a Boston newspaper that concentrated on the coaching business, in 1828. "Here, the whole population is in motion, whereas, in old countries, there are millions who have never been beyond the sound of the parish bell." Both stages and respectable inns proliferated along the Boston Post Road to exploit this burgeoning tourist economy.

Unlike some other historic American roads, such as Mississippi's

Coach travel flourished on the Boston Post Road in the late 1700s and early 1800s, adding to an already thriving inn business. But by the mid-nineteenth century, the railroads had made stagecoach lines all but obsolete

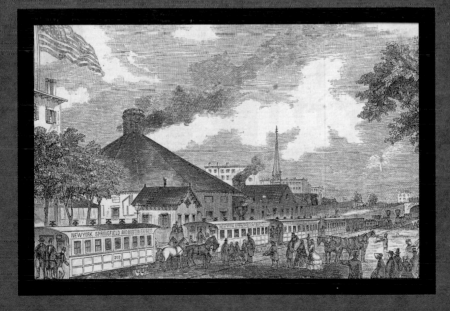

Natchez Trace and trails through California's gold rush country, the Boston Post Road provided relatively secure transit. "Not in the . . . road's history was horseman or stage stopped for the purposes of robbery . . . ," Holbrook asserted with some disappointment. "[T]his record was not for lack of rogues, as witness the periodic robberies of Yankee banks and individuals. It was rather that in New England men started early to use drafts and bills of exchange, which were not easily negotiable, if at all." Americans in the West, on the other hand, tended to pack bags of gold and bars of silver on stagecoach rides.

However, the route from Manhattan through Massachusetts did boast its share of eccentrics. There was Pease, of course. Later would come the abolitionist John Brown, who operated a wool warehouse in Springfield, Massachusetts, before storming west to clash with proslavery forces in Kansas; and showman Phineas T. Barnum, who discovered the midget Charles Sherwood Stratton—soon to become world-renowned as "General" Tom Thumb—while on a visit to Bridgeport, Connecticut. Barnum subsequently returned to Connecticut to raise a gaudy mansion and plow his fields using a circus elephant instead of horses or mules.

Last, but certainly not least, was a natty stage driver with the unlikely name of Ginery Twichell.

Born in 1811 at Athol, Massachusetts, Twichell had quit school when he was sixteen and worked a handful of odd jobs before signing on with a farmer who, as a sideline, operated a stage wagon between the town of Worcester and the northern extremes of Worcester County. So taken was Twichell with this enterprise that when he turned twenty-one, he bought the farmer's line and proceeded to drive his competitors out of business. Then he expanded the reach of his coaches, secured postal contracts, bought more and larger wagons, and by 1846 was known throughout the region for the efficiency and speed of his service. But that year, Twichell outdid even himself when he volunteered to carry some foreign news dispatches from Boston to New York.

Apparently, Manhattan's fiercely competitive *Herald* and *Tribune* newspapers were both aching to know the contents of these dispatches, which were scheduled to arrive by steamship in

January of that year. The *Herald* had gone so far as to hire a special train to carry their news from Boston down to Norwich,
Connecticut, where it would be ferried across the Sound to Long
Island and then sped on horseback to New York. Looking for
even quicker delivery, *Tribune* editor Horace Greeley turned to
Ginery Twichell. Could the famed express rider outdo the
Herald's elaborate arrangements? Twichell said he could—and he
did, at one point riding sixty-six miles through a heavy snow-
storm to Hartford, where he took a train to New Haven, then sad-
dled up again and finished his assignment, as one account of the
adventure phrased it, *"considerably* ahead of the *Herald* couriers."

A Sense of Rebirth

TWICHELL'S WILD RIDE gave hope to Yankees who
were fearful of losing post road coach travel to the
increasing competition of railway companies. But sadly,
this victory of horse over iron horse was only a last
gasp for the industry that Levi Pease and so many others had
helped to build. Although stagecoaches would remain a viable
means of transport in the American West for another four decades,
by the 1850s, newspaper editorialists across New England were
already lamenting the obsolescence of their local stagecoach lines.
Mail was going by train now. Most people were going by train, too.
Even Twichell, synonymous with the high times of the Boston Post
Road, found his future with the steam locomotive: He was elected
president of the Boston & Worcester line in 1857 before going on
to become a member of the U.S. Congress.

Not until a century later, when trucks began to replace trains
in postal deliveries and automobiles became a plague upon the
planet, did the old highways from New York to Boston start to look
at least as busy as they had once been. Who's to know what another
hundred years might bring to the Post Road?

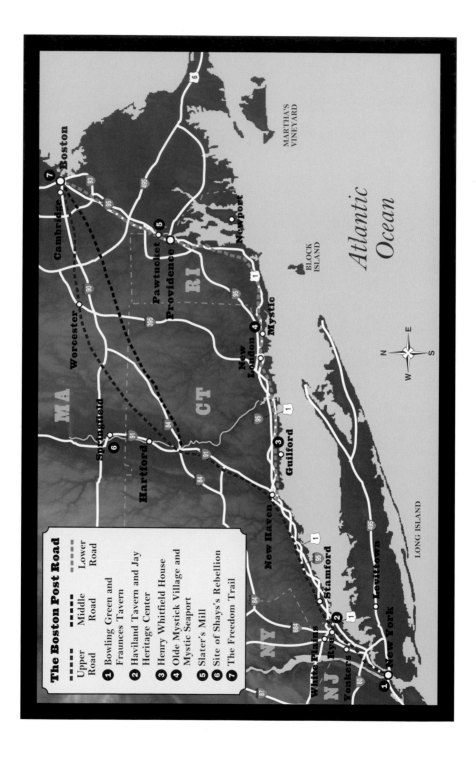

The Boston Post Road

Upper Road   Middle Road   Lower Road

1 Bowling Green and Fraunces Tavern
2 Haviland Tavern and Jay Heritage Center
3 Henry Whitfield House
4 Olde Mystick Village and Mystic Seaport
5 Slater's Mill
6 Site of Shays's Rebellion
7 The Freedom Trail

The Boston Post Road Today

In our technologically advanced world, when letters can be delivered as fast as one can type, it may be difficult to imagine a time when mail was carried on horseback between New York City and Boston. But New England's three principal Post Road routes—and most notably the Upper and Lower Roads—are eloquent reminders of those days. What remains of them can be found along Interstates 90, 91, and 95.

NEW YORK CITY TO NEW HAVEN

On the south end of Manhattan Island, colonial mail runs began at **Bowling Green** (Broadway at Battery Place), which became New York's first park in the mid-eighteenth century. On their way to Boston, post riders traveled past the **Fraunces Tavern** (54 Pearl Street), a favorite watering hole for early politicians. (Historical lithographs inside the tavern depict Post Road culture.) A stop might be made in the area of today's **South Street Seaport Museum** (along Water Street, between John Street and Peck Slip), where visitors today can wander among Federal-style warehouses and past other displays highlighting New York's nineteenth-century maritime history.

Standing smack dab on the old Post Road is **St. Paul's Chapel** (Broadway and Fulton Street), built in 1766, Manhattan's sole remaining pre–Revolutionary War church. George Washington went there to pray for guidance after he was sworn in as the nation's first president in 1789. Also on the road is the **Abigail Adams Smith Museum** (421 East Sixty-first Street). Full of antique furnishings, this house was owned in the 1790s by the daughter of President John Quincy Adams—though she never actually slept there—and later served as a hotel for post riders. The Post Road continued through a portion of what is now Central Park, at the western edge of which stands the **New-York**

Historical Society (170 Central Park West, between Seventy-sixth and Seventy-seventh Streets), which houses vintage furniture, maps, and carriages, as well as memorabilia from the Post Road, including paintings and an original milestone. At Manhattan's north end, mail carriers often stopped at the **Morris-Jumel Mansion** (Edgecombe Avenue at West 160th Street), which served as Washington's headquarters during the Battle of Harlem Heights, before being used as a tavern.

Twenty five miles north of New York City, in the town of Rye, Washington also booked a room at the **Haviland Tavern** (1 Purchase Street), which is now the Rye Historical Society, replicating colonial lifestyles. Across town on the Post Road is the **Jay Heritage Center** (210 Boston Post Road), a mansion built in 1838 by Peter Jay. The home is being restored to preserve its historical significance: The estate was the site of the boyhood home of Peter's father, John Jay, the nation's first chief justice of the Supreme Court.

The Post Road continued along what is now Interstate 95 to **New Haven,** Connecticut, home of **Yale University,** founded in 1701 and alma mater of such memorable Americans as Nathan Hale, Cole Porter, Noah Webster, and President William Howard Taft. From there, the Upper and Lower Post Roads diverged.

The Upper Road

Take I-91 north from New Haven to **Hartford,** the Constitution State's capital, founded in 1636. The Visitors Bureau there sponsors a self-guided tour through local historical sites. Featured are the **Old State House** (800 Main Street), the earliest state capitol building, and the **Center Church and Ancient Burying Ground** (Main and Arch Streets), which marks the site of Hartford's first church, with a neighboring graveyard that contains headstones dating back to 1640.

On I-91, near the Connecticut border is **Springfield,** Massachusetts home to the country's first federal arsenal. The farmers' insurrection known as Shays's Rebellion attempted to seize that facility in January 1787, but its members were repulsed by militiamen. The **Springfield Armory** (1 Armory Square) contains an exhibit on the evolution of firearms, some of which were used during the Revolution, while the **Connecticut Valley Historical Society Museum** (Edwards and Maple Streets) features furniture and art, including re-creations of a Federal-period dining room and two nineteenth-century tavern rooms.

About halfway to Boston and just north of I-90 is **Worcester,** founded in 1722. Few places along the Post Road had so many claims to fame. Deborah Sampson, the first woman to serve in the American armed forces hailed from here: In 1782, she enlisted in the Revolution wearing men's clothes and calling herself "Robert Shurtleff." Worcester also hosted the first national Women's Suffrage Convention in 1850. The **Worcester Historical Society** (30 Elm Street) preserves the city's history. But for a in-depth look back at America, take in the **American Antiquarian Society** (185 Salisbury Street), which is stuffed with early documents on literature, culture, and other subjects.

THE LOWER ROAD

From New Haven, this route follows I 95, close to the Connecticut shore, passing through **Guilford,** renowned for its varied collection of authentic early homes. Along an extant patch of the Post Road, you can see the lavishly decorated **Thomas Griswold House** (171 Boston Street), built in 1774 and surrounded by a barn, a blacksmith shop, and gardens that contain only plants dating from before 1820; the **Hyland House** (84 Boston Street), a red saltbox house from 1660, which features fireplaces big enough to walk into, centuries-old furniture, and an herb garden; and the **Henry Whitfield House** at 284 Old Whitfield Street. Built in 1639, the Whitfield is the oldest stone residence still standing in New England and is now a museum exhibiting three centuries' worth of furnishings.

Continue east to Mystic and its **Olde Mystick Village,** an appealing assemblage of eighteenth-century-style shops and eateries. Fast forward from there to the nineteenth century at **Mystic Seaport,** the nation's largest maritime museum, where you can tour schooners and four hundred smaller vessels from the 1800s.

As you enter Rhode Island, take U.S. 1 toward Newport, once ranked with Boston and New York as the nation's top ports. The **Point District** is a restored collection of colonial homes along

Newport's shore. Nearby, the **Brick Market** (Thames Street at Washington Square) is a former theater, town hall, and headquarters for slave-trading that now houses the **Museum of Newport History.** Guided walking tours start from the Brick Market, May to October, and you don't want to miss touring the **Wanton-Lyman-Hazard House** (17 Broadway), built in 1675 and the site of the 1765 Stamp Act Riot. The **Redwood Library** (50 Bellevue Avenue), built in 1748, is the nation's oldest working library, while the **Friends Meeting House** (21 Farewell Street) dates back to 1699, when it served as the local Quaker meeting place. Before you leave Newport, you might do as post riders did and quench your thirst at the **White Horse Tavern** (Marlborough and Farewell Streets), which bills itself as the oldest continuously operating pub in the U.S., established in 1673.

Along the Post Road in northern Rhode Island, the town of Pawtucket thrived during the 1790s with its **Old Slater Mill** (67 Roosevelt Avenue). The first American factory to produce cotton yarn using water-powered machines (thus launching the Industrial Revolution in this country), the mill has been restored, and now offers demonstrations of spinning and weaving, as well as informative slide shows.

BOSTON

The end of the line for all of these Post Roads, downtown Boston is one huge lesson in American history. Everywhere you look you'll find a building or a crossroads that is familiar from your schoolbooks. **Faneuil Hall** (Fanueil Hall Square at Merchants Row) opened in 1742 as a market and meeting hall. It burned to the ground nineteen years later, but was soon replaced, becoming a center where both politicians and peddlers could gather (inspiring a local poet to write: "Here orators in ages past have mounted their attack/Undaunted by proximity to sausage on the rack"). The hall's third floor features a collection of historic military arms and memorabilia, while a second-floor gallery features portraits of famous Americans. The ground level, along with adjacent **Quincy Market,** is given over to cafés, shops, and street vendors—a splendid place for people-watching.

The two-and-a-half-mile **Freedom Trail** begins at the Visitor Center in Boston Common (at Tremont Street and Temple Place) and leads you past more than a dozen important sites from colonial and Revolutionary times. Included are the **Old South Meeting House** (310 Washington Street), where plans for the Boston Tea Party were solidified; the **Boston Massacre Site,** where in March 1770 British redcoats clashed with townspeople; the surprisingly humble **Paul Revere House** (19 North Square), built in 1680; and the **Old North Church** (193 Salem Street), Boston's oldest church building (erected in 1723) and the starting point for Revere's celebrated 1775 ride to warn minutemen at Lexington and Concord of approaching British troops.

Two other essential stops on any Beantown history tour. The **Granary Burial Ground** (at Tremont and Bromfield Streets), where you'll find the graves of many patriots, among them Samuel Adams and John Hancock, along with the last resting place of Judge Samuel Sewall, the only jurist to admit publicly that he was mistaken to condemn women during the Salem witch trials. Finally, you'll want to spend some quiet time at **Boston Common** (bound by Beacon, Charles, Boylston, Tremont, and Park Streets). Once considered a Boston hinterland, this has been a beloved public park since 1634. On the grounds where jugglers and sermonizers perform today, redcoats camped during the Revolution and troops were mustered during the Civil War.

To learn more about the Boston Post Road, call the New-York Historical Society, 212-873-3400; the Newport Historical Society, 401-846-0813; and Boston's Freedom Trail, 617-242-5642. —*Ellen L. Boyer*

The Great Wagon Road

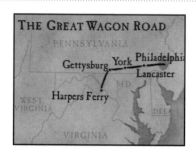

THE GREAT WAGON ROAD

Gettysburg York Philadelphia
Lancaster
Harpers Ferry

PENNSYLVANIA

MD.

WEST VIRGINIA

DEL.

VIRGINIA

ROCKS SAILED THROUGH the air, hitting the prisoners on their backs, their arms, their legs, each strike a dull fleshy thump answered by a low groan. The guards had hoped to avoid exactly this sort of violence as they carted their captives down the Great Wagon Road from Philadelphia. But they had apparently not realized how angry some patriots would be at the men in custody. The crowd hurled insults with the same vehemence that they cast stones.

From the Revolutionary War through the Civil War, this long route between the North and the South carried patriots, presidents, and even a prophet or two.

The prisoners were denounced as monarchists, traitors, cowards—any of which might have been considered a criminal offense in that fall of 1777, as colonial America struggled to win its independence from Great Britain. In truth, they were merchants and businessmen.

What had these burghers done?

Nothing. And that was precisely the problem. They were pacifists, Quakers who refused to take up arms in the cause of America's incipient liberty. Violence was against their religion. So while other Pennsylvanians had embraced the Revolutionary War and adopted Thomas Jefferson's Declaration of Independence, the Quakers continued to favor peace and even maintained trade with the British. This led the revolutionists to suspect that if they scratched a

William Penn received the charter for Pennsylvania from England's King Charles II in repayment of a debt, and he wanted his colony and his planned city of Philadelphia to be havens of tolerance.

Quaker, they would find a Tory, a loyalist to the Crown. When John Pemberton, a prominent Philadelphia Quaker, published a strong pacifist statement, which was circulated in December 1776, those fears seemed only to be confirmed.

Shortly after that statement appeared, the Continental Congress, meeting in Philadelphia's Independence Hall, decreed that the American colonies should disarm and incarcerate all residents "notoriously disaffected" against the Revolutionary cause. Pemberton and sixteen other Quakers from the City of Brotherly Love were arrested and, in September 1777, taken under armed guard to Virginia, where it was thought they could be safely held and silenced until the Revolution was won.

Being paraded through the countryside in a wagon and stoned by passersby would have been an ignominious experience for any-body. For members of the Society of Friends (Quakers), however, such treatment was especially galling. After all, Quakers had enjoyed tremendous wealth and influence in Philadelphia, thanks to William Penn, a leading Quaker himself, who had received the char-ter for Pennsylvania from King Charles II in 1681—payment for a loan that Penn's father had made to Charles, the famed restorer of the British monarchy. Most of Penn's initial real-estate investors in his New World territory had been Quakers, and a majority of the merchants and traders who had helped build Philadelphia on the banks of the Delaware River were, as well. Now, seventeen of their fellows had been denounced as Judases and sent off down the Wagon Road. This was an affront—one hardly mitigated by the fact that Congress had also been forced out of Philadelphia, fleeing down that same rural highway under threat of capture by British forces. (Congress would find a new home in York, Pennsylvania, while the British occupied Philadelphia for most of a year.)

Within eight months of their internment, and after repeated requests to the Pennsylvania government, the well-behaved dis-senters were allowed to return home. All was forgiven, and the Quakers went unmolested for the rest of the war. President George Washington later asserted that "there is no denomination among us, who are more exemplary and useful citizens [than the Quakers]." By then, though, the Quaker expulsion from Philadelphia had already earned a sad but unforgettable chapter in the long history of the Great Wagon Road.

Serving farmers, merchants, soldiers, settlers bound for the South and West, and religious missionaries hot to sow the seeds of Christianity among Native Americans, the Wagon Road was an essential avenue of commerce and transportation and eventually stretched from southeastern Pennsylvania to eastern Georgia—a distance of eight hundred miles. "In the last sixteen years of the colonial era," historian Carl Bridenbaugh wrote in *Myths and Realities: Societies of the Colonial South,* "southbound traffic along the Great Philadelphia Wagon Road was numbered in tens of thousands; it was the most heavily traveled road in America and must have had more vehicles jolting along its rough and tortuous way than all other main roads put together."

The route's most-frequented and best-recalled section led from Philadelphia through mountainous western Virginia, where it shared much of its length with the Wilderness Road, a trail followed by innumerable Kentucky-bound pioneers of the eighteenth century. Yet the Wagon Road lost little of its identity in that shared course. It is remembered with pride as the road on which stalwart Conestoga wagons were introduced. The path taken by many nineteenth century African American slaves escaping Southern plantations via the Underground Railroad. And the route along which Union and Confederate troops marched toward what would be the single bloodiest battle of the Civil War.

The highway's very name speaks of its historical importance. This wasn't just any wagon road. This was the *Great* one.

THE PHILADELPHIA EXPERIMENT

WITHOUT WILLIAM PENN, the Great Wagon Road probably would not have seen the early swell of traffic that it did. Born in London, England, in 1644, the son of a renowned British admiral, Penn was considered an innovator and independent thinker even as a young man, especially when it came to religious matters. Rather than declare fealty to the Church of England, as would have been conventional, Penn was seduced by the teachings of an iconoclast named George Fox—founder of the Society of Friends—who contended that ministers and public rites were unnecessary in establishing communication between the soul of man and the spirit of God. For his nonconformity, Penn was expelled from Christ Church College, Oxford, in 1662. He went on to travel, preach, and write on behalf of Fox's Quaker doctrine and religious tolerance, but he paid a price: He was imprisoned four times for his beliefs.

We can only guess what went through the mind of King Charles II when Penn, having inherited his father's financial claim against the Crown, petitioned that the debt (worth £16,000) be paid through a royal grant of land in the New World. Britain had been struggling to tighten control over its American colonies; giving Penn responsibility for a new province had to have struck at least some clearheaded strategists as courting disaster. Still, Penn received his charter for Pennsylvania and promptly got busy creating what he envisioned as "the seed of a nation" and a "holy experiment": a semiutopia complete with a liberal frame of government, open courts, and the guarantee of religious freedom. Penn also started offering property for sale, both within his planned city of Philadelphia and in the surrounding territory. His enthusiasm for his experiment proved infectious. In 1682 alone, the same year that Penn first visited his colony, twenty-three ships full of immigrants sailed for Pennsylvania.

Penn had originally intended to place the capital of his province in the area of what is now Chester, Pennsylvania, but when he learned that he had let too much of that vicinity's land fall into private hands, he decided to relocate Philadelphia up the Delaware River. His intention was to erect a city that synthesized urban needs and rural aesthetics. To accomplish this, Penn established a rigid gridiron pattern that "provided easily divisible real estate," according to *Pride of Place: Building the American Dream*, by architect Robert A. M. Stern. "It also inhibited the catastrophic spread of fire and disease that had been fostered by the narrow, crooked streets of Europe's medieval cities." In order to

Faces of freedom: the Amish
and Mennonite flocked to
Pennsylvania seeking religious
tolerance and remain there
today in great numbers.
Independence Hall bcoame a
symbol of freedom for a young
nation.

preserve a modest sense of nature in the hamlet, Penn designed a central square (now occupied by City Hall), along with four other symmetrically distributed squares, and he spelled out how he would ideally like to see homes oriented: "Let every house be placed, if the person pleases, in the middle of its plat, as to the breadth way of it, so there may be ground on each side for gardens or orchards, or fields, that it may be a green country town, which will . . . always be wholesome."

Just as Rhode Island founder Roger Williams had drawn residents to his colony earlier in the century with the promise that they could worship as they chose, so Penn's religious tolerance attracted a diverse and substantial flock to Pennsylvania. Germans began arriving there in 1683; by 1709, almost fourteen thousand of them (including Amish and Mennonites) had entered the province. On their heels came Scottish Presbyterian families who had worked the linen trade in Ireland before being forced out by English taxes. The next immigrant waves brought Baptists, Catholics, and, naturally, more Quakers.

At the end of the 1600s, Philadelphia boasted a population of about four thousand; by 1790, it had grown into a metropolis of more than fifty-four thousand (the largest in North America until New York eclipsed it in 1820), with whale-oil street lamps, sporting clubs, blue-stocking literary societies, and a tax-supported nighttime crime watch. Even before the Revolution, in fact, Philadelphia had surpassed New York and Boston as the continent's premier trade center.

Many Europeans who had hoped to find their destiny in Pennsylvania, however, didn't stay there long enough to witness this growth. Some were discouraged from settling by high land prices. Others were pushed out by what seems a recurring theme in American history: mounting discrimination against non-English newcomers. No less than the great publisher and politician Benjamin Franklin, who himself had been an emigrant to Philadelphia (from Boston in 1723), bought into these ugly prejudices in 1751, when he wrote: "Why should Pennsylvania, founded by the English, become a colony of aliens, who will shortly be so numerous as to Germanize us, instead of our

Anglicifying them, and will never adopt our language or customs any more than they can acquire our complexion?"

Folks started to look south, to the wild reaches of Maryland and Virginia, for new and cheaper land. In 1732—as Parke Rouse Jr. details in his history *The Great Wagon Road: From Philadelphia to the South*—Lord Baltimore, the proprietor of Maryland, issued an open invitation to northerners angling for homes south of Philadelphia. He proclaimed that his colony, "being Desireous to Increase the Number of Honest People," would give to any family two hundred free acres between the Potomac and Susquehanna Rivers. This land, Rouse adds, would "be exempt from the payment of quit rents for three years after settlement and then at a rate of only four shillings sterling per hundred acres. Single persons were offered a hundred acres on the same terms." The enticement worked. Within the next quarter-century, Maryland's population would quadruple, to 130,000.

The route that these pioneers took—the future Great Wagon Road—led them west from Philadelphia through the Pennsylvania towns of Lancaster, York, and Gettysburg. It then headed south across the Maryland panhandle and skirted the eastern slopes of the Appalachian Mountains all the way through western Virginia, following part of an ancient Indian trail called the Great Warpath. Eventually, the Wagon Road continued south across the Carolinas to Augusta, Georgia.

Once, this course had been trampled only by Native Americans such as the Cherokee, the Iroquois, and the Shawnee, along with buffalo, deer, and other game. But a series of negotiations between colonial governors and Indian sachems, conducted from the 1720s through the 1740s, cleared the way for whites to use the trail in relative safety.

It remained safe until the French and Indian War (1754–63), when the Wagon Road saw its first use by military detachments (some under the command of George Washington), most of them headed south or west to secure British settlements against assault by Indians who had allied themselves with the French Crown. Resentful of English colonists pushing into native lands west of the Appalachians, the Shawnee and others used the war partly as an excuse to wreak vengeance on settlers who had staked out property along the Wagon Road just east of those mountains.

THE COMING OF THE CONESTOGAS

THE CONCLUSION OF THE FRENCH and Indian War brought relief to frequent travelers on the Wagon Road and ushered in a period of concerted improvement for the thoroughfare. By 1765, what had been a narrow and sometimes hard-to-distinguish pathway was being cleared to accommodate horse-drawn vehicles. Although recent wars had drained state government coffers of money that might have gone to improvements, county courts took responsibility for maintaining their segments of the road at public expense. After they had finished with their harvests for the year, local farmers were often hired to fill mudholes and spread fresh gravel over the roadbed. Conditions remained far from ideal, especially when winter rains and snow made mush of the route, but use of the Wagon Road was at an all-time high.

Try to picture what traffic on this road was like in the late eighteenth century. The common traveler would have gone afoot, carrying his worldly goods in a pack slung over his shoulder. If it was a Sunday, there might have been entire families riding horseback into town for church services, the father leading, with his youngest child gripping his waist and bouncing on the rear of the steed. On their way, these families probably would have encountered two-wheeled, one-horse carts, many of them homemade with wooden axles and wheels that were simply cross sections of huge tree trunks. They might have had to pull off the road and wait while cattle or sheep were herded toward Philadelphia, then a principal livestock market. Likely, they would also have come across packhorse trains carrying hardware, medicine, rum, sugar, or other manufactured goods from town to trade in the country for produce. These processions usually comprised ten or twelve horses, each carrying up to six hundred pounds, following a lead horse and rider. Each horse's bridle would be tied to the saddle of the animal in front, and they would all be wearing bells, so that the train driver could find his horses if they strayed while grazing.

Perhaps the most impressive sights on the road were the Conestoga wagons. Developed in the Conestoga Valley of Pennsylvania's Lancaster County, these capacious, well-balanced craft became popular after about 1750. With a large boatlike body and a swaybacked canvas or homespun cover that hung over the front and rear (making the wagon look like an old-fashioned woman's bonnet on wheels), the Conestoga might be thought of as the heavy-duty truck of its day. It kept its cargo in place and was considered remarkably sturdy. A hinged tailgate made for easy loading from the rear; feed boxes hung off the sides for horses; and the wagoner steered from a "lazy board" mounted over the left front wheel. "From this," claims Rouse in *The Great Wagon Road*, "developed the American practice of driving vehicles from the left."

Conestogas weren't cheap. They sold for around $250, and a

Horse Sense

When it came to the job, Conestoga drivers may have been the proverbial strong, silent types. In *The Great Wagon Road: From Philadelphia to the South*, Parke Rouse Jr. tells of these captains of the highway.

The wagon driver usually commanded a team of four or five horses, requiring constant attention and a firm hand on the "jerk line," which connected with the bit of the left wheel horse, or team leader. By this line the wagoner controlled his horses, walking alongside them or riding a seat behind the left front wagon wheel.

More important than the jerk line were the commands, which were those used by English countrymen. . . . "Haw" meant turn left, while "gee" meant turn right. No other commands except "whoa" were needed. The large, strong wheel horses set the pace and provided braking power through their strong hindquarters on downhill grades. On steep plunges, the driver might insert a chain from the wheels to the coupling poles to provide a brake.

buyer would have to invest $200 more in every horse needed to pull the thing. However, immigrant families embarking for settlements in Virginia or South Carolina could fit everything they owned in these wagons, with ample room to spare. Some commercial versions, designed to move loads of goods to and from towns, grew to be twenty-six feet long and eleven feet high and required half a dozen horses to pull them. Most were piloted by big-drinking, hard-fighting men whose size suggested that they could probably pull the wagons themselves.

For more than half a century, Conestogas dominated the Wagon Road. After 1800, though, they contended increasingly with passenger and mail coaches. These new breeds of conveyance were much lighter and faster than the ungainly Conestogas. The problem was, muddy ruts and bogs slowed stagecoaches even more readily than they did heftier wagons.

Roads obviously had to be improved before passengers could get the most out of the five cents a mile they paid for stagecoach service. One solution was to place wooden poles close together over large mudholes, but the resulting corrugated surface was uncomfortable for riders, who feared that all the jolting would knock loose either their teeth or their senses. Covering sections with planks was also tried on the Wagon Road south of Philadelphia, as it had been

Fightin' Words

Where did the derogatory term "Georgia cracker" originate? Apparently on the Great Wagon Road. John Lambert, an Englishman familiar with travel along the southern section of this thoroughfare, wrote in 1814 that the wagoners of Georgia "are familiarly called *crackers* (from the smacking of their whips, I suppose). They are said to be often very rude and insolent to strangers and people of the towns whom they meet on the road, particularly if they happen to be genteel persons."

The Great Wagon Road was the busiest thoroughfare in the colonies. Inns sprang up along its length to accommodate coach travelers, and the Conestoga wagon got its start hauling goods to new markets. All the activity meant steady work for blacksmiths.

The Inn Thing

As travel increased along the Great Wagon Road, roadside inns proliferated. But the weary traveler had to be mindful that inns could vary widely in quality.

For the paltry sum of three shillings a day, most inns provided guests a place to sleep, three meals, beer between those meals (since many inns were simply taverns with rentable rooms), and a fire where they could warm their feet on a snowswept winter's eve. Provisions, though, were often of questionable quality, and you could expect that the tea and coffee would prove unpalatable. (The story is told of an eighteenth-century congressman who spat out what he was served in one inn. "Sir," he directed the innkeeper, "if this be tea, bring me coffee. And if this be coffee, bring me tea!")

Sleeping arrangements could prove troublesome. Beds were awarded on a first-come, first-served basis, and if there were no more beds available—or if no one was willing to share the bed they already had—latecomers would have to spread their blankets on the inn's floor or find a place in the adjacent haybarn. The barn was often the most peaceful place to be, explained Parke Rouse Jr. in *The Great Wagon Road*, since drunken guests and brawling tended to be commonplace: "Travelers along the Great Road occasionally found a whole tavern in an alcoholic uproar with rooms, stairs, and innyard filled with drunks."

Accommodations tended to improve the farther north you went. Travelers in the South often complained of bedbugs, a shortage of towels and tablecloths, and of having to wash in a stableyard watering trough, rather than finding washbasins and jugs in their rooms. Hostelries closer to Philadelphia—especially those managed by Germans—represented the cream of the crop, with praiseworthy and plentiful food.

As eighteenth-century German traveler Johann David Schoepf wrote in his book *Travels in the Confederation, 1783-84*, inns functioned as the community centers of small towns, and thus were usually decorated with public notices. "It is not always the custom to hang shields [signs] before taverns, but they are easily to be identified by the great number of miscellaneous papers and advertisements with which the walls and doors of these publick houses are plastered; generally, the more the bills are to be seen on a house, the better it will be found to be."

on the Boston Post Road. Predictably, it had the same result: The planks rotted. Not until the 1820s, when toll-road (turnpike) developers started to take over significant portions of the Wagon Road and resurface it in stones or gravel, did stagecoaches finally realize their potential for speed.

By that time, Americans were streaming along the Great Wagon Road. Many were heading south, because gold had been discovered on Georgia's Cherokee lands in 1828. Others went west, into the Ohio and Mississippi river valleys and on to Texas, which would declare its independence from Mexico in 1836. As early as 1834, a railroad line connected Philadelphia and Lancaster, Pennsylvania. Within the next four decades, trains would supplant stage and wagon travel, sending the Great Wagon Road into decline. Yet those 40 years would bring almost as much drama to this highway as had the previous 150.

THE MARTYR

DRAWN BY TWO WHITE horses, an open wagon bearing the prisoner pulled up beneath the new scaffold where he was to be hanged. For a tense moment, infantrymen standing about the platform were unsure of how to proceed. Then the jailer came to their rescue, asking the condemned man to step down. Everyone watched as the black-suited captive—tall, gaunt, and bearded like some Old Testament prophet—rose from the seat he had been given on his own coffin and, with his hands tied behind his back and his feet in red felt slippers instead of boots, jumped off the tailgate into the grass.

John Brown seemed well resolved to his death.

He was certainly more at peace that day, December 2, 1859, than most folks in Charlestown, Virginia (now part of West Virginia). The city buzzed with trepidation about Brown's execution there. In the years leading up to the Civil War, Brown, an unsuccessful businessman from New England, had come to embody the spirit of militant abolitionism. He believed that he was God's agent on Earth, sent to purge America of its slaveholding traditions. Toward this end, he and five of his sons had journeyed to Kansas in 1855, hoping to make that territory safe for antislavery settlers. But their campaign had resulted in violence, including an incident during which proslavery men were dragged from their houses and hacked to death with broadswords. Then, on the night of October 16, 1859, Brown and a band of twenty-one men, including five blacks, had seized the government armory, arsenal, and engine house at Harpers Ferry, on the Potomac River just east of the Great Wagon Road. They had taken hostages (among them, George Washington's great-grandnephew) and planned to incite a nationwide slave rebellion. Instead, militiamen under Robert E. Lee captured the fifty-nine-year-old Brown, who was subsequently convicted of treason and sentenced to hang.

Even as Brown ascended the steps of his gallows, people in the watching crowd worried that he might somehow escape. The army was apprehensive, too, and had taken extraordinary precautions. Fifteen hundred troops had been brought in for the hanging (among them, a twenty-one-year-old actor and Virginia militiaman by the name of John Wilkes Booth), and a massive brass cannon was aimed squarely at the scaffold, ready to shred John Brown's body with grapeshot if his supporters tried to save him at the last minute. They didn't. Nor, to the dismay of many observers, did the fiery abolitionist make any last statements. However, Brown did slip a note to his jailer before the noose was dropped over his head. It read, in part: "I John Brown am now quite *certain* that the crimes of this *guilty land* will never be purged *away*; but with Blood."

Brown's words proved prophetic. Within a year and a half, South Carolina's Fort Sumter fell before Confederate invaders, and the United States—less than a century old—split asunder.

Not only would the country be divided for four years; so would families and friends. "Despite the South's desire to call it a War Between the States," wrote historian C. Vann Woodward, "it *was* a civil war." It was a war sparked by deep-seated differences between the social and economic structures of the North and South, especially on the question of slavery. It was a war fought brother against brother; a war that would kill more men than had died in all previous American wars *combined.*

Rumblings of the trouble to come had been heard along the Great Wagon Road for at least two decades, as more and more African Americans fled north up the legendary Underground Railroad to freedom. This railroad had nothing actually to do with trains, nor did it follow a single route. Rather, it was a collection of overland and sea paths by which men, women, and children could escape the system of slavery on which plantation owners and others in the South had depended for two hundred years. There were many "conductors" on this railroad, people who spoke out fervently as abolitionists, or were just sympathetic to the cause, and who directed or hid slaves on their way north. Some—like former slaves Frederick Douglass and Harriet Tubman—are familiar; most did their work without the recompense of fame.

Although blacks represented less than 3 percent of the Pennsylvania population in 1861 (compared with 33 percent or more in southern territories), that state had some of the most active antislavery groups in the nation, thanks to its complement of Quakers. Based on their belief that every human soul was equal and deserving of dignity, the Quakers had protested against slavery ever since the seventeenth century, and by 1782 all Quaker-owned slaves had been set free. It was only to be expected that Quakers would be active in the Underground Railroad during the Civil War, operating escapee stations at both Gettysburg and York, Pennsylvania, and helping slaves flee up the Wagon Road, in defiance of Confederate efforts to close that thoroughfare at the Potomac.

Although the road took slaves to a new life, it also took soldiers to a far-grimmer fate. Ulysses S. Grant, the cigar-chewing Union army general, dispatched federal troops down the highway to attack Staunton, Lexington, and other rebel towns in western Virginia. But it was the three-day Battle of Gettysburg, July 1–3, 1863—a battle that neither side had planned to fight—that really brought the Civil War to the Great Wagon Road.

As history tells it, the conflict began when a Confederate infantry brigade, intending to commandeer a supply of shoes that was rumored to be stored in the village of Gettysburg, ran into a Union cavalry contingent west of town. Soon, every military division in the area closed on the battle site, taking up positions and scaring the bejesus out of area residents.

After two days of clashes, Union forces held a strong position, yet Confederate General Robert E. Lee was determined to win by striking at his opponents' center. His men launched a furious cannon barrage at the federals, only to be answered by Union shelling. At one point, some 250 guns were firing at once—a deafening fusillade. Then, suddenly, the Union guns fell silent. It was only a move to conserve ammunition, but the Confederates took it to mean they had destroyed the Union batteries, and they advanced quietly from their hiding places. One Yankee officer, quoted in Geoffrey C. Ward's *The Civil War*, described the scene:

> More than half a mile their front extends . . . man touching man, rank pressing rank. . . . The red flags wave, their horsemen gallop up and down, the arms of [thirteen] thousand men, barrel and bayonet, gleam in the sun, a sloping forest of flashing steel. Right on they move, as with one soul, in perfect order without impediment of ditch, or wall, or stream, over ridge and slope, through orchard and meadow, and cornfield, magnificent, grim, irresistible.

When the Confederates got closer, the Union troops opened fire. "We could not help hitting them with every shot," remembered a federal officer. The rebels fell in clumps, and still they kept coming. Some were able to pierce the Union line before they retreated, to be met by a disheartened Lee, who told them, "It was all my fault." (Lee later offered to resign over the Gettysburg debacle, but Jefferson Davis, president of the Confederacy, refused to let him go.)

Losses at the Battle of Gettysburg were terrible. More than forty-five thousand men—almost a third of the troops involved— were killed, wounded, or went missing, twenty-eight thousand of them from the South. As a Union man from New Jersey recalled it, "[The dead lay] upon the open fields . . . in crevices of the rocks, behind fences, trees and buildings; in thickets, where they had crept for safety only to die in agony; by stream or wall or hedge, wherever the battle had raged or their weakening steps could carry

John Brown,
failed businessman but
passionate abolitionist,
was active in helping
slaves up the Wagon Road
to freedom. When he
seized a government arse-
nal at Harpers Ferry, he
was captured and hanged.

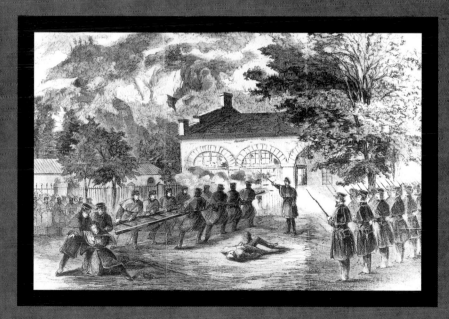

them." Whatever optimism the Confederacy had had about invading and subduing the North was lost in those three days.

No one could make such a wound in the history of a nation disappear. On November 19, 1863, however, President Abraham Lincoln tried to begin the healing process with his address at the dedication of a new Gettysburg cemetery. Perhaps his conclusion is the most poignant part of that speech:

> The world will little note, nor long remember what we say here, but it can never forget what they did here. It is for us the living, rather, to be dedicated here to the unfinished work which they who fought here have thus far so nobly advanced. It is rather for us to be here dedicated to the great task remaining before us— that from these honored dead we take increased devotion to that cause for which they gave the last full measure of devotion—that we here highly resolve that these dead shall not have died in vain; that this nation, under God, shall have a new birth of freedom; and that government of the people, by the people, for the people, shall not perish from the earth.

Unfortunately, the Great Wagon Road was another casualty of the times. Train travel made it more or less obsolete in the post–Civil War period, and it wasn't until the twentieth century that this road—like the Boston Post Road—gained new life under the wheels of automobiles. As one speeds down its length today, it's easy to miss that age when the fastest vehicle here was a Conestoga wagon.

The Great Wagon Road Today

Whether they were looking for religious freedom, virgin land, or an escape from slavery, travelers made their way along the Great Wagon Road for more than two hundred years before the introduction of automobiles. Today, it is much faster going. To follow the route's northern section—from Philadelphia to Harpers Ferry— take U.S. Highway 30 west through Pennsylvania to Chambersburg, then follow Interstate 81 south into West Virginia, swinging east on state Route 51 to U.S. 340 and on to Harpers Ferry.

PHILADELPHIA

A wide variety of churches reflects the City of Brotherly Love's early significance as a refuge from religious persecution, a place where people were free to worship in their own way. George Washington and John Adams both patronized the city's first Roman Catholic Cathedral, **St. Mary's Church** (252 South Fourth Street), founded in 1763, and it was there that the first public religious commemoration of the Declaration of Independence was held. An even older Catholic institution, rather hidden away, is **Old St. Joseph's National Shrine** (321 Willings Alley), erected in 1733. Built between 1727 and 1754, **Christ Church** (Second and Market Streets) counted not only Washington among its worshipers, but also Benjamin Franklin, Betsy Ross, and even Thomas Jefferson. The Anglican church also contains a historic font: Given to the Philadelphia church, it is the font in which city founder William Penn was baptized in England. The nearby **Arch Street Friends Meeting House** (320 Arch Street), the largest of its kind in the country—and still in use—was built in 1804 on land donated to the Quakers in 1693 by Penn himself.

During a single day's touring, you can take in some of the most important sites from the founding days of the United States. Occupying several central-city blocks and managed by the National

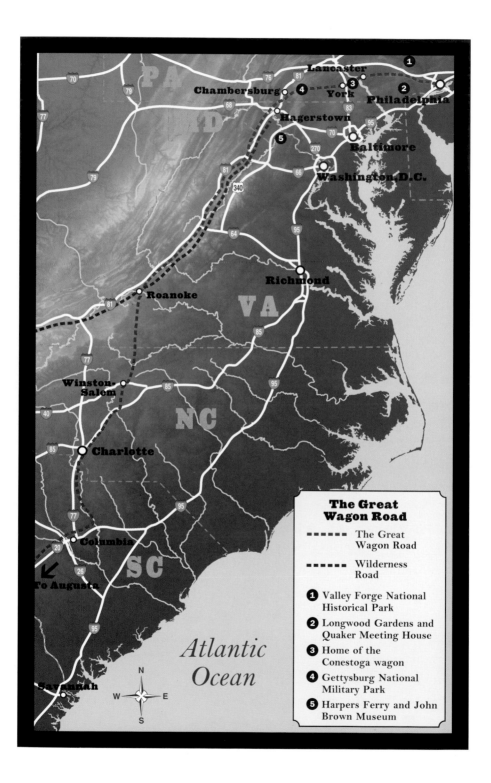

The Great Wagon Road

- - - - - - The Great
Wagon Road

- - - - - - Wilderness
Road

1 Valley Forge National
Historical Park

2 Longwood Gardens and
Quaker Meeting House

3 Home of the
Conestoga wagon

4 Gettysburg National
Military Park

5 Harpers Ferry and John
Brown Museum

Park Service, **Independence National Historic Park** (Second to Sixth Streets, between Market and Walnut Streets) contains **Independence Hall,** built in 1732 and the place where the Declaration of Independence was adopted on July 4, 1776; the **Liberty Bell Pavilion,** which houses that famous national symbol, commissioned in 1751 to commemorate the fiftieth anniversary of Penn's Charter of Privileges (it cracked during its first test); and **Old City Hall,** which was home to the U.S. Supreme Court from 1791 to 1800.

Typical of Philadelphia's pre–Revolutionary War residences is the **Betsy Ross House** (239 Arch Street), which contains tools of the type that would have been used by the woman who may or may not have sewn the first flag of the United States. **Elfreth's Alley** (off North Second Street, between Race and Arch Streets) is reputed to be one of the oldest continuously inhabited streets in the nation. The homes along its length were constructed between 1720 and 1800. One of the buildings holds Elfreth's Alley Museum, which exhibits period furnishings.

Finally, visit the Germantown district, north of city center, where you'll find the **Stenton Museum** (Eighteenth Street, between Courtland Street and Windrim Avenue) and one of the Conestoga wagons that used to roll along the Great Wagon Road. The nearby **Cliveden House** (6401 Germantown Avenue) harbored British forces in 1777, during the Battle of Germantown, Washington's last conflict before wintering at Valley Forge. Many of the home's original furnishings are still there to be appreciated.

DOWN THE ROAD

Drive eighteen miles west of downtown Philadelphia, along Lancaster Pike, to reach **Valley Forge National Historical Park.** It was to this area that Washington brought his Continental army during the brutal winter of 1777–78. The general had intended to reorganize his forces here; instead, he spent much of his time just trying to put food in front of his ten thousand men, approximately one-quarter of whom died during those bitter months. Today, you can view films about camp life, watch costumed reenactments of training maneuvers, and tour Washington's Headquarters.

In the town of **Kennett Square,** Pennsylvania, walk through the picturesque **Longwood Gardens** (three miles northeast of town on U.S. 1). But of greater historical import is **Longwood Quaker Meeting House,** a quaint structure that stands just outside the garden's trail. Here, nineteenth-century Quakers devoted to the cause of abolitionism plotted to help Southern slaves flee north via the Underground Railroad. The nearby **Longwood Cemetery** pays silent tribute to their efforts.

Enter the heart of Pennsylvania Dutch country at **Lancaster,** where the **Amish Farm and House** (2395 Lincoln Highway East) gives visitors a taste of this old Germanic culture through lectures and tours of nineteenth-century buildings. The town's central market is staffed by Amish, who tend to their produce in much the same way as did their ancestors.

York, which served as the nation's capital during British occupation of Philadelphia, is less than an hour's drive west of Lancaster. At the **Historical Society of York County** (250 East Market Street), visit landmarks that help illuminate York's history, including the **General Gates House,** the **Golden Plough Tavern,** and the **Bobb Log House.** It was in York where America's Articles of Confederation were adopted in 1781 (only to be replaced by the Constitution in 1789). The **York County Colonial Court House** (West Market Street and Pershing Avenue) has an audio-visual presentation on the subject, as well as the original printer's copy of the Articles. Quaker assemblies still gather at York's **Friends Meeting House** (135 West Philadelphia Street), which dates from 1766.

More than sixteen hundred monuments commemorate the 1863 Battle of Gettysburg at the fifty-seven-hundred-acre **Gettysburg National Military Park.** Inside the visitor center you will find the **Museum of the Civil War,** featuring one of the world's largest collections of Gettysburg relics, as well as the Electric Map, an intriguing orientation to the battle. At the nearby **Cyclorama Center,** a 360-foot circular painting (completed in 1884) depicts Pickett's Charge, the battle's climactic clash. The **Soldiers' National Cemetery** holds more than thirty-five hundred graves from Civil War times, and was where Abraham Lincoln delivered his Gettysburg Address.

Since the Underground Railroad once followed portions of the Great Wagon Road, **Harpers Ferry,** in West Virginia, is an essential stop on any tour of this historic route. The town has been restored to its nineteenth-century form at the **Harpers Ferry National Historic Park** (on U.S. 340 at the confluence of the Potomac and Shenandoah Rivers). Sites include the reconstructed **John Brown's Fort,** located on Arsenal Square, near where the abolitionist made his last stand against federal troops in 1859, and the **John Brown Museum** (on Shenandoah Street), which devotes a film to Brown's life and his cause.

To better acquaint yourself with life and lore along the Great Wagon Road, contact Philadelphia's Independence National Historical Park, 215-597-8974; the Gettysburg National Military Park, 717-334-1124; and the Harpers Ferry National Historic Park, 304-535-6298. —*Ellen L. Boyer*

The
Wilderness Road

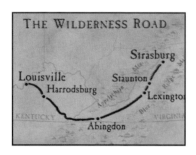

THE WILDERNESS ROAD

Strasburg

Louisville   Staunton
  Harrodsburg   Lexingto

KENTUCKY   VIRGINIA
        Abingdon

ARLY IN THE SUMMER of 1769, a hunting party of six white men, accompanied by ten or fifteen heavily laden packhorses, forded the Holston River in what would one day be the northeast corner of Tennessee. From there, they trekked west through laurel thickets and chestnut tree stands, catching and skinning what game they could find, until they reached a Native American trail known as the Great Warpath, an age-old route on the east flank of the Appalachian Mountains that linked the confederated Iroquois tribes of western New York with the Cherokee in the South. This trail, the hunters knew, led toward a defile in the Cumberland Mountains, part of the Appalachians, by which they intended to enter the untamed territory of Kentucky. Nothing about the men seemed to distinguish them from so many others who roamed the borderlands of colonial America. They hailed from settlements along the upper end of North Carolina's Yadkin River. Each carried a flintlock rifle, powder horn, bullet pouch, and hunting knife. Provisions for a long adventure were secured atop their horses, leaving the hunters free to defend themselves against Indian attacks. Each man boasted some wilderness experience. However, only one was a true

Building on animal trails and well-worn Native American paths, Daniel Boone, the eighteenth century's archetypal backwoodsman, helped blaze the first important road west for early settlers.

Daniel Boone and his five companions got their first look at Kentucky after breaching the Cumberland Gap in 1769. More recently, Tom Bodett got a view of Virginia's Shenandoah Valley.

woodsman, bold enough to tackle the frontier and skilled enough to weather its hazards unscathed—and unscalped.

His name? Daniel Boone.

Then thirty-five years old, Boone literally had been talked into leading this expedition by John Findley, a loquacious Irish trader with whom he had soldiered in 1755 as part of a British-led force organized during the French and Indian War to push French

> "[DANIEL] BOONE, the typical frontiersman, embodied in his own person the spirit of loneliness and restlessness which marked the first venturers into the wilderness."
>
> —THEODORE ROOSEVELT,
> *The Winning of the West*

troops out of western Pennsylvania. During lulls in that campaign— which culminated in the bloody Battle of the Monongahela—Findley had excited Boone's imagination with tales of a paradise called *Kanta- ke* (an Iroquois term denoting meadows or fields). Fourteen years later, while he was peddling household wares in North Carolina, Findley came upon Boone's cabin on the Yadkin and resumed his hyperboliz- ing where he had left off. By this point, though, he could add consid- erably to his depictions of Kentucky, having spent more than a little time there—part of it as a captive of the Shawnee Indians. As Boone listened, his blue-gray eyes wide with interest, the Irishman limned a land rugged but exquisite in terrain, with an abundance of bear, buf- falo, and deer. The more Findley spoke, the more Boone was con- vinced that he should initiate a hunt into Kentucky, with Findley serving as guide.

The hunt would also allow Boone to explore farther west, as he had been eager to do for some time. His previous foray over the Appalachians, during the fall and winter of 1767–68, had been spoiled by inclement weather. A second try was definitely in order.

So it was, as summer splashed across eastern Tennessee, that Boone, his brother-in-law John Stewart, Findley, and a trio of camp helpers approached a **V**-shaped notch high in the Appalachians that was soon to be famous around the world: Cumberland Gap. About 500 feet deep, flanked by a sheer rock face on the north and a smaller stone knob on the south, the Gap was so narrow in places that it barely allowed room for an old Native American pathway, which stretched toward Kentucky and beyond.

Thanks in large part to Boone's efforts, this mountain pass—located near where the borders of Tennessee, Kentucky, and Virginia now meet—would serve in the late eighteenth century as the principal gateway to the West. Perhaps as many as three hundred thousand pioneers would funnel through the Gap before easier routes opened in the north.

Yet the Gap was merely the most memorable feature along the Wilderness Road, the storied course that helped spread American colonization beyond the Appalachians. This road carved a broad arc, nearly a thousand miles long. Its eastern portion substantially followed the Great Warpath, beginning at the Potomac River town of Watkins Ferry (near Martinsburg, West Virginia, today), then swinging south between Virginia's Blue Ridge and Allegheny Mountains to the present site of Kingsport, Tennessee. The western arm of the Wilderness Road, and the portion most often associated with that name—and with Boone—led due west from Kingsport, through Cumberland Gap, and picked up a short stretch of another Native American trace (known as the Warriors' Path) before veering northwest to Hazel Patch, Kentucky. There, it split. Its eastern fork headed north to the Kentucky River site of Boonesborough, named in honor

The Roots of Bluegrass?

John Findley, the backcountry peddler who convinced Daniel Boone to set off on his 1769 hunt into Kentucky, has also been credited with introducing to the region its now famous bluegrass. The seeds of this grass—a native of England, where it's known as "timothy"—may have been transported within the English hay Findley used to pack his trade goods at Lancaster, Pennsylvania. "[When he threw] the packing aside after reaching his destination, the seed sprouted and grew," John Mack Faragher conjectures in *Daniel Boone: The Life and Legend of an American Pioneer.* "Other traders surely did the same. The action of buffalo, deer, and other grazing animals then spread the seed to other clearings and licks."

of its founder; the more-traveled west fork meandered through Kentucky to the Falls of the Ohio, where the city of Louisville would grow.

"To sketch the annals of the Wilderness Road," remarked Tennessee historian Robert L. Kincaid, "is to portray an epochal migration. It may be called the grandfather of the roads which connected the East with the West."

Certainly no other trail could claim to have better spurred the early development of Kentucky and the Ohio River valley. But the route's importance didn't end then. During the Civil War, Union and Confederate troops traveled its length, facing each other in battles all over western Virginia. And by the close of the nineteenth century, entrepreneurs were building industrial and commercial centers along it, confident that they would someday be the pride of the South.

BEATEN PATHS

ENTURIES BEFORE CHRISTOPHER Columbus stumbled onto the New World, Native Americans had carved an intricate network of paths up and down what is now the eastern United States. These trails carried hunters searching for food, traders on missions of commerce, and warriors bent on conquest or retribution. As Europeans delved deeper into the American countryside, they came upon these roads and made them their own.

In the fall of 1671, a small force, under the command of Virginia colonists Thomas Batts and Robert Fallam, was sent west from Virginia's Fort Henry. Its charge: to find "the ebbing and flowing of the Waters on the other side of the Mountains," with the expectation that any rivers would facilitate trade throughout the continental interior. Batts and Fallam made it as far as the valley of the Ohio. More important, they found the Great Warpath, which would prove a boon to travel along the eastern side of the Appalachians.

Almost three years later, Gabriel Arthur became the first white man, reportedly, to tread the length of Cumberland Gap. Arthur had been dispatched from Fort Henry in May 1673 as part of a

When early pioneers traveled the Wilderness Road, it was barely more than a footpath through the forest in many spots. Like the Native American Great Warpath, part of it followed Virginia's Blue Ridge Mountains.

scouting group led by South Carolina planter James Needham. The contingent also included eight Appomatoc natives as hunters and guides. Early in the trek, they were fortunate to meet a friendly company of Tomahitan (Cherokee), who ushered them over the Great Smoky Mountains and on to the Cherokee capital of Chota, in eastern Tennessee. Sadly, Needham would get no further. After reporting back in person to his superiors at Fort Henry, the planter was returning to Chota when he and his primary guide, a choleric Appomatoc called, variously, Indian John or Hasecoll, fell to quarreling. Growing irate, Hasecoll suddenly grabbed a gun and shot Needham to death. Then—in a scene that must have left all who witnessed it with a lifetime of nightmares—he ripped out Needham's heart, shook it defiantly at the eastern horizon, and declared his hatred of Englishmen.

When word of this got back to Chota, Arthur, having stayed behind, was almost burned at the stake in a sympathetic act of rebellion. But he survived, thanks to the intervention of a Tomahitan chief, and became something of an adopted member of the tribe. Arthur was later led to Ohio on a war expedition, only to be taken prisoner by the Shawnee, who released him on the condition that he help them establish trade with the English. That agreed, they pointed Arthur to a trail they called Athawominee—the "Path of the Armed Ones," or Warriors' Path—which they said would take him home. Arthur followed this track south along the western edge of the Appalachians and, just as he had been assured, arrived in East Tennessee by way of a cleft in the Cumberland Mountains. By June 1674, he had made his way safely back to Fort Henry, with reports of his travels.

Arthur's superiors quickly understood the commercial value

> "STAND AT CUMBERLAND GAP and watch the procession of civilization, marching single file—the buffalo following the trail to the salt springs, the Indian, the fur-trader and hunter, the cattle raiser, the farmer—and the frontier has passed by."
>
> —FREDERICK JACKSON TURNER,
> *The Significance of the Frontier in American History*

of Cumberland Gap, as a conduit to Native Americans wanting weapons and blacksmith goods, even if they didn't yet comprehend the role it could play in moving settlers to the frontier. But at the time—and for the next century—moving either products or people west of the Appalachians was more easily theorized than realized.

GROUNDS FOR DISPUTE

FROM THE LATE SEVENTEENTH through much of the eighteenth century, Great Britain, France, and Spain constantly butted heads over control of North America. Britain figured it held the most solid claim, having stacked its colonies up and down the Atlantic seaboard. Since nobody then understood how wide North America was, the original charters of Massachussetts, Connecticut, Virginia, the two Carolinas, and Georgia all blithely granted them title to every square inch of dirt between the Atlantic and the Pacific. This rankled Spain, which had wrapped its tentacles around Florida and Mexico and was itching to expand its empire further. Following Francisco Vásquez de Coronado's explorations into the American Southwest (1540–42) and Juan Rodríguez Cabrillo's inspection of the California coast (1542), the Spanish Crown made clear its interest in all lands west of the Rocky Mountains, though it did little to exercise its hegemony there for the next two hundred years.

Meanwhile, France—which already dominated eastern Canada—sent adventurers Louis Jolliet and Jacques Marquette (in 1673) and René-Robert Cavelier, Sieur de La Salle (in 1682), to probe the vast region drained by the Mississippi River and its tributaries. Paris then declared its mastery over the whole Mississippi valley. French fur trappers swept in, and military outposts were erected to fend off rival claimants.

That none of this jockeying for position took into account the presence of Native Americans seemed only normal in that day and age. European powers simply assumed that the Indians' title to the land of their forefathers would ultimately be forfeit—if not with their cooperation, then by coercion. To stave off war, the natives struck treaty after treaty with the Europeans, ceding to colonists huge chunks of western land. Optimists hoped these concessions would keep the peace; but they served only to increase the Europeans' appetite for greater sway over the continent.

Among the English, that hunger reached fever pitch in 1749, after Pierre Joseph Celoron, Sieur de Blainville, departed Quebec to claim for France all lands as far south as New Orleans. Sensing violence in the wind, a leader of the Seneca—one of six powerful Indian nations democratically united under the Great Law of the Iroquois, or Haudenosaunee ("People of the Longhouse")—proposed that both the French and English withdraw from the hotly contested Ohio River valley, leaving the Iroquois to govern it as a buffer zone. Neither Paris nor London, however, seriously entertained that idea. Instead, they chose to prosecute what history now remembers as the French and Indian War (1754–63), which would incidentally help clear the way for westward expansion.

The war was a most unconventional conflict. Both sides engaged Indians as allies, for they were savvier than Europeans in matters of woodland combat. Colonial governments offered bounties to men who collected the scalps of enemy natives (fueling future arguments that whites were at least partly responsible for spreading the practice of scalping among indigenous peoples). Although it was fought on the Native American frontier, nobody believed the war was waged on the natives' behalf. Most of the Indians were struggling for their own independence as much as for any distant king. They raided white settlements with a vehemence fed by the fear that no matter which side prevailed, Native American cultures were threatened.

Sure enough, after the war ended and France was expelled (at least temporarily) from territories east of the Mississippi, British authorities sought to mollify the Indians by proclaiming that white settlement west of the Appalachians would be forbidden until Indians agreed to border adjustments. But this was nothing more than an expedient. The victorious English still openly coveted western lands, and with the war having fueled their anti-Indian sentiments, they would be even less willing than before to respect native rights there.

Land speculators and colonial officials of the mid-eighteenth century were already rather adept at violating those rights. Soldiers were

often paid with "land warrants" that permitted them to locate and register claims to contested frontier properties. After the French and
Indian War, Colonel George Washington convinced the beleaguered
colony of Virginia that it should pay its veterans' pensions with these
land warrants rather than with cash. Based on rank and term of service, each vet could expect between fifty and three thousand unbroken
acres in the west.

At the same time, investors organized land companies that surveyed and laid out backcountry tracts for prospective settlements, then
enticed enough people onto those tracts that they could make a case
for ownership. After all, went an oft-repeated assertion, the wilderness
was worthless until inhabited. Shouldn't those folks fearless or foolish
enough to tame it receive the land as reward for their risk?

It was an employee of one such land company, a former physician
from Virginia named Thomas Walker, who made the first fully
recorded discovery of Cumberland Gap during a survey mission in
1750. He dubbed it "Cave Gap," for a large cave that yawned in the
north face of the pass. Walker reserved the name Cumberland—after
the duke of Cumberland, then a hero because of his victory over
Scottish Jacobites—for a river he found immediately west of the Gap.
Later, hunters gave the same name to the mammoth pass and the
mountains that framed it.

BORN TO THE BACKWOODS

FOREMOST AMONG THOSE hunters stood Daniel Boone, a
man whose myth has, unfortunately, cast him as far shal-
lower and less interesting than he was in real life.

He was born in Exeter Township, near present-day
Reading, Pennsylvania, on October 22, 1734. His father, a weaver
named Squire Boone, had arrived in America from England twenty-
one years before, followed closely by most of the remainder of his
family. In 1720, Squire married a strong-willed woman, Sarah
Morgan, with whom he would produce eleven children.

As Daniel once recalled, he was just a boy when he acquired
a "love for the wilderness and hunter's life" that frequently led him

to neglect chores around the family farm. His father gave him his first "short rifle gun" when he was only twelve or thirteen, and within a couple of years Daniel had achieved a marksman's eye. Many an hour he spent shooting animals or birds for food, chatting up backwoodsmen, and meeting a polyglot mixture of Indian hunters. Perhaps it was those early encounters that led him to his unusual (for the time) lifelong tolerance of Native Americans. While tales suggest that he did in many an Indian, Boone himself claimed to have killed but three—and those in self-defense.

He grew comfortable with the solitude of the wilds and extraordinarily skilled at finding his way through their darkest reaches. (Asked in his senescence whether he had ever lost his way, Boone replied, "No, I can't say as ever I was lost, but I was bewildered once for three days.") Eventually, he would be recognized as a "long hunter," one of a limited breed of men who fancied spending years at a crack wandering the outback in pursuit of deer, the skins of which were in high demand.

In 1751, Boone moved with his family to the banks of the Upper Yadkin River, in the western part of North Carolina. As John Mack Faragher describes it in *Daniel Boone: The Life and Legend of an American Pioneer*, it was an ideal spot for the young hunter.

> Bears were so numerous, it was said, that a hunter could lay by two or three thousand pounds of bear bacon in a season. The tale was told . . . that nearby Bear Creek had taken its name from the season Boone killed ninety-nine bears along its waters. The deer were so plentiful that an ordinary hunter could kill four or five a day, and it was said that Boone and a companion took thirty between sunup and sundown near the head of the Yadkin.

Boone was attracted to more than animal tracks, though. Approaching his twentieth birthday, he had nearly reached his full measure, a powerful gent with broad shoulders and thick legs. At about five feet eight inches tall and 175 pounds in weight, he might not have been as imposing as Fess Parker, the actor who portrayed him in a popular television series, but Boone was nonetheless considered handsome. He had prominent cheekbones, dark hair that he plaited with bear grease in Indian fashion, and pale, penetrating eyes that gazed out from beneath the brim of a smart beaver-skin hat he wore. (Contrary to some depictions of him in a fur cap, "Boone always despised them and kept his hat," according to Faragher.) Women noticed him—one in particular, the tall, buxom, raven-tressed Rebecca Bryan, whose Welsh Quaker clan lived not far from the Boones. The pair became aware of each other in 1753, when Rebecca was fifteen. They wed three years later, after Daniel's militia service at the Battle of the Monongahela.

Being Boone's wife was not easy. Over the first twenty-five years of marriage, Rebecca delivered ten children—six sons and four daughters—several of whom would perish in advance of their parents. Living on the Yadkin, she had to put up with highwaymen and assorted other outlaws, the recurring threat of Indian assaults, and the very real chance that her husband wouldn't return from one of his adventures. (Folklore has it that in the early 1760s, after Boone had been absent on a hunt for two years, Rebecca was actually convinced that he had met his maker. Grief-stricken and lonely, she had an affair with one of Boone's brothers, producing a daughter she named Jemima—whom she was suckling when Boone returned! Boone's reaction suggests a frontier morality somewhat more pragmatic than our own. "So much the better," he is supposed to have said. "It's all in the family.")

> ASKED LATE IN LIFE whether he had ever lost his way, Daniel Boone quipped, "No, I can't say as ever I was lost, but I was bewildered once for three days."

A RESTLESS SPIRIT

REBECCA'S CONCERN FOR HER plight can only have grown throughout her life with Daniel: with each passing season, Boone talked more enthusiastically about pioneering some place even more remote than North Carolina.

By the mid-1760s, new residents were streaming down the

eastern arm of the Wilderness Road—the former Great Warpath—
swelling the population of the Upper Yadkin to four times what it had
been fifteen years before. Daniel was feeling downright crowded.
("Boone used to say to me," a Carolina resident once boasted, "that
when he could not fall the top of a tree near enough his door for fire-
wood, it was time to move to a new place.") Boone also complained
that local game was running thin, making it difficult for him to meet
his financial obligations. Following his father's death in 1765, responsibility for the welfare of the extended Boone family had fallen to him,
and he had given intense thought to where he might relocate at least
his generation of the clan. Florida, a British possession since the
French and Indian War, seemed to offer opportunities. However, one
visit there persuaded him that the only successful hunting was being
done by the clouds of insects infesting the swamps.

It was in this restive state that Boone's old war buddy, John
Findley, found him in the winter of 1768–69. No wonder the Irishman
had little trouble talking Boone into a Kentucky hunt. They left the
Yadkin in the following May and were gone two years, crossing
Cumberland Gap, hiking up the Warriors' Path, and generally marveling at what the country offered. The expedition wasn't profitable; the Shawnee caught and

> THE HIDE OF A DOE fetched fifty
> cents or more, while a buck's skin
> was worth no less than a dollar,
> inspiring the term *buck* as slang for
> American currency.

stripped Boone of every single fur he had collected. They may also
have killed John Stewart, his companion and brother-in-law. But
Boone's opinion of the place suffered little as a consequence.
Describing this expedition to John Filson (author of the biography
that first made the backwoodsman a mythic figure), Boone remembered that "we found everywhere abundance of wild beasts of all sorts,
through this vast forest. The buffaloes were more frequent than I had
seen cattle in the settlements, browsing on the leaves of the cane, or
cropping the herbage on those extensive plains, fearless, because igno-
rant, of the violence of man."

Even before he left Kentucky, Boone was hankering to go back.
("I returned home to my family," he recalled many years afterwards,

Natural Bridge, south of Lexington, Virginia: Backwoodsmen once crossed it on foot, and its beauty so awed Thomas Jefferson that he privately purchased the land from the British in 1774.

"with a determination to bring them as soon as possible to live in Kentucke, which I esteemed a second paradise, at the risk of my life and fortune.") He didn't wait long to satisfy this dream. In 1773, he convinced Rebecca and several families of their acquaintance to pull up stakes and follow him across the Appalachians. They went without government sanction and despite warnings of violence from both the Cherokee and Shawnee. The result: Boone's oldest son, James, and several other boys of the party were captured, tortured, and killed by Indians, convincing the emigrants to retreat east of Cumberland Gap until safer entry into the territory could be assured.

Not until 1775 could Boone begin to make that possible.

Just the year before, Lord John Dunmore, the last royal governor of Virginia, had sent militiamen into Ohio country to provoke a war with the Shawnee, Ottawa, and other tribes. Defeated, the natives finally ceded to colonists hunting rights in Kentucky and unhindered access to the Ohio River. Hoping to capitalize on this easing of tensions, a land-speculation partnership called the Transylvania Company negotiated a treaty with the Cherokee in March 1775. In exchange for £10,000 worth of trade goods, this agreement gave the company ownership of about two-thirds of Kentucky and a giant swath of Tennessee.

The legalities here were disputable, since England still forbade colonization west of the Appalachians and the claim on Kentucky wasn't exclusive to the Cherokee. Yet the head of the Transylvania Company, a retired North Carolina judge named Richard Henderson, was satisfied enough that he hired Boone and thirty axmen to hack a trail over Cumberland Gap and on to the Kentucky River.

That path would become the western arm of the Wilderness Road.

THE UNSTOPPABLE CURRENT

IN BOONE'S CONTINUOUS PUSH toward the west, there could be seen a·certain fatalism. Even he once remarked upon it: "Sometimes I feel like a leaf carried on a stream. It may whirl about and turn and twist, but it is always carried forward." After his demise in 1820, others would loudly sing his praises—the poet Lord Byron in an unfinished epic released across

America in 1822; James Fenimore Cooper in his Natty Bumppo tales (including *The Last of the Mohicans*, 1826), so obviously inspired by Boone's adventures. But Boone cast himself as less the hero than "an instrument ordained to settle the wilderness." He was just there to give folks what they wanted—passage to the wide-open spaces.

There wasn't a whole lot to "Boone's Trace," as his passage into Kentucky was originally known. It joined sections of the moccasin-groomed Warriors' Path with minor trails tramped down by countless buffalo and new stretches carved out of heavy canebrake. Not until twenty years after it was started was the road smooth enough and sufficiently wide to accommodate decent-sized wagons. Yet shortly after Boone and his trailblazers finished their work, a report to Lord Dunmore stated that "at least five hundred people

The Long Hunter

Foraging for game "by himself, so the tales suggested, was the way [Daniel] Boone preferred it. He might spend several weeks hunting and trapping with no companions save his dog and horse. He could construct a little 'half-faced camp,' a three-sided shanty covered with brush, the open end facing the fire, and there he would take his evening meals. . . . In the nineteenth century his love of isolation was criticized by many as an indication of an antisocial nature, and Boone's family responded defensively. 'His wanderings were from duty,' declared one niece, arguing that 'no man loved society better, nor was more ardently attached to his family.'

Yet Boone actually relished these opportunities to be alone. . . . He frequently carried along a copy of the Bible, or a book of history, which he loved, or *Gulliver's Travels*, his favorite book, to read by the light of the campfire. Then, leaving the fire burning, he would bed down on a cushion of hemlock or dried leaves, head to the backlog, feet to the fire to prevent the rheumatism that was the constant complaint of old hunters, moccasins tied to his gun, standing primed and ready should Indians or outlaws attack."

(John Mack Faragher, *Daniel Boone: The Life and Legend of an American Pioneer*, 1992)

are preparing to go out [to Kentucky] this Spring from Carolina besides Numbers from Virga. to Settle there."

By 1800, after the United States was free of Britain's grip and Kentucky had won admission as the new country's fifteenth state—

The Trials of Daniel Boone

Of the great names which in our
  faces stare,
The General Boon, backwoodsman
  of Kentucky,
Was happiest amongst mortals
  anywhere;
For killing nothing but a bear or
  buck, he
Enjoyed the lonely, vigorous,
  harmless days
Of his old age in wilds of deepest
  maze.

When Lord Byron penned those elegaic lines in his 1820s poem *Don Juan*, he had never even met Daniel Boone. He was simply using him as a literary contrast with more warlike breakers of the American frontier. He didn't know—or didn't care—that, far from living in peace and plenty, Boone was actually spending his old age in pain and sadness.

No sooner had Boone moved his family to Boonesborough in the fall of 1775 than his mettle was sorely tested. Shawnee Indians kidnapped his daughter Jemima and two of her girlfriends, and Boone had to engineer a rescue. Three years later, he himself was kidnapped by the Shawnee and escaped only after negotiating a false surrender of the fort at Boonesborough. Though Boone sought over and again to explain his tactic, many of his contemporaries never forgave him for what they considered a cowardly act or feared was a collaboration with the British to drive American settlers out of the West. Over the next dozen or so years, Boone relocated his family several times around Kentucky and present-day West Virginia; was robbed of funds entrusted to him by investors planning to buy land warrants in Virginia; lost a brother and a son to Indian battles; was captured briefly by British forces during the Revolutionary War; lost money in various land-speculation and trading ventures, then lost still more in a scheme to supply militia companies in western Virginia; and finally went back to full-time hunting.

By the late 1790s, John Filson, a former Pennsylvania schoolteacher, had published his book the first west of the Alleghenies—tens of thousands of pioneers a year were wearing ruts in the Wilderness Road.

They were a hardy bunch—Germans, Englishmen, and Scottish-Irish immigrants whose predecessors had landed in North

The Discovery, Settlement, and Present State of Kentucke . . . Containing the Adventures of Col. Daniel Boon (1784), which spread Boone's renown worldwide, and Kentucky had named one of its counties in honor of the old woodsman. But such accolades wouldn't put food on Boone's table, wipe out old debts, or soothe the rheumatic disorders—caused by his years of tromping through woods in damp moccasins—that now stiffened his joints. So in 1799, his lands in Kentucky gone and many of his early dreams vanished with them, Boone accepted an invitation from the Spanish governor of Missouri country to take possession of a large tract of bottomland on the north bank of the Missouri River, just west of Saint Louis.

Unfortunately, President Thomas Jefferson's 1803 acquisition of the Louisiana Territory—more than eight hundred thousand square miles between the Mississippi and the Rocky Mountains—threw Boone's Missouri claims into dispute.

Only an act of Congress in 1814, a year after his wife, Rebecca, died, prevented Boone and his kin from losing their land. The decision, a congressional committee report of the time made clear, was a compassionate one, recognizing Boone as "an aged, infirm, and worn-out man, whose best days have been usefully devoted to the settlement and prosperity of the Western Country, and whose only remaining earthly hope is that the benevolent interposition of the national Legislature in his behalf may, in his extreme old age, gladden his drooping heart, and raise him from poverty and distress."

In 1817, after making his last long hunt along the Missouri River, Daniel Boone fell ill. He died in 1820, a month shy of his eighty-sixth birthday, and was buried next to Rebecca on his daughter Jemima's farm in Charette, Missouri. In 1845, the pair who had moved so often in life were moved in death—to a cemetery in the Kentucky capital of Frankfort.

America a century before; meditative Quakers, long-bearded Dunkers, and celibate Shakers who, in 1805, commmenced building the village of Pleasant Hill in central Kentucky. These early migrants were lucky to make ten miles a day down Virginia's segment of the Wilderness Road, then they crawled northwest to Boonesborough or farther west to Harrodsburg, Louisville, and other towns being established closer to the Ohio River.

In their wake came enterprising merchants, wanting to sell them ammunition, hardware, or overnight lodgings. Horse breeders and buyers were soon to follow, attracted by an early bit of Kentucky legislation (introduced by Daniel Boone) that encouraged horse breeding in the territory. Criminals, too, inevitably worked their way down the road. A pair of the most infamous were the Harpe brothers—Micajah ("Big Harpe") and Wiley ("Little Harpe")—whose murderous depredations on this route in the 1790s ended only after Big Harpe was shot and beheaded, his skull then mounted on a sapling in Hopkins County at a lonely spot still called Harpe's Head. The first steamboat pushed into Louisville in 1811, frightening residents, who believed it was a sea monster.

> "TO SKETCH THE annals of the Wilderness Road is to portray an epochal migration. It may be called the grandfather of the roads which connected the East with the West."
>
> —ROBERT L. KINCAID,
> *The Wilderness Road*

Communities along the Wilderness Road grew in the first half of the nineteenth century. Improvements to the route eased the lives of its frequent travelers. And President Andrew Jackson's Indian Removal Act, passed in 1830, drove Native Americans—considered a perpetual menace to white habitation—from their homelands in the South. Though the U.S. Supreme Court tried to halt it, the Cherokee, Shawnee, and others were forced over the "Trail of Tears" to relocate in Kansas and the Indian Territory (Oklahoma).

Increased river traffic and the construction of the National Road across Ohio and Indiana diminished the importance of the Wilderness Road, and it took the Civil War to put it back in the public spotlight. The competing forces of Abraham Lincoln and

Belle Grove Plantation served as the headquarters of Union General Philip Sheridan during the Battle of Cedar Creek. Louisville, Kentucky, close by the Falls of the Ohio River, marked the western reaches of the Wilderness Road.

Jefferson Davis marched up and down the route, doing battle at places such as Cedar Creek, in Virginia's Shenandoah Valley, where Confederate General Jubal Early won a surprise attack against Union troops in September 1864, only to have his forces crushed in a counterassault engineered by General Philip Sheridan.

Both the Union and the Confederacy feared that Cumberland Gap could be used as the doorway for armies bound north or south, so they struggled to control it. The Gap changed hands four times during the war. General Ulysses S. Grant, riding the Wilderness Road to Lexington, Kentucky, in 1864, was so impressed by the Gap's strategic possibilities that he told companions, "With two brigades of the Army of the Cumberland I could hold that pass against the army which Napoléon led to Moscow."

The Promised Land

Moses Austin, a Missouri mine owner (and father of future Texas Pioneer Stephen F. Austin), traveled west along the Wilderness Road in 1796. He was astonished by both the volume of traffic on the route and the faith of the families—many of them clad in rags unequal to the task of keeping out the winter chill—that better lives inevitably awaited them in Kentucky. He wrote in his journal:

Ask these Pilgrims what they expect when they git to Kentuckey and the Answer is Land. have you any. No, but I expect to git it. have you any thing to pay for land, No. did you Ever see the Country. No but Every Body says its good land. can any thing be more Absurd than the Conduct of man, here is hundreds Travelling hundreds of Miles, they Know not for what Nor Whither, except its to Kentucky, passing land almost as good and easy obtain.d, the Proprietors of which would gladly give on any terms, but it will not do its not Kentuckey, its not the Promis.d land, . . . and when arriv.d at this Heaven in Idea what do they find? a goodly land I will allow but to them forbiden Land. exhausted and worn down with distress and disappointment they are at last Oblig.d to become hewers of wood and Drawers of water.

Two decades later, a different sort of conqueror moved in on the Gap: Alexander Alan Arthur, a distant Scottish relative of President Chester Alan Arthur and a visionary who saw in the Cumberlands the germ of a commercial empire. Well connected with monied interests in Great Britain, he set about drumming up funds for development of major industries in the area. He spoke persuasively of mining coal and iron ore from the surrounding mountains, of cutting timber and selling it at an impressive profit, and even of constructing a new town adjacent to the Gap—"Middlesborough" (or Middlesboro, as it is spelled today). Before the economic depression in the mid-1890s strangled off his European financing and sent his plants and factories into a slow paralysis, Arthur had laid train lines, erected residential centers, and found investors enough to put up a seven-hundred-room resort hotel and spa that he believed would attract another flood of travelers down the Wilderness Road.

Much has changed since that era. Daniel Boone, as depicted in classrooms today, seems tediously heroic, bereft of the weaknesses and desires that would give flesh to his legend; more often than not he is confused with the later Indian fighter Davy Crockett, who did affect a coonskin cap. Most of the Wilderness Road now lies buried beneath broad highways. Only the occasional driver who is patient enough to stop and read historical markers gleans any sense of the triumphs or the tragedies that made the original road to the West such a prize.

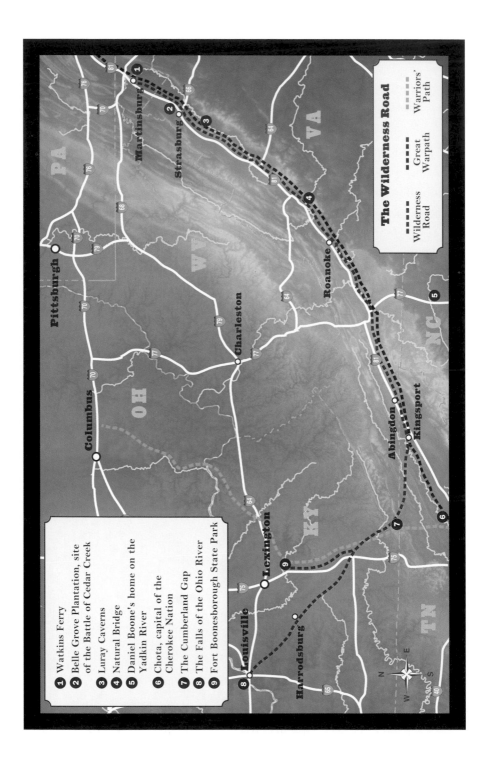

The Wilderness Road

Wilderness Road
Great Warpath
Warriors' Path

1 Watkins Ferry
2 Belle Grove Plantation, site
  of the Battle of Cedar Creek
3 Luray Caverns
4 Natural Bridge
5 Daniel Boone's home on the
  Yadkin River
6 Chota, capital of the
  Cherokee Nation
7 The Cumberland Gap
8 The Falls of the Ohio River
9 Fort Boonesborough State Park

The Wilderness Road Today

Three hundred years of frontier heritage unfold along the five-hundred-mile Wilderness Road. Where once there were forest paths, today asphalt pavement and historical markers trace much of the way. Follow Interstate 81 south through western Virginia, then head west from Abingdon along U.S. Route 58 to the Cumberland Gap. In Kentucky, sites along the old trail are accessible from U.S. Route 25 and Interstate 75.

VIRGINIA

The Old Dominion's western extreme abounds in early Americana. Start in Middletown, at the north end of the Shenandoah Valley, where you'll find **Belle Grove Plantation.** Built in 1794, this mansion displays period artifacts and shows Thomas Jefferson's architectural influence in its Palladian-style windows and columns. It was near Belle Grove that Union army troops defeated Confederate forces in the Battle of Cedar Creek (1864). Ten minutes south is **Strasburg,** known for its legion of antiques stores. Founded by Germans in 1740, Strasburg's proximity to the Valley Pike and Manassas Gap railroad made it a strategic prize during the Civil War. Drop into the **Strasburg Museum** (on King Street) to learn about the area's growth, or follow a self-guided tour between local landmarks. Still farther south, in the town of Luray, are the impressive **Luray Caverns,** discovered in 1878 and featuring an organ that uses the stalactites as sound resonators.

The college town of **Staunton** is the birthplace of Woodrow Wilson, twenty-eighth president of the United States. It's also home to the excellent **Museum of American Frontier Culture,** which includes on its property four working farmsteads from the eighteenth and nineteenth centuries; employees tend to chores as frontier Shenandoah Valley residents once would have. An even more photogenic place is **Lexington** (twenty miles south of Staunton), site of **Washington and Lee University,** founded in 1749. On its grounds sits the **Lee Chapel and Museum,** final resting place of Confederate General Robert E. Lee. (The remains of Lee's beloved horse, Traveller, are buried just outside.) Not far away, the **Stonewall Jackson House** (8 East Washington Street) keeps alive the memory of that ill-fated Confederate commander (he died after being mistakenly shot by his own men during the Battle of Chancellorsville). Fourteen miles south of Lexington looms the **Natural Bridge,** a stone splendor once traveled by pioneers, now crossed by U.S. Route 11. This natural span so struck Jefferson that he purchased it from the British in 1774. If you scrutinize the stone, you can see where George Washington once inscribed his initials.

A final stop on Virginia's portion of the trail—and a refueling point for Daniel Boone and other early travelers—is **Abingdon,** where a self-guided walking tour will weave you past historical homes, craft shops, and the renowned and still very active **Barter Theatre** (279 Barter Drive), founded in 1933.

KENTUCKY

U.S. Route 58 West leaves Abingdon and enters Kentucky at the **Cumberland Gap,** through which snaked Boone's famous path. Visitors to the national historical park that now encompasses the mountain pass can camp, attend living-history demonstrations, and hike on an original fragment of the Wilderness Road. In the park's southeast corner, and accessible via one of the park's tours, is **Middlesboro,** once a bustling trading center, now a leading producer of coal.

Head west to I-75 and then north about sixty-five miles to **Fort Boonesborough State Park.** Founded in 1775 and once a promising outpost—the first of several Southern settlements named in honor of Kentucky's best-known woodsman—Fort Boonesborough went on to suffer from various Indian attacks and was eventually abandoned. In 1974 the fort was reconstructed and today stages demonstrations of pioneer crafts making. To see an even older (and more successful) habitation, make a southwest loop on state Route 152 about thirty miles to **Harrodsburg,** founded in 1774. A replica of the stockade around which this town developed is now busy with docents interpreting regional history. Just to the northeast is the **Shaker Village of Pleasant Hill** (3501 Lexington Road). Founded in 1805, this was once the third-largest Shaker community in America, but its decline began before the Civil War, as members died out without new ones to replace them. By the twentieth century, the Shakers were gone, but their village has been handsomely restored.

Louisville, some fifty miles northwest of Harrodsburg, was the goal of many a hiker over the Wilderness Road. Established on the Ohio River in 1778, the city has since become associated with whiskey factories, the famous Louisville Slugger baseball bat (made here since 1884), and, of course, the **Kentucky Derby,** a mile-and-a-quarter horse race that—except for during a World War II ban—has been run every year since 1875.

For more information about Virginia sites along the road, contact Shenandoah Valley, 540-999-3500; or the Lexington Visitor Center, 540-463-3777. In Kentucky, call the Cumberland Gap National Historic Park, 606-248-2817; and the Daniel Boone National Forest, 606-745-3100. —*Ellen L. Boyer*

The River Road

RIVER ROAD
Natchez
Woodville
Oakley Plantation
LOUISIANA
MISS.
Destrehan
New Orleans

STEAMBOATS—THOSE LONG, narrow, multidecked side- or sternwheelers that Mark Twain likened to "wedding cake[s] without the complications"—dominate our image of the Mississippi River in the nineteenth century. However, long before such smoke-belching behemoths arrived on the scene, North America's greatest waterway was thick with boats of a smaller, though hardly less colorful, stripe, piloted by men whose ferocity and rambunctiousness would become legendary.

Established by hell-raising Mississippi boatmen, this pathway helps preserve memories of a time when New Orleans was clinging to its French heritage.

Some of the early boatmen were from Daniel Boone country, Kentucky. Others hailed from elsewhere in the valleys of the Ohio or Mississippi Rivers. But the residents of towns on the lower Mississippi referred to them all—with no minor measure of revulsion—as "Kaintucks." Tradesmen, they were, ferrying furs, livestock, and farm produce from way up north to the great port of New Orleans, the "Crescent City," where the cargo could be sold or else hefted aboard sailing ships bound for Europe or South America. Taking the same products overland would have been cost-prohibitive and far more time-consuming.

The only problem was, after they had ridden down the Mississippi to New Orleans, most of these boats had no means to get back upriver. They had no engines of any kind and were far too

As the refined folks of New Orleans discovered, the boatmen who floated goods down the Mississippi—and then had to make their way back upriver on foot—were a lusty, raucous bunch.

heavy for men to pole or pull against the current. So, once emptied of cargo, the wooden vessels were scrapped for building materials. (A number of New Orleans's most historic structures still contain the planking that once served in boat hulls.)

And what of their crews? Well, they might stay in La Nouvelle Orleans, as the port city's French founders had called it, partaking of the romantic gumbo of high-life and low-life that distinguished Louisiana's capital from the continent's more pretentious or prudish cities. Or, they could walk home, up winding pathways—known collectively as the River Road—that paralleled the Mississippi and eventually intersected two hundred miles upriver with a notorious robbers' route that came to be called the Natchez Trace.

A MOSQUITO FLEET

IN THE SEVENTEENTH-CENTURY, French explorers observed Native Americans plying the waters of the Mississippi River in a light, shallow-draft sort of dugout canoe made of cypress, which the outsiders dubbed a "pirogue" (pronounced *pee-roh*). As France began to establish its authority over the Mississippi region—first by franchise with a conniving investment company (masterminded by Scottish financier John Law) and then through the crown's governance—its representatives in the New World adapted the canoe design to their own uses, creating much bigger dugouts or piroguelike craft shaped of cypress planks.

Boats had to grow still larger and more efficient, however, as settlements along the Mississippi increased in number and size. American immigrants had been moving beyond the Appalachian Mountains for years before the Revolutionary War. But after peace between the new United States and Great Britain was restored, the pace of westward migration picked up substantially. In the 1770s, there were approximately twelve thousand settlers in the territories of Ohio, Kentucky, Tennessee, and Mississippi. By 1800, the count had risen to almost four hundred thousand, and a census for 1820 shows the population of that area at more than a million and a half—quite enough to attract entrepreneurs interested in building up trade between the agrarian north and the merchants of Dixie.

At least a dozen types of boats transported goods south along the Ohio and Mississippi Rivers, each one more outlandish-looking than the last. The flatboats, however, predominated. These flat-bottomed, rectangular craft—basically floating boxes—were sometimes

Look Away, Dixieland

As with many historical nicknames, there seems to be more than one source for the term *Dixie*. Some authorities claim it derives from the Mason-Dixon Line, a state boundary shared by Pennsylvania and Maryland. Established in the 1760s by British surveyors Charles Mason and Jeremiah Dixon to settle old border disputes once and for all, the Mason-Dixon Line has since become the symbolic border between the American North and South.

But in his wonderful book *The French Quarter: An Informal History of the New Orleans Underworld,* Herbert Asbury offers another genesis. Asbury recalls that when the hell-raising flatboatmen of the nineteenth century spoke of "Dixie," it was in specific reference to New Orleans, not the South as a whole. He explained the nickname's roots thusly:

A few years after Louisiana became a part of the United States, at a time when the American monetary system was in a chaotic condition, one of the New Orleans banks began issuing ten-dollar notes, one side of which was printed in English and the other in French. On the latter, in large letters, was the French word for ten, *dix.* Since the proper pronunciation of French was not one of the accomplishments of the river men, one of these notes was known simply as a "dix"; collectively they were "dixies," a name that soon applied to the city of issue as well.

Use of the term spread after 1859, when Ohioan Dan Emmett (who also composed "Old Dan Tucker" and "Blue-Tail Fly") wrote his most famous song, "Dixie," originally titled "Dixieland." During the Civil War, the Confederacy adopted "Dixie" as its anthem (adding some Union verses that have since been forgotten). The tune's opening lines are still familiar worldwide:

I wish I was in the land of cotton;
  Old times there are not forgotten.
Look away, look away, look away,
  Dixieland.

Flatboats were the workhorses of the Mississippi.
The U.S. completed the Louisiana Purchase in the
Cabildo, which once housed the Spanish governing
body of New Orleans and the state supreme court.
St. Louis Cathedral and Jackson Square sit at the
heart of the Vieux Carré, the French Quarter.

huge, from fifty to more than one hundred feet long, and fifteen to twenty-five feet wide. They were constructed of heavy timbers and planks, with a cargo hold (about four feet high) wedged between the hull and deck. Most carried from thirty to one hundred tons of freight and crews of four to six men. Rude shelters on top allowed those hands to come in out of the rain, but there were only open pens for horses, sheep, hogs, and other livestock being taken to market. Using a tillerlike oar at the stern and two smaller oars, or "sweeps," on either side, men steered these vessels around rocks and pushed them clear of mudflats.

Only slightly less prevalent on the rivers were keelboats. Fourteen to eighteen feet wide, and ranging in length from forty to eighty feet, they were narrow in the beam, with pointed bows and sterns. (Much larger versions, called "packet boats," could also be spotted on the Ohio River.) A roof covered the greater part of the deck; a windlass—handy in yanking the boat off sandbars— was standard equipment at the prow; and sweeps at port and starboard might protrude a full twenty feet, requiring two men each as operators.

Keelboats could carry perhaps seventy tons of freight, at most. Yet they had a distinct advantage over bulkier flatboats, in that they were able to travel against the current. The four-inch keel-like timber that ran lengthwise along the bottom of its hull gave this craft its name and increased its maneuverability. Because keelboats sat higher in the water than flatboats, they could be pulled on towlines by crewmen who hiked onshore up the River Road to Baton Rouge, Louisiana, and then bushwhacked from there. If the riverbed was shallow and hard, the men could even pole the boat upstream. In *The French Quarter: An Informal History of the New Orleans Underworld*, author Herbert Asbury describes the choreography necessary to accomplish this task:

> For this work poles eighteen to twenty feet long were used, with a wooden crutch or knob on one end and an iron shoe on the other. Ten to twenty men on either side of the boat set the iron shoes against the bottom of the river, and the crutches or knobs against their shoulders, and walked toward the stern, thus

propelling the boat upstream. As each pair reached the stern, they ran back over the top of the cargo box to the bow, so that with a crew of twenty men there were always sixteen poling and four returning to the bow. The sweeps were usually employed only as a supplementary source of power, for it was almost impossible to find men strong enough to make much headway against the current with the sweeps alone.

To make fifteen miles a day using this method was considered positively herculean. As a result, while a trip downriver from Louisville, Kentucky, on the upper Ohio River, took about four weeks, poling a loaded keelboat north over the same course often required three to five months. No wonder many river traders of that time chose to ditch their rigs in Louisiana after a single use and hike home. The typical cost of a boat—$1 to $4 a foot—just wasn't enough to make it worth reusing the damn thing.

Trade on the Mississippi, in this era of man-powered boats, followed the rhythm of the river. Kaintucks would schedule their New Orleans voyages during the high-water seasons—November to January and March to May—when travel was easiest. But no matter when they departed, there were always dangers awaiting them. Some were environmental, such as rapids, boulders, and downed trees in midstream, their thick branches threatening to swat crewmen from the edges of boats. Or thunderstorms and hurricanes nearer the Gulf of Mexico. Other risks came from human sources.

Especially in the initial decades of this river commerce, Native Americans posed a threat. As if they were on some Disney ride gone horribly out of control, Kaintucks frequently faced blind turns in waterways where natives would fire at them from a tree-lined bank or charge them in packs of canoes. Other native schemes also proved effective. Asbury remarked that "one of the favorite practices of the Indians was to don ragged American clothing, cover their faces with flour, and hail the flatboats from the water's edge, simulating white men in distress and pleading for help." Those pilots most green or gullible were likely to have their goods and their lives taken—not necessarily in that order.

Pirates presented another menace, with the worst of their lot concentrated in the Kentucky section of the Ohio River. These malefactors came up with every imaginable ploy to draw boats close to shore. They stuck false warnings in channels. They lured thirsty souls with signs offering cheap drink and still cheaper entertainment. In difficult waters, pirates even advertised the services of experienced navigators—who were all too ready to run the boats aground, where the bandits could capture the crew and plunder the

The Kaintuck President

During Abraham Lincoln's first presidential campaign in 1860, his staff didn't present him as the Illinois lawyer he was, but rather as the ideal candidate of the time—someone who had risen from humble roots, a man born in a log cabin and grown into the "Woodchopper of the West." They might have noted that he was also a former Mississippi River flatboatman.

In his much-acclaimed 1995 biography, *Lincoln,* historian David Herbert Donald recalls how, in his nineteenth year, Kentucky-born Abe left his family home on Little Pigeon Creek, in southern Indiana, lured away briefly by tales—tall and otherwise—of life on the Father of Waters:

In 1828, when James Gentry, who owned the local store, decided to send a cargo of meat, corn, and flour down the rivers for sale in New Orleans, Lincoln

accepted the offer to accompany his son, Allen, on the flatboat, at a wage of $8 a month. They made a leisurely trip, stopping frequently to trade at the sugar plantations along the river in Louisiana, until the dreamlike quality of their journey was rudely interrupted. "One night," as Lincoln remembered, "they were attacked by seven negroes with intent to kill and rob them. They were hurt some in the melee, but succeeded in driving the negroes from the boat, and then 'cut cable' 'weighed anchor' and left." New Orleans was by far the largest city the two country boys had ever seen, with imposing buildings, busy shops, and incessant traffic. Here they heard French spoken as readily as English. In New Orleans, Lincoln for the first time encountered large numbers of slaves. But neither boy made any record of their visit to the Crescent City; perhaps it was too overwhelming.

hold at leisure.

Among the most successful of these brigands was a giant of a man called Colonel Plug (who claimed to have been an American army officer during the Revolutionary War). Plug was famous—or, rather, infamous—for hiding himself aboard flatboats at night. When the vessel cast off again, he would bore holes in the hull enough to start it sinking—conveniently opposite to where his henchmen were prepared to stage a rescue. Except that the sole person ever rescued was the colonel; everyone else was left to drown, as Plug's confederates plucked the boat clean of merchandise. Only once did Plug miscalculate as to how much water he should let into a boat—a fatal error, as it turned out, for he went down with the craft before his men could reach him.

UNDER THREE FLAGS

A CCEPTING A CERTAIN AMOUNT of peril as inevitable in their chosen profession, the Kaintuck boatmen kept right on bringing their wares to anchor along New Orleans's Tchoupitoulas Street, the main riverfront road. Their numbers increased in the early nineteenth century, as the Crescent City became a prosperous market for cotton, sugar, and slaves, attracting legions of slick opportunists and middle-class workers, all of them ripe to purchase products being floated downriver. According to Mary Ann Sternberg's *Along the River Road: Past and Present on Louisiana's Historic Byway,* in 1802 "New Orleans recorded 265 flatboat arrivals; four years later, there were 1,223." Adds Herbert Asbury, "Sometimes there were so many of these craft in port that it was possible to walk a mile without leaving their decks."

Of course, by then, New Orleans had gone through far more dramatic changes. Louisiana as a whole was no longer French-dominated, as it had been until King Louis XV ceded French lands west of the Mississippi to Spain in 1762, during the French and Indian War. Nor was it Spanish, for Napoléon Bonaparte had won the territory back through the Treaty of San Ildefonso in 1800, though he didn't exercise his sway there for two more years. Instead, all of those once-French lands—almost nine hundred thousand square miles, stretching from the Mississippi to the

New Orleans on the Brink

Americans who traveled to the Crescent City soon after it became U.S. territory generally looked forward more than New Orleanians did to the inevitable mixing of French and Yankee cultures. Among the enthusiasts was Baltimore architect Benjamin Latrobe, who rebuilt the U.S. Capitol after its destruction by British forces during the War of 1812. Visiting in 1819, Latrobe wrote in his diary:

Americans are pouring in daily, not in families, but in large bodies. In a few years, therefore, this will be an American town. What is good & bad in the French manners, & opinions must give way, & the American notions of right & wrong, of convenience & inconvenience will take their place.

When this period arrives, it would be folly to say that things are better or worse than they now are. They will be changed, but they will be changed into that which is more agreeable to the new population than what now exists. But a man who fancies that he has seen the world on more sides than one can-not help wishing that a *mean*, and *average* character, of society may grow out of the intermixture of the French & American manners.

Such a consummation is per-haps to be more devoutly wished than hoped for. There is a lady, and, I am told, a leading one among the Americans, who can speak French well, but is deter-mined never to condescend to speak to the French ladies in their language, altho' in New York she prided herself on knowing their language. Many of the leading Gentlemen, when not talking of tobacco or cotton, find it very amusing to abuse & ridicule French morals, French manners, & French houses. In truth there is evidently growing up a party spirit, which in time will give success to the views of the Americans, & everything French will in 50 years disappear. Even the miserable patois of the Creoles will be heard only in the cypress swamps.

(Benjamin Henry Boneval Latrobe, *Impressions Respecting New Orleans: Diary and Sketches, 1818-20*)

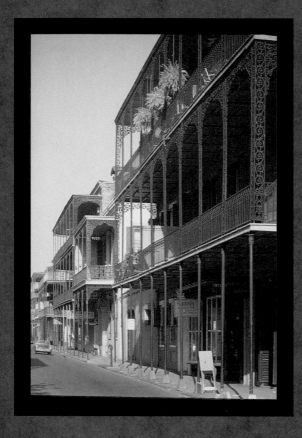

Upper-floor galleries and ornate ironwork mark the architecture of the French Quarter. With a victory at the Battle of New Orleans, Andrew Jackson rode a wave of popularity that took him to the White House.

Rocky Mountains—had come into American possession, thanks to what has been called the most amazing real-estate deal in history: the Louisiana Purchase of 1803. Through President Thomas Jefferson's quick action, the United States bought command over New Orleans and the vast river system on which it so depended for only fifteen million dollars (about four cents an acre).

Most Americans lauded the deal, but aristocratic New Orleans Creoles (a term then referring just to whites of European colonial parentage—French or Spanish) were not happy with this turn of affairs. Not in the least. After all, when they thought of Americans, what came to mind were the Kaintucks, whom they considered buckskin-wearing, whiskey-swilling barbarians. (Creole parents actually cast Kaintucks as hobgoblins, scaring children into obedience by telling them that if they weren't careful, the Kaintucks would get 'em!) They had no desire to see more such coarse individuals storming over the levees and disrupting their elegant gatherings.

Despite the oppressive humidity in summer and the swarms of yellow fever–spreading mosquitoes, the Creoles had made New Orleans, just a hundred miles from the mouth of the Mississippi, into a redoubt of French-style gentility. Magnificent balls and banquets crowded the social calendar. Women dressed in the height of fashion, with Parisian gowns and whalebone corsets. Behind the wrought-iron gates of the Vieux Carré (the Old Square, now familiar as the French Quarter), wealthy families decorated their mansions with art from the Orient, European carpets and chandeliers, and decanters of exquisite French wines.

Weather and insects aside, New Orleans was not without its troubles. The whole social order was supported by slaves, many imported from overseas (at least before Louisiana became the eighteenth American state in 1812), who ensured that plantation crops would be sown on time and Creole children properly cared for. And that order would be clearly upset by the slave rebellion of 1811—the largest ever in North America, according to historians—during which some five hundred angry rebels marched south along the River Road toward the Vieux Carré. It took the intercession of troops from Baton Rouge and militiamen from

New Orleans to stop the city from being sacked. Sixteen of the black leaders were executed and their heads mounted on pikes along the River Road to discourage further violence.

Outsiders sometimes had harsh words for the Crescent City lifestyle. Territorial Governor William C. C. Claiborne wrote President Jefferson that Louisianans were "uninformed, indolent, luxurious—in a word, ill-fitted to be useful citizens of a Republic." But as far as New Orleanians were concerned, they occupied a hard-won paradise. To them, the notion of their city's culture being endangered by vulgarians swarming in from the United States—much as the Visigoths had once overrun the refined Roman Empire—was abhorrent. They would give the cold shoulder to Americans even after January 8, 1815, when U.S. Major General Andrew Jackson, commanding troops assisted invaluably by New Orleans militiamen, former Haitian slaves fighting as free men of color, and Gulf Coast pirates under Jean Lafitte, won a major victory against British forces trying to capture New Orleans. (Only later, as Jackson was planning to depart for Natchez by way of the River Road, did he receive word that his fighting had been for naught: The British had signed the Treaty of Ghent, ending the War of 1812, two weeks before the Battle of New Orleans.)

Kaintuck Etiquette

Considering the behavior of the many Kaintucks they had encountered, residents of New Orleans could have been excused for their reluctance to accept other Americans as neighbors. "As a class," Asbury wrote of the Kaintucks, "they were probably the roughest, toughest, and most ferocious of all the pioneers who helped carve an empire from the western wilderness."

When not working their boats or guzzling their weight in alcohol, Mississippi boatmen of the early 1800s liked to fight. The dirtier, the better. There was a champion on every craft, and he proudly wore a red turkey feather in his cap or hair to show everyone else how ready and willing he was to whop them within an inch of their lives. Should two or more flatboats or keelboats tie up on a night at the same river town, it was guaranteed that some beefy pair would soon be biting, gouging, kicking, and stabbing each other. Again, Asbury sets the scene:

> Before a fight began, certain established conventions were observed. Facing each other in the ring formed by their fellows, the gladiators strutted about, leaped into the air, cracked their heels together, and shouted their war-cries, each striving to outdo the other in ferocity of expression and in his claims of an extraordinary ancestry.
>
> "I am a child of the snapping-turtle!"
>
> "I was raised with the alligators and weaned on panthers' milk!"
>
> "I can outrun, outjump, outshoot, throw down, drag out, and lick any man in the country!"
>
> "I'm a roaring rip-snort and chock-full of fight!"
>
> "I'm a pizen wolf from Bitter Creek and this is my night to howl!"
>
> "I can wrastle a buffalo and chaw the ear off a grizzly!"
>
> . . . When they had tormented each other into furious rages, the fight was on, and it didn't stop until one or the other of the combatants had cried enough. If a man's tongue was yanked out, or if he had been otherwise rendered incapable of speech, his friends might shout the humiliating word on his behalf.

Almost as much as they enjoyed a good brawl—and tearing up a town in the process—weary boatmen fancied a roll with some woman of bounteous curves and easy virtue. New Orleans was the Mississippi's undisputed capital of sin. However, satisfaction could also be found upriver in Natchez-under-the-Hill. Occupying a mile-long shoreline flat below Natchez proper, this was a memorably squalid district of half-sunken sidewalks, dirty children, and almost every conceivable sordid enterprise. For men who hadn't yet made their money on the river, or who had already spent everything while heading up the River Road, over-rouged prostitutes beckoned from casement windows. Deeper-pocketed sorts might amble over to Madame Aivoges's bordello, which tradition holds was the swankest in town, a place where callers were checked out thoroughly through a peephole in the front door before ever being allowed into the perfumed inner sanctum.

And there were always the floating whorehouses. The most storied of these was owned by Annie Christmas, a six-foot-eight-inch, 250-pound—and rather hirsute—hellion. When Annie wasn't working a flatboat, lifting flour barrels onto her shoulders as if they were made of cotton candy, she would shave her mustache, slip into a dress, and run a ship of women up the river. Folklore has it that Annie could be as daunting a lover as she was a stevedore, and that every cruise, she would offer a keg of whiskey to whichever of her girls could entertain the most men in the shortest period. The prize, as might be expected, usually went to Annie herself.

ROLLING ON THE RIVER

IN THE FALL OF 1811, the first "wedding cake without the complications" set out to navigate the Mississippi: The steamship *New Orleans,* sailing from Pittsburgh, reached its namesake city by early January 1812, introducing a new era of speed to river travel. For a while, steamboats, flatboats, and keelboats managed to coexist, the steamboats pulling their ungainly, unpowered cousins whenever they needed to return north. By the 1850s, however, flatboats were a rare sight.

The River Road had a longer life. Although it was damaged severely by heavy use during the Civil War (or "The War between the States," as it's known in the South), the road bounced back, just as it did every time it was washed out by high waters. On late summer evenings in the 1890s, it was busy with young couples promenading, children at play, or grandparents visiting their neighbors. Until 1935, it continued to be the principal overland route between New Orleans and Baton Rouge. Today, like the river itself, it seems a thing of the past, a charming reminder of simpler days, when flatboats rather than oil tankers sailed by—and you made sure to stay clear of any Kaintucks with red turkey feathers in their hats.

Mississippi boatmen faced a number of hazards: floating debris and pirates on the trip downriver to New Orleans, and swamps infested with snakes and alligators on the way back up the River Road and the Natchez Trace.

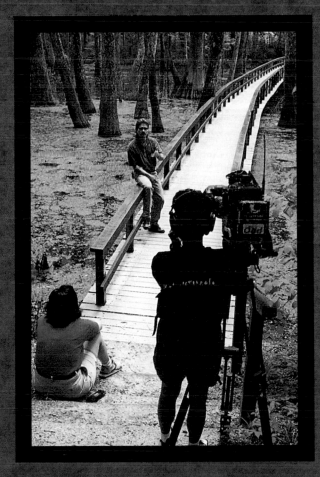

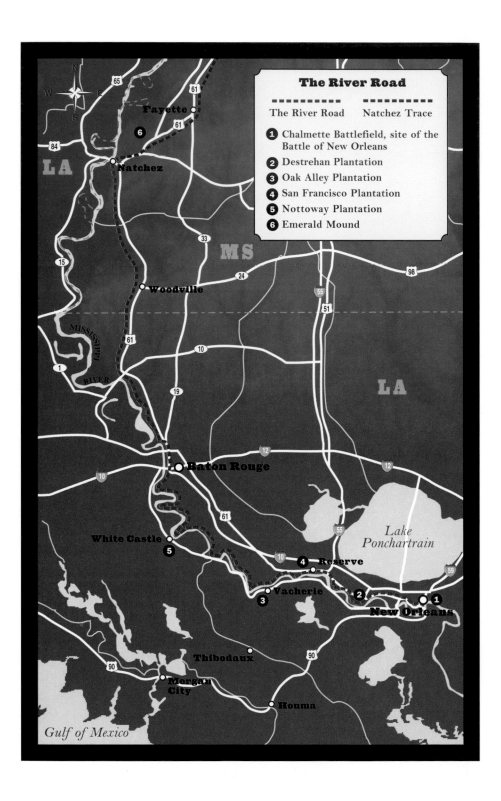

The River Road

- - - - - - - - - - -   - - - - - - - - - - -
The River Road   Natchez Trace

1 Chalmette Battlefield, site of the
Battle of New Orleans

2 Destrehan Plantation

3 Oak Alley Plantation

4 San Francisco Plantation

5 Nottoway Plantation

6 Emerald Mound

The River Road Today

Time and more direct freeways have diminished its importance, yet the River Road still beckons the traveler, with its array of classic Southern plantations and the opportunity it offers visitors to wind leisurely up the Mississippi. The road begins in uptown New Orleans, near the Audubon Zoological Gardens, and follows the Mississippi as far as the Louisiana capital of Baton Rouge (about a hundred miles), where U.S. Route 61 leads inland to Natchez, Mississippi. Although the River Road runs along both sides of the Mississippi, its east side is the more scenic. The road's numerical designation is inconsistent between parishes (counties); on the east bank, for instance, it follows Louisiana Routes 48, 628, 44, 942, 141, and 327. If you think you've diverged from the historic route, stop and ask.

PLANTATION TOURING

There are many stunning examples of plantation architecture along the River Road. But some houses stand out from the rest. **Destrehan** is the oldest extant plantation home in the Mississippi River valley, built between 1787 and 1790 and located at 13034 River Road, approximately half an hour from downtown New Orleans. **San Francisco Plantation** shows unusual Classic Revival and Bavarian design influences. Built in 1856 and initially called St. John de Marmillon, it was dubbed Sans Fusquin—French slang for "Down to my last red cent"—by the second owner, who overspent to redecorate it. The third owner anglicized the name to San Francisco. **Nottoway Plantation** (1859) is the largest antebellum plantation house in the South—sixty-four rooms and fifty-three thousand square feet. **Oak Alley Plantation** (1839) may be the most romantic of all these homes, taking its name from the twin rows of live oaks, dripping in Spanish moss, that line the way from the river to the house.

NEW ORLEANS

History fairly oozes from the banks of the Crescent City—so called for its shape, nestled as it is between the Mississippi and Lake Pontchartrain.

Jackson Square, named in honor of Andrew Jackson—American commander at the Battle of New Orleans—rests at the heart of the Vieux Carré, or French Quarter, the original city center. Once a military drill field known as the Place d'Armes, this tiny square (bound by Decatur, St. Peter, Chartres, and St. Ann Streets) now hosts artists, musicians, and vendors. St. Louis Cathedral, the oldest continuously operating cathedral in the United States (and the third church on this site, dating from 1794), stands photogenically at the back of Jackson Square, flanked by the Cabildo (701 Chartres)—the eighteenth-century Spanish seat of government in New Orleans (where the Louisiana Purchase was completed on December 20, 1803)—and the Presbytère (751 Chartres), once a home for priests, later a courthouse. Bordering either side of Jackson Square are the impressive red-brick Pontalba Apartments, believed to be the oldest apartment structures in the New World. Surrounding the square are numerous strollable streets, thick with an ethnic brew of cafés. On the riverbank nearby, the two-century-old French Market (several blocks along Decatur Street) entices with decadent scents of Creole cookery and fresh produce. Not far away, at the corner of St. Louis and Chartres streets, sits the Napoleon House. A cluttered drinking spot and restaurant, it takes its name from an 1821 plot to rescue the French emperor from his exile on the island of St. Helena and install him in this former residence. (Unfortunately, Napoléon died of cancer just three days before the rescue ships were to sail from New Orleans.) Royal Street is decorated with art galleries and antique shops from end to end, and the Historic New Orleans Collection contains antique documents and paintings of the region, as well as modern photographs.

From the French Quarter, take the St. Charles Avenue streetcar—the oldest continuously operating streetcar line in the nation—to the Garden District. Rich in blooming magnolias and azaleas, this area is where prosperous Americans, shunned by the nineteenth-century Creole aristocracy, built their Italianate and Greek Revival mansions using wood salvaged from the flatboats. Structures of special note include Colonel Short's Villa (1859), which sits behind a wrought-iron fence of intertwined cornstalks and morning glories, and the **Louis S. McGehee School** (1872).

Nightlife in New Orleans begins and ends at dawn. Jazz originated here, so there are plenty of opportunities to get an earful dur-
ing a visit. You won't want to miss attending a concert in
Preservation Hall (on St. Peter Street, between Bourbon and Royal
Streets), a rather dilapidated-looking building next to **Pat
O'Brien's,** the French Quarter's most popular bar, with a seductive
courtyard and rowdy indoor piano bar. Wilder times can be had
along Bourbon Street, where the **Old Absinthe House** (240
Bourbon Street)—perhaps the oldest bar still operating in
Louisiana—is said to have hosted Andrew Jackson and the pirate
Jean Lafitte, as they discussed their strategy for the Battle of New
Orleans. (To learn more about their plans, drive or ferry east of
downtown to the **Chalmette Battlefield**, where films, park ranger
talks, and exhibits help bring to life that brief confrontation with
the British.)

For more information, contact the River Road Historical
Society, 504-764-9315; the Louisiana State Museum, 504-568-6968;
or the New Orleans Welcome Center, 504-568-5661. —*Ellen L. Boyer*

The Natchez Trace

RESIDENTS OF NATCHEZ could have been excused for showing either curiosity or horror—or both—as they watched the pair of shabby strangers lug a hefty lump of dried blue clay through their streets in October 1803. After all, it wasn't every day that men came calling on this wealthy Mississippi cotton-growing town with a preserved human head tucked beneath their arms.

The pate in question belonged to Samuel Mason, a notorious robber and murderer who had preyed for years upon travelers of the Natchez Trace, a 450-mile-long backwoods route connecting Natchez, Mississippi, and Nashville, Tennessee. Mason, it was said, had been born in Virginia in 1750, had fought for American freedom during the Revolutionary War, and later served as a Kentucky justice of the peace. A tall and husky gent, his handsomeness sullied only by a projecting front tooth that gave him a wolfish grin, Mason was a late convert to criminality. He was already in his forties when he claimed his first victim—a Carolina outlaw who paid with his life for his temerity in eloping with Mason's daughter. After that, however, Mason rapidly made up for lost time, leading his three sons and other hoodlums in raids on Trace riders and riverboatmen alike.

Land pirates? Assassins? Malevolent innkeepers? No wonder early travelers along the road between Natchez and Nashville called it "the Devil's Backbone."

Natchez-under-the-Hill was a freewheeling, bawdy part of town, but the Natchez Trace—leading to Nashville—was downright life-threatening. Even famed explorer Meriwether Lewis didn't survive his trip on the Trace.

Although periodically captured—and even once flogged and pilloried in Natchez—Mason proved irrepressible, a remorseless rebel who could usually evade Natchez or New Orleans authorities by simply slipping west across the Mississippi River into what was then still Spanish territory.

His reign of terror persisted until 1803, when William C. C. Claiborne, newly appointed governor of Mississippi Territory (and future governor of Louisiana), finally offered a two-thousand-dollar reward for Mason—dead or alive.

Collection of that reward was what had brought the two strangers and their clay-encased cranium into Natchez. The pair introduced themselves to the local magistrates as James Mays and John Setton. Their story was that they had found Mason hiding in a swampy area near Lake Concordia, west of the town. While the bandit slept one night, the two men tomahawked his head clean off his shoulders and encased it in clay to prevent putrefaction. Their gruesome souvenir confirmed Mason's death. So where was their blood money?

A Trail of Many Names

Only since the 1820s has the Natchez Trace been known by that name. Prior to then it was called the "Path to the Choctaw Nation" along its southern portion and the "Chickasaw Trace" throughout its northern course. When it became a widely used thoroughfare by the Tennessee and Kentucky boatmen on their return business trips from New Orleans through Natchez to Nashville and by the post riders for the delivery of the mail between Nashville and Natchez, it was officially called the "Road from Nashville in the State of Tennessee to the Grindstone Ford of the Bayou Pierre in the Mississippi Territory." It was only after all of its busiest activity had subsided that it picked up the name which has passed down to us through history.

(James ‘A. Crutchfield, *The Natchez Trace: A Pictorial History*, 1985)

It was at this point that the door to the magistrates' chambers flew open and in stormed a man history records as one Captain Stump from Kentucky, his brow furrowed with confusion and anger. Stump charged that he had spotted, among the bounty hunters' horses, two steeds that recently had been stolen from him on the Trace. While explaining all of this to the Natchez magistrates, in hopes of retrieving his property, Stump peered, fixing his eyes on the stranger who had introduced himself as Setton, and suddenly blurted out, "Why, that man's Wiley Harpe!"

Outside of Samuel Mason's, few names could have had a more chilling effect on America's early frontier settlers. The dark-haired, tawny-skinned Harpe brothers—Micajah ("Big Harpe") and Wiley ("Little Harpe")—had moved west from North Carolina with their two sisters in the 1790s and built up a reputation for heinousness that was familiar along both the Wilderness Road and the Natchez Trace. "They not only robbed their victims," wrote Jonathan Daniels in *The Devil's Backbone: The Story of the Natchez Trace.* "They also added torture and mutilation to murder. They were early practitioners of a special art in disposal of the bodies of those they killed. They ripped open their bellies, removed the entrails, and filled the cavities with stones. Then they sank them in swamps or steams."

Big Harpe was eventually felled by a bullet in Kentucky, after which his head was severed and mounted in the fork of a tree, where it remained for years. But Little Harpe had escaped to rampage in Mississippi—often, rumor had it, in league with Samuel Mason. Now it appeared that Little Harpe—after doing in his erstwhile partner for cold hard cash—had waltzed right into the arms of the law at Natchez. Two criminals for the price of one!

The man called Setton denied that he was Wiley Harpe, and it took some time before a flatboatman from Tennessee, John Bowman, could be found to make a positive identification. "If he's Little Harpe," Bowman contended, "he'll have a scar under the left nipple of his breast, because I cut him there in a difficulty we had, one night in Knoxville." Setton's shirt was ripped off. The scar was there.

Several versions are told of what happened next, but they all end with Wiley Harpe and "James Mays"—revealed as another desperado, Samuel Mays—being hanged at Greenville, just up the Trace, on February 8, 1804. In what seems to have been a particularly grisly tradition of the Old South, Little Harpe's head, like his elder brother's, was cut off and staked on the Trace, where years of rot and rain stripped it to a grinning skull.

That skull should have been a clear warning: Beware all ye who pass by here. During the years of its heaviest use—from the 1780s through the 1820s—the Natchez Trace played an important part in the movement of people and trade goods between Kentucky and New Orleans. A number of prominent figures from America's past left their mark on this forest path, among them Andrew Jackson, Aaron Burr, and Meriwether Lewis, of the Lewis and Clark Expedition fame. But it served too as the haunt of scoundrels— enough of them that the United States government felt it necessary to issue warnings to travelers along its course.

Of all the major trails that helped Americans win the West, the Natchez Trace may have been the most infamous.

DISPUTED TERRITORY

CONNECTING THREE IMPORTANT watercourses—what we know today as the Cumberland River, the Tennessee River, and, of course, the Mississippi—the Trace was probably trod by natives of the Mississippian culture for centuries before the Spanish explorer Hernando de Soto happened upon it in 1541.

The Mississippians had risen to power in the American southeast around A.D. 700, erecting towns many acres in size as well as massive earthen temple mounds. The center of their culture was located near present-day Saint Louis, at a huge city called Cahokia—most distinctive for a ten-story-high royal mound, built for their absolute leader, the Great Sun—but examples of Mississippian mounds and villages dotted the Natchez Trace. De Soto, who had participated in Francisco Pizarro's conquest of the Inca Empire in the early 1530s, was interested not so much in studying the natives as in subjugating them and stealing their young women, so he did not understand the import of the times. Yet he apparently witnessed the waning days of the Mississippian culture and the rise of several other tribes, including three—the Choctaw, the Chickasaw, and the Natchez—that would play crucial parts in the life of the Trace.

More than a century and a half later, the French—whose adventurers Jolliet, Marquette, and La Salle had done their best to map the Mississippi River valley—established Fort Rosalie (later renamed Fort Panmure by the British) at the present-day site of Natchez. It was a strategic spot, right on the river, in the heart of the lands of the Natchez (whom the French believed they had subdued after a 1716 uprising), and at the southern end of what would become known as the Natchez Trace. By way of that path, the French figured they could expeditiously reach the neighboring Choctaw, their friends in the New World and their potential allies in any imminent hostilities.

However, the Choctaw couldn't save the rapacious French from the Natchez in 1729. Upset at French demands that they abandon prized portions of their land (including a few of their ceremonial mounds), the proud Natchez attacked Fort Rosalie. About 250 men were killed in the skirmish, and 300 women and children were taken prisoner. French vengeance was swift. And terrible. Enlisting the Choctaw in their cause, French forces essentially destroyed the Natchez nation. Despite flags of truce from the Natchez, the French butchered as many natives as they could and sold hostages into West Indian slavery.

That violence precipitated worse. In 1736, the French demanded that the Chickasaw turn over some Natchez braves under their protection. Not taking kindly to such orders, the Chickasaw defeated an advance force of the French near what is now Tupelo, Mississippi, and then forced a second wave of troops to retreat all the way to Mobile, on the Gulf Coast. Following these incidents, France's control over the area was more a matter of rhetoric than reality. By 1763 and the close of the French and Indian War, there were many in Paris who were happy to see the region—and its problems—given over, along with France's other claims east of the Mississippi River, to Great Britain.

Centuries before the white man, natives of the Mississippian culture built ceremonial mounds and vast cities like Cahokia. In the heydey of the Natchez Trace, crude cabins served as "stands," where travelers could eat and rest.

Although King George III's government officially forbade settlement on other British lands west of the Appalachian Mountains, it encouraged people to move into the verdant Natchez district—perhaps in hopes of building a first line of defense there against the Spanish, who had gained control over New Orleans by treaty in 1762. "The majority of those who came [to Natchez] were men of intelligence and character," wrote nineteenth-century historian John Francis Hamtramck Claiborne in *Mississippi, as a Province, Territory, and State.* He added, however, that "bad men, outlaws, and fugitives from justice came likewise." And that would become the hallmark of the Trace.

At the northern end of the path, a settlement party sponsored by Richard Henderson—the judge who earlier had hired Daniel Boone to cut the western arm of the Wilderness Road into Kentucky—began arriving in 1779 at a point on the Cumberland River. Led by James Robertson and John Donelson, the party hastily raised a stockade and christened it Nashborough (later, Nashville), in honor of North Carolina patriot Francis Nash.

After the Revolution, more colonists seeped into the lower Trace region, as well. There were still threats to their fledgling towns—from natives, who made no secret of their displeasure with the white man's increasing presence on their lands, and from the Spanish, who reoccupied Natchez in 1781 and didn't fully cede to the United States its rights to the area until 1795. (The last Spanish flags were not lowered at Natchez until the Mississippi Territory was created three years after that.) Yet traffic was already brisk along the trail. According to *The Devil's Backbone,* in 1790 "at least sixty flatboats stopped at Natchez with the crops and goods of Kentucky, Pennsylvania, Ohio, Tennessee, and Virginia. And . . . Spanish authorities there reported at least 250 men returning northward over the Natchez Trace."

Many of these travelers were Kaintucks, who, after slogging north along the River Road and fortifying themselves with food and drink at the King's Tavern in Natchez (and perhaps with female companionship in Natchez-under-the-Hill), were ready to brave the monthlong journey to Nashville. It was a rough venture, the narrow trail leading through swamps and marshes, with

alligators lying in wait. Crossing the Tennessee River meant bat-
tling swift currents in chest-high water. Inns, or "stands," as they
came to be known here, were not common on the Trace until the
early nineteenth century; before that, men had to pitch camp in
the open, leaving themselves vulnerable to disease-carrying mosquitoes—not to mention the human vultures that prowled the
hardwood forests.

FOR A LADY'S HONOR

I T'S ONLY FITTING THAT this frontier route would play
a large part in the life of Old Hickory, the country's first
frontier president. Born in South Carolina in 1767,
Andrew Jackson joined the militia at thirteen to fight in
the Revolution, only to be captured. A year later, he was
orphaned and taken under the wing of a well-to-do uncle. In
Presidential Anecdotes, Paul F. Boller writes that residents of
Salisbury, North Carolina, where the future president spent part
of his boyhood, remembered him as "the most roaring, rollicking,
game-cocking, horse-racing, card-playing, mischievous fellow,
that ever lived in Salisbury." By 1788, when he decided a move
to distant Nashville would do him good, Jackson had already
fought a duel and gained ambition as a lawyer.

Tall, with intense, steel-blue eyes and an abundant head of dark
red hair, Jackson had frequently attracted women in the past. In
Nashville, he drew one more than others: Rachel Donelson Robards,
comely daughter of the late Nashville cofounder, John Donelson,
and wife of Lewis Robards, a Kentucky businessman (a slave trader,
some said) who had wed Rachel in 1785. To many, their marriage
looked ideal—except that Robards turned out to be a jealous, spite-
ful man. Not long before Jackson's arrival in Tennessee, Robards
had kicked Rachel out of their Kentucky home, convinced that she
was having an affair with a gentleman whose only crime had been
to show her inordinate politeness. She left Kentucky to live with her
widowed mother in Nashville, and Jackson met her there when he
became one of Mrs. Donelson's boarders.

The area around Natchez abounds with scenic beauty and wildlife. It also features elaborate plantation homes, such as Longwood—the largest octagonal home in America. The Civil War prevented its completion, and it stands today unfinished, frozen in time.

It didn't take long for Robards to direct his ire at the young attorney, as well. Hearing rumors of Jackson's interest in his spouse, Robards insisted that Rachel rejoin him in Kentucky. Their reconciliation was brief, however, and Jackson was called upon by Rachel's family to bring her back to Tennessee. He subsequently whisked her to Natchez, where she might find respite from Robards' jealousy, then followed the Trace back to Nashville.

But Robards was not easily fended off. In December 1790, he sought permission from the Virginia legislature (Kentucky was then still a part of Virginia) to divorce, accusing Rachel of adultery. Jackson, at first anxious to put a pistol to Robards' head and make him retract his allegations, chose instead to make the most of what he took to be a legitimate divorce: He proposed to Rachel, and the pair wed in Natchez in 1791, then rode north along the Trace with a large company. Not until two years later did Jackson learn that no divorce had ever been granted and that Robards was only then suing for divorce on the grounds that his wife had been living in sin with Andrew Jackson for two years!

As soon as the real divorce came through, the Jacksons

Making a Stand

Most of the traveler accommodations, or "stands," built along the Natchez Trace were rudimentary. Some were positively ramshackle, and remained so even as the trail matured and improved. In his book *The Natchez Trace: A Pictorial History*, James A. Crutchfield quotes a minister complaining in 1816 that some of these "hotels are made of small poles, just high enough for you to stand straight in, with a dirt floor, no bedding of any kind, except a bearskin, and not that in some of these huts. You feel blank and disappointed when you walk in and find a cold dirt floor, naked walls, and no fire. Camping out is far better than such conditions."

remarried. But gossip about Rachel's adultery circulated for years and received national attention in the presidential race of 1828. During that campaign, supporters of incumbent John Quincy Adams—perhaps giving birth to the shameful tactic that continues to this day, of launching personal attacks against candidates *and* their spouses—sought to counter Jackson's credentials as a lawyer, legislator, and hero of the Battle of New Orleans with charges that he was a bigamist and wife-stealer. "Ought a convicted adulteress and her paramour husband to be placed in the highest offices of this free and Christian land?" asked a pro-Adams newspaper in Ohio.

Democrat Jackson went on to win that election—and become the first president from the emerging West—but Rachel died less than three months before his inauguration. "May God forgive her murderers," Jackson said at his wife's funeral, referring to the slanderers who he believed had hastened her demise, "as I know she forgave them. I never can."

PASSAGE TO INTRIGUE

THE YEARS BETWEEN Andrew Jackson's arrival in Tennessee and his election as president were those of the Natchez Trace's greatest importance. During that time, the U.S. government began making treaties with the Choctaw and the Chickasaw, the idea being that troops would follow to widen the Trace and build bridges, wherever necessary. These improvements would not only make it easier for flatboatmen, itinerant preachers, land speculators, and slave traders to use the trail, they would also speed the delivery of mail and commercial goods over the Trace. At the same time, new hostels opened to serve travelers. Many of those stands were just collections of rude cabins, while some weren't even that luxurious. Their operators offered hot meals and, in the best circumstances, conversation. In 1810, according to *The Devil's Backbone*, there were "at least seven inns on the Natchez road," which meant that in most cases, they were days apart. By 1815, the *Louisiana and Mississippi Almanac* listed forty stands.

One of the most eminent travelers on the Trace in those years was an accused murderer—though not cut from the same cloth as Samuel Mason or the Harpes. Aaron Burr was, rather, recently retired as vice-president of the United States. Under indictment for killing Alexander Hamilton, the country's first secretary of the treasury, in a duel, Burr decided to head west in 1805. He visited Kentucky, New Orleans, and Natchez, then moved up the Trace to Nashville (a lengthy journey he dismissed as a "wilderness jaunt"). Sources said that Burr needed money and that he hoped to involve himself in lucrative schemes born of the vast acreage that President Thomas Jefferson had added to the country through the Louisiana Purchase. Others insisted he was planning to recruit an army in the West, wrest Texas and Mexico from Spain, and promote himself as emperor of a new nation. Acting out of that latter fear, the American government had the previously popular Burr arrested on suspicion of treason. He was briefly held at Natchez, escaped there, and was recaptured farther south. A trial in Virginia ultimately acquitted Burr of the charge.

Enticing more people—especially more prosperous ones—up the Natchez Trace led unfortunately but inexorably to a proliferation of murderers and "land pirates" along its course. In 1803, Governor Archibald Roane of Tennessee explained his concerns in a letter to the U.S. secretary of war. "The road passing through the Indian Country from Natchez to Nashville," Roane wrote, "has for some time past been infested with a gang of Bantitti [sic], whether White men or Indians, or both, has not been fully ascertained." Assaults were soon so commonplace that Jefferson began offering a four-hundred-dollar reward to anyone who could apprehend such malefactors.

Danger didn't come only from those who roamed the Trace, however. Even stand owners might loot or kill their lodgers. Historian Jonathan Daniels recorded a bit of folklore about one hostel of horrors:

> [It] concerns the son of parents who made a business of robbing and murdering their guests. After leaving home, the son came back older, bearded, and a prosperous brigand in his own right. He planned a playful return. Not telling his ma and pa who he was, he talked of his riches and he got his skull cracked while

he slept. Later a neighbor, whom the young man had let in on the joke, asked about the son. Sick and frightened, the old folks went secretly and dug up the body where they had buried it. On his breast they found the birthmark that their son had borne since his mother, who helped kill him, had suckled him long before.

When Captain Meriwether Lewis succumbed under mysterious circumstances at a stand on the Natchez Trace, it was bruited about that he had met a similar fate, that he had been murdered by villainous hands. Some people still believe that.

The circumstances of Lewis's death can be boiled down to these:

In mid-September 1809, the man who (with his associate William Clark) had become a national hero for his 1803–06 explorations over the Rocky Mountains and down the Columbia River to the Pacific Ocean, arrived by boat at Chickasaw Bluffs, today the site of Memphis, Tennessee. He had traveled from Saint Louis, where he now held office as the governor of upper Louisiana (Missouri), and was bound for the nation's capital in Washington. He carried with him his edited journals of the Lewis and Clark Expedition, which he intended to deliver to his publishers in Philadelphia, as well as official records that he wished to present to the bureaucrats who, since the recent inauguration of President James Madison, had begun to protest Lewis's expenditures and even question his integrity—something that never would have happened under his patron, Thomas Jefferson.

At the time, Meriwether Lewis, though only thirty-five, was not well. Either in body or mind. He had become a heavy drinker and may have been suffering from malaria, for which he took medicines laced with morphine and opium. He was "certainly in a deep depression," relates Stephen E. Ambrose in *Undaunted Courage*, his exhaustive study of the Lewis and Clark Expedition. "Twice [during his river trip] he tried to kill himself—whether by jumping overboard or with his pistol is not known—and had to be restrained by the crew." When Lewis arrived at Chickasaw Bluffs, he was in such a state that a local army commander resolved to "detain him there until he recovered, or some friend might arrive in whose hands he could depart in safety." He was put under a twenty-four-hour suicide watch.

Within a week, however, the governor had started to recover, and he was impatient to continue east. He could have boated down-river to New Orleans and from there sailed to Washington, but with British warships lurking along the Atlantic coast, he decided it would be less dangerous to travel overland, beginning on the Natchez Trace. So, together with two servants and Major James Neely, a government Indian agent, Lewis set off southeast from Chickasaw Bluffs at the end of September. They joined the Trace at Chickasaw Agency, near Tupelo, with Lewis appearing "at times deranged in mind," according to a later report by Neely. After two days of rest, they headed north along the Trace, crossing the Tennessee River on October 8 or 9. Shortly thereafter, thunder-storms caused the party to lose a couple of their pack horses, and Neely went looking for them; Lewis continued on with the servants, promising to wait for the major at the first stand he could find.

Late in the afternoon of October 10, 1809, Lewis arrived—apparently alone—at Grinder's Stand, a log cabin inn about seventy miles shy of Nashville, operated by former North Carolinians Robert E. Grinder and his wife, Priscilla Knight Grinder. Mr. Grinder was away, but Mrs. Grinder greeted Lewis and asked if he would just need accommodations for one. No, he replied, two ser-vants were trailing behind. When they arrived, Lewis, who by then had partaken of a bit of the Grinders' whiskey, asked the servants for his gunpowder; he received only an indistinct answer—no doubt they, too, had heard of the explorer's suicide attempts.

Lewis acted agitated as Priscilla Grinder prepared dinner. "Sometimes he would seem as if he were walking up to me," she recalled in years to come, "and would suddenly wheel round, and walk back as fast as he could." Lewis couldn't even enjoy his meal, springing up after only a few bites and talking to himself in a heated manner. Once he was calm again, he lit a pipe and sat in a chair by the cabin door. "Madam, this is a very pleasant evening," he told her. She was not convinced.

Later, after the servants had gone to a barn to sleep and Priscilla Grinder had retreated to a bed in an adjacent kitchen-house, she heard

Steamboat travel on the Mississippi River put an end to the usefulness of the Natchez Trace. The same relentless march of progress has transformed Nashville from a frontier fort to a modern city and the capital of country music.

the governor pacing in her cabin and conversing aloud, "like a lawyer," she said. This was followed, shortly before sunrise, by the loud bark of a pistol and the sound of something falling on the floor, followed by the exclamation: "O Lord." Soon, there was a second pistol shot.

Within minutes, Lewis staggered outside, calling, "O madam! Give me some water and heal my wounds!" When Priscilla Grinder didn't respond—perhaps fearing what she might discover—Lewis wandered about for a few minutes, tried to get a drink from an empty bucket, and finally repaired to his room, where he was found by his servant after first light, still conscious, a piece of his forehead blown away and another bullet wound in his side. He asked for water, which he was given this time, and then told the servant, "I am no coward; but I am so strong, so hard to die." As Ambrose tells it in *Undaunted Courage*, Lewis went on to say that "he had tried to kill himself to deprive his enemies of the pleasure and honor of doing it."

Two hours more—"just as the sun rose above the trees," Priscilla Grinder recalled—and Meriwether Lewis was gone.

In the nearly two centuries since, there have been sinister elaborations to this tale: stories of Lewis fearing for his life at Grinder's Stand; of his turning away other potential lodgers at gunpoint; of mysterious moccasin tracks around the cabin; and of Robert Grinder

Relative Safety

It's curious to think that many Americans who had been fearful of traveling over the Natchez Trace thought nothing of later hopping a steamboat on the Mississippi River. As Jonathan Daniels points out in *The Devil's Backbone: The Story of the Natchez Trace*, "Steamboats did not mean safe travel, however comfortable and elegant they were. Murders on the Trace never compared in quantity with deaths on the river. In the forty years after Nicholas Roosevelt steamed down between the river's astonished shores, more than four thousand people were killed or maimed in steamboat accidents or explosions on the Mississippi."

returning that night to murder Lewis for his money or because he found the explorer in bed with his wife. Ambrose insists that such conjecture is "not convincing." Yet macabre folklore has a life of its own. A *long* life.

HISTORY RECLAIMED

A S IT DID TO THE River Road, the introduction of steamboats on the Mississippi River dealt a significant blow to the usefulness of the Natchez Trace. The death knell came in 1820, when a new highway—Andrew Jackson's Military Road—shaved more than two hundred miles off the trip between New Orleans and Nashville. Although some portions of the Trace were kept up for local transportation, much of it fell into disuse and was reclaimed by the surrounding wilderness. There was fighting along its course during the Civil War—at Natchez, Port Gibson, Tupelo, Franklin, and Nashville—but the Trace itself wasn't really involved. People started to forget about this road that had once carried Old Hickory's army back from its victory in New Orleans; had led the Choctaw and Chickasaw away from the lands of their forefathers, into Oklahoma relocation areas; and would forever be associated with the Harpe brothers and their dastardly disciples.

Not until the early twentieth century was interest in the Natchez Trace revived. Articles about the Trace began appearing in magazines, inspiring a preservation campaign spearheaded by the Daughters of the American Revolution and the Daughters of the War of 1812. This campaign was picked up by President Franklin Delano Roosevelt, who included the establishment of a Natchez Trace Parkway as one of the job-creation projects of his New Deal. There was more than a little justice in that. After all, it was one of FDR's ancestors—Nicholas Roosevelt—who had doomed the Trace in 1811 by building and navigating the *New Orleans*, the first steamboat to ply the waters of the Mississippi.

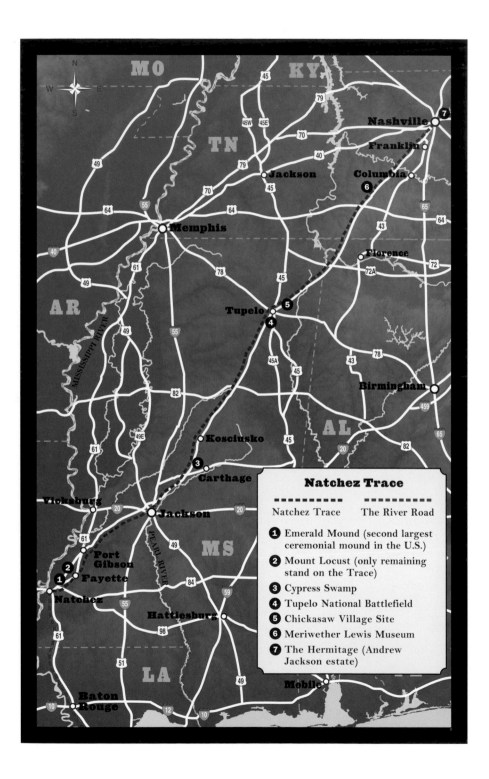

The Natchez Trace Today

Murder, mystery, and mayhem went along for the ride with early travelers of the Natchez Trace. Today, however, you'll face nothing more daunting than scheduling visits to all the museums and historic sites that exist along this trail of the Kaintucks. To trace what's left of the Trace, follow Highway 61 north from Natchez. This runs into the Natchez Trace Parkway—one of the most popular units in the National Park Service system—which crosses Mississippi, going through Jackson and Tupelo, skims the northwest corner of Alabama, and leads finally into Tennessee.

MISSISSIPPI

Begin your trip at the town of **Natchez,** the rest, refueling, and recreational stop for anyone traveling up the River Road from New Orleans. You can get a taste of this town's Kaintuck-era debauchery in the renovated historic district known as Natchez-under-the-Hill, where **King's Tavern** (619 Jefferson Street) is believed to be the oldest building, constructed before 1789. Then sample Native American culture at the **Grand Village of the Natchez Indians** (400 Jefferson Davis Boulevard), home to a museum, reconstructed huts, and renovated ceremonial mounds, all of which help tell the story of this once-important tribe, destroyed by the French in the early eighteenth century. To learn more about local Native Americans, drive eleven miles northeast of Natchez to **Emerald Mound,** the second-largest native mound in the country.

Colonial Natchez comes to life in the preserved luxury of its antebellum homes, including **Auburn House** (Duncan Street at Auburn Avenue), built in 1812; the **Monmouth Plantation** (36 Melrose Avenue), built in 1818 and once the residence of General John A. Quitman, a Mexican War hero, governor, and U.S. congressman; and **The House on Ellicott's Hill** (North Canal at Jefferson Street), which dates back to 1798.

More recent but no less historic is **Longwood** (on Lower Woodville Road), the largest octagonal house in the country. Construction began on the house in 1860, but the outbreak of the Civil War and the death of the home's owner, Dr. Haller Nutt, prevented its completion, leaving it as a preserved work in progress.

Just fifteen miles northeast of Natchez, restored **Mount Locust** is the only stand (inn) remaining where it once stood on the Trace. An on-site exhibit depicts the history of this place, which was probably built as early as 1780 as a one-room cabin.

Located in the Mississippi capital of **Jackson,** roughly eighty miles north of Natchez along the Parkway, is the **Mississippi Crafts Center.** Artists there integrate the past with the present by continuing the Choctaw Indian traditions of pottery making, wood carving, and basket weaving. Nearby, take in **Cypress Swamp,** through which thick-skinned Kaintucks once hiked amid bald cypresses and alligators. Another natural attraction is **Dogwood Valley,** host to an exquisite collection of that flowering tree and through which visitors can take a simple fifteen-minute walk along a sunken portion of the Old Trace.

Continue northeast on the Natchez Trace Parkway to **Tupelo** to experience some more native history at the **Chickasaw Village Site.** Interpretive panels, audio stations, and other exhibits there document the life of the Chickasaw tribe. Meanwhile, Mississippi's final Civil War confrontation, fought in July 1864 (and resulting in the defeat of the Confederate cavalry under Major General Nathan B. Forrest), is remembered at the **Tupelo National Battlefield** (West Main Street).

TENNESSEE

Follow the Parkway through Alabama and on to the Tennessee town of Hohenwald, where you'll find the **Meriwether Lewis Museum.** The famed cross-country explorer is buried there, beneath a broken column that symbolizes his untimely and mysterious death—either by murder or suicide. Located close to the site of Grinder's Stand, where Lewis perished in 1809, the log cabin museum contains material relevant to his last days.

On the banks of the Cumberland River at Nashville rests **Fort**

Nashborough, the original settlement for Tennesee's capital city. The log fort has been reproduced as it would have appeared in its 1780 heyday, when it withstood Indian attacks. But the historical star of Nashville has to be **The Hermitage,** Andrew Jackson's estate, just northeast of downtown. After purchasing 625 acres of land in 1804, Old Hickory proceeded to erect a Federal-style abode here. It was completed in 1821, partially burned in 1834 during Jackson's second term as president, and rebuilt in the Classical style two years later. Visitors can roam the grounds with an audio-guide that leads them through the mansion (which contains many of the original furnishings), the property's log houses, and the adjacent slave quarters, as well as a museum and an amphitheater that presents a film about this Natchez Trace nomad-turned-politician. Jackson and his wife, Rachel, are buried in the estate's garden.

For more information, contact the Natchez Trace Parkway Visitors Center, 601-680-4002. —*Ellen L. Boyer*

The Mormon Trail

L OCKED WITH HIS BROTHER HYRUM and two associates in an upper room of the jailhouse at Carthage, Illinois, Joseph Smith, a prophet to his followers, but a reprobate and a polygamist to many others, had plenty of time to ponder what had brought them there in the summer of 1844—and might soon lead to their deaths.

It had all started with the angels.

Smith was born in Sharon, Vermont, on December 23, 1805.

Like those who fled religious persecution in Europe for America, the Mormons looked to the West for salvation. These Latter-day Saints fled the East to find not just land, but a New Jerusalem.

Fourteen years later, as the story goes, while working on his father's farm in Palmyra, New York, he received his first spiritual visitation. At the time, a religious revival movement was recruiting converts across the Northeast. As anxious as the next man for salvation, but troubled by the claims and counterclaims of proselytizers, Smith is said to have knelt one day in a grove behind his family home and prayed for divine guidance. Suddenly, a towering pillar of light rose before him. Inside it, by Smith's account, were two figures who counseled him against joining any sects—"All their creeds were an abomination"—and told him, instead, to prepare for an important assignment.

Over the next eleven years, Smith regularly experienced visions,

Joseph Smith, founder and spiritual leader of the Latter-day Saints, prophesied an itinerant life for his followers. Persecution finally led to the Mormon exodus from Nauvoo, Illinois, in 1846.

during which he was told that the church of Christ had been withdrawn from Earth and that God had selected him to restore it. In an especially important encounter, Smith maintained that an angel had let him in on an important secret:

> He called me by name and said unto me . . . that his name was Moroni, that God had work for me to do; and that my name should be had for good and evil among all nations, kindreds, and tongues. He said there was a book deposited, written upon gold plates, giving an account of the former inhabitants of this continent and the source from which they sprang. . . .

In 1827, Smith reportedly dug this sacred chronicle out of a slope in western New York and spent the next three years deciphering its "curious" hieroglyphics "by the gift and power of God." According to the plates, Native Americans were really "Lamanites," the descendants of emigrants from Israel who had settled in America six centuries before Christ. Furthermore, Jesus Christ had appeared in his resurrected body to the inhabitants of the New World after his crucifixion—and he would come back to the continent once a new, "true" church was established there. Smith would be that church's prophet.

The gold plates vanished after Smith's work with them was done; he said an angel spirited them away. Then in 1830, he published his translation of their text as the Book of Mormon and founded the Church of Jesus Christ of Latter-day Saints for people who took faith in the book's promises. Smith attracted followers with his particular synthesis of revivalist showmanship (total immersion and speaking in tongues) and old-time religious elements (the promise of an imminent Second Coming and prophets who communicated directly with God).

In the beginning, Smith's flock could be counted on two hands. Within a year, however, he had gathered several hundred Latter-day Saints (he chose that name to distinguish them from the "former-day saints" of the Old Testament). The church's detractors, or gentiles, as the Mormons called them, denounced Smith as a lunatic or a fraud and his book as blasphemous. Like tent revivalists of their time, wrote poet John Greenleaf Whittier, the Mormons "speak a language of hope and promise to weak hearts, tossed and troubled."

Rather than fight the nonbelievers, Smith and company took flight in 1831 to Kirtland, Ohio (now a Cleveland suburb), where they erected their earliest temple. Again, they drew criticism for their smug belief that they, alone, were God's chosen people. They also attracted the law, thanks to Smith's well-intentioned but unwise dabbling in the local banking business, which ended in bankruptcy. In 1838, with criminal charges and angry mobs at their heels, the remaining faithful fled once more, this time to western Missouri.

Smith had great hopes for the Show Me State. After all, according to him, it was holy ground—the place where Adam and Eve had lived in exile from the Garden of Eden and where Cain killed Abel. But local clergymen, like their brethren in Ohio, attacked the beliefs of Smith's followers. "The Mormons," blustered one Presbyterian minister, "are the common enemies of mankind and ought to be destroyed." Slaveholders opposed the Mormons' abolitionist convictions; others accused them of stealing, inciting Indian violence, and even printing counterfeit currency. Riots, nocturnal floggings, and murders ensued, with the Mormons the target of the persecution. Smith was tarred and jailed. Finally, the governor of Missouri, Lillburn W. Boggs, frantically dispatched some six thousand state militiamen to the area in October 1838, insisting that "the Mormons . . . must be exterminated or driven from the state if necessary for the public peace."

"WE SHALL BE BUTCHERED"

THE EARLY MORMONS must be given points for tenacity. They lived from eviction to eviction in the upper Midwest, trusting that Smith—even when he languished in police custody or stunk of tar—would somehow lead them to salvation. If that couldn't be found in Ohio or Missouri, there was always hope of it in the next state over. Or the one beyond that. Years before, in fact, Smith had prophesied that the

Mormons would embrace this itinerancy until they came to their new Promised Land, "where the city of the New Jerusalem shall be prepared, that ye may be gathered in one."

Even the "war" declared by Governor Boggs didn't shake their faith. They picked up their belongings and, during the winter of 1838–39, trailed their leader east across the Mississippi River, to the small, slightly decrepit town of Commerce, in western Illinois. Smith renamed the place Nauvoo, which he insisted meant "beautiful location, a place of rest" in Hebrew. Within half a decade, the Mormons had built it into the state's second-largest city (after Chicago), with some twenty thousand inhabitants and an impressive hilltop temple. More people arrived every month, and missionaries spread the Mormon word overseas, in western Europe.

Tired of the abuse inflicted upon him and his flock by America's civil laws and by meddlesome neighbors, Smith took advantage of Illinois's deep political divisions and got permission to set up his community as a more-or-less autonomous principality. He actually had license to countermand state court orders and liberate Mormons who were wanted by outside law-enforcement agencies. (One of those wanted men was Smith, himself—particularly after then ex-governor Boggs was pumped full of buckshot in Missouri, a crime for which Smith protested his innocence.) To protect his city-state, the prophet established his own militia, the Nauvoo Legion, a well-armed, well-drilled private army of four thousand men, "whose parades were so gorgeous with blue coats, white trousers, jackboots, feathers, and the music of Captain Pitt's Brass Band," wrote Wallace Stegner in *The Gathering of Zion: The Story of the Mormon Trail,* "that passing steamboats tied up at the landing to watch."

Joseph Smith, then only thirty-nine, had essentially created a clean, well-ordered theocracy, with himself on its throne. And still he wasn't satisfied. So in 1844, although he had repeatedly demonstrated his contempt for outside authority, Smith announced his intention to run for the presidency of the United States. This, as far as nonbelievers were concerned, was the height of arrogance. But it wasn't gentiles who proved the most significant threat to Smith's standing; it was dissenters within his own flock. The reason? Polygamy.

Mr. Smith Goes to Washington?

Had Joseph Smith lived long enough to actually mount a campaign for the White House in 1844, he certainly would have been the darkest of dark-horse candidates. He wasn't well known beyond the Mormon community, and that particular race would have pitted him against two celebrated opponents: Democrat James K. Polk, former governor of Tennessee and speaker of the U.S. House of Representatives; and Henry Clay, a renowned Whig senator and one-time secretary of state, who also happened to be the most famous Kentuckian since Daniel Boone. Even a third contender, New York's James G. Birney, making his second bid for the presidency on the antislavery Liberty Party ticket, might have counted on winning more votes than Smith, simply by virtue of name recognition.

But the Mormon prophet's interest in the growing westward movement was directly in line with the country's mood.

For the first time in a presidential contest, territorial expansion was the major issue of the campaign. Politicians delivered fustian speeches about "manifest des-tiny," the annexation of Texas (an independent slave-holding republic since 1836), and the extension of the country's western border to the Pacific Ocean.

Polk was an enthusiastic expansionist; Clay, less so. But Smith had been telling his religious followers to go west for years. "And from this place," he prophesied long before the Mormons faced their troubles in Missouri, "ye shall go forth into the regions westward; and inasmuch as ye shall find them that will receive you, ye shall build up my Church in every region, until the time shall come when it shall be revealed unto you from on high, where the city of the New Jerusalem shall be prepared, that ye may be gathered in one."

In the end, of course, Polk won a slim victory, and during his single term in office he successfully prosecuted the Mexican-American War (1846–48) as a means of acquiring California and much of the Southwest as new U.S. territory. Still, it is intriguing to wonder whether Joseph Smith, delivering an expansionist message said to come from God himself, might have accelerated that process.

The Mormon, California, and Oregon Trails followed much the same route until they diverged near Fort Bridger, Wyoming. Fort Laramie was an outpost of civilization after weeks of travel across the plains. Many Saints made the trek pulling handcarts—and made it more swiftly than wagons.

The prophet had begun secretly touting plural marriage as a "divine command" in about 1831 (though it wouldn't be publicly admitted until 1852, according to Stegner.) As biographer Fawn M. Brodie noted in *No Man Knows My History*, Smith—judging by pictures, a smooth-shaven, not unattractive man, with lush brown hair—had taken forty-nine wives (some of them already married to his acolytes) before his untimely demise. Amazingly, he kept this secret until 1844, when influential Mormons opposed to the practice began turning against Smith, insisting that he confess or be exposed as just another man with typically human weaknesses and flaws. Despite the threat this posed to someone who claimed to be God's anointed tribune, Smith refused to repudiate his actions. When the apostates retaliated by printing newspapers full of stories detailing his polygamy—as well as alleging that he had abused the Nauvoo city charter and used church funds improperly—Smith ordered their printing press destroyed. But the damage had been done. A new tide of anti-Smith, anti-Mormon bile flooded the area around Nauvoo.

Fearing civil war, Governor Thomas Ford of Illinois convinced a reluctant Smith to give himself up in Carthage on June 24, 1844. "We shall be butchered," Smith predicted. Ford assured them they would be safe and had Smith, his brother Hyrum, and two others immediately confined to an upstairs cell of the jail.

Three days later, however, as the afternoon light was fading, Smith heard shouting and shots outside his cell door. At first, he thought the Nauvoo Legion had come to rescue him. Instead, it was a lynch mob wearing blackface. Smith grabbed a six-shooter that had been smuggled into the cell and began firing as the mob crashed through the door. But the odds didn't favor the Mormons. Smith saw his three comrades collapse under the mob's blows and bullets. And finally, his revolver empty, the prophet wheeled around to jump from the chamber's window; below him waited a hundred more of his enemies.

Some say that, as he sprang, a bullet caught Joseph Smith in the back. Others claim that he cried out, "Oh, Lord, my God!" while he tumbled to earth. What is known for sure is that, as he lay broken and twitching in the yard, four men fired pistols into his body until they were certain he would never get up again and that no angel was going to come to his aid.

SUCCESSION AND MIGRATION

THE ASSASSINATIONS ROCKED the church. Mormons resigned themselves to being booted out of Illinois, as they had been from so many other places. Stegner writes that there was "a streak of puritan masochism in many early Mormons—one feels that without tribulation they would hardly have felt confident of their identity as Saints."

But tribulation and dissent also led to splinter sects. The most potent of these—and the only one active today—was the Reorganized Church of Jesus Christ of Latter-day Saints, opposed to polygamy and led by Smith's surviving first wife, Emma, and their son Joseph.

The void left by Smith brought on a brief skirmish for power. Finally, Brigham Young stepped forward to fill the prophet's shoes. At forty-three years old, Young was a stocky, golden-haired former Vermont farmer and carpenter, as rude-born and home-educated as Joseph Smith had been. A practiced speechifier, occasionally pungent and fiery in his language, Young claimed a long, distinguished history with the church. He had done missionary work in the East and Midwest, had fought off rioting gentiles in Missouri, and was one of the dozen apostles appointed by Smith himself. Now he was the Mormons' new patriarch.

Even before Smith's death there had been talk of another pilgrimage further west; now it became a holy mission. The Republic of Texas, Mexican-held California, the new Oregon Territory, and Vancouver Island (now in British Columbia, but then a part of Oregon and coveted by both the United States and Britain) had all been mentioned as destinations. Young took his time deciding. He didn't wish to move his followers just for the sake of movement; he wanted to find them an *ideal* spot. If they were ever to enjoy a new Zion, he reasoned, it would have to be someplace free of troublesome gentiles. The West still offered plenty of open territory. Yet only after reading the reports of explorer John Charles Frémont, who had journeyed west in the early 1840s and found the valley of the Great Salt Lake fit for "civilized settlement," was Young convinced of their goal.

In 1845, the Illinois legislature revoked the city charter of Nauvoo. By then, much of the organization for a migration had been completed. Wagon shops in town had manufactured hundreds of vehicles, firearms and oxen had been purchased, and women had worked thick calluses in their fingers making tents and blankets. Early the next year, amid rumors that nonbelievers were mounting an assault on the town, the Mormon exodus commenced.

Brother Brigham—described in *The Gathering of Zion* as a man "as practical as Joseph was visionary, as efficient in administration as Joseph was fertile in invention"—had carefully mapped out their route. He had also set a regimen for his people to maintain as they snaked across the Great Plains and climbed over the western mountains. "At 5:00 in the morning," the patriarch instructed, "the bugle is to be sounded as a signal for every man to arise and attend prayers before he leaves his wagon. Then cooking, eating, feeding teams, etc. till seven o'clock, at which time the camp is to move at the sound of a bugle. Each teamster to keep beside his wagon with his loaded gun in his hands or in his wagon, where he can get it at any moment."

The Mormons would not all go at once. First, they would ferry (or walk, as the winter ice thickened) over the Mississippi River to a staging camp, passing Joseph Smith's old home on their way and perhaps making an offering to his widow, who refused to enlist in this exodus. From there, they would depart at regular intervals in neat companies supervised by a hierarchy of captains and lieutenants. Small teams went ahead to set up rest stations, plow fields, and sow seeds in order to make the trek somewhat easier. Each new company was expected to replant fields for the next caravan, as well as build bridges and construct reusable rafts. "If you do these things," Young promised, "faith will abide in your hearts; and the angels of God will go with you, even as they went with the children of Israel, when Moses led them from the land of Egypt." On March 1, 1846, two thousand Mormons began rolling west in some five hundred wagons.

Meanwhile, a separate contingent of 238 Latter-day Saints from the East had left New York City on February 4, sailing aboard the charter ship *Brooklyn*. Their shepherd was Samuel Brannan, a big, broad-shouldered, loudmouthed, twenty-six-year-old Irish newspaperman from Maine. While Young wagoned west, Brannan planned to swoop around Cape Horn and into San Francisco Bay, a voyage of some eighteen thousand miles. The germ of a town there—then known as Yerba Buena, "good herb," but soon to be San Francisco—was governed benignly by Catholic Mexicans and would serve perfectly, Brannan thought, as the starting point for a Mormon takeover of Northern California. Should Young decide to come clear out to the Pacific coast, rather than settle anywhere before, the entrepreneurial Brannan intended to make his fellow Mormons welcome in the territory—and maybe make some money off them at the same time.

DESTINY MADE MANIFEST

AMERICANS HAD BEEN MOVING westward across the continent since the 1830s. Hundreds of thousands set off with their covered wagons from the town of Independence, in the western Missouri district the Mormons had once called home, and traveled up the Oregon Trail to the Columbia River; or they took a cutoff that led them into California. Alternately, they might head southwest from Independence, down the Santa Fe Trail and into the future state of New Mexico. Whichever route they took, the point is that they went. In wave after wave. Residents of the young United States seemed to have an insatiable, bone-deep desire to sniff out and occupy every new horizon.

However, Brigham Young's people were not your everyday land seekers. For one thing, they didn't necessarily volunteer. Rather, they went under pressure from both their religious elders and their tormentors back east. Wallace Stegner points out, further, that they differed from most travelers, who moved with scant provisions and less purpose:

In 1847, Brigham Young and his first party of Mormon pioneers reached "Zion": the valley of the Great Salt Lake. Over the next two decades, the disciplined migration of some seventy thousand Mormons followed in their wake.

[Mormons were] the most systematic, organized, disciplined, and successful pioneers in our history, and their advantage over the random individualists who preceded them and paralleled them and followed them up the valley of the Platte came directly from their "un-American" social and religious organization. Where Oregon emigrants and argonauts bound for the [California] gold fields lost practically all their social cohesion en route, the Mormons moved like the Host of Israel they thought themselves. Far from loosening their social organization, the trail perfected it.

A common misconception is that these religious pilgrims hacked out their own, completely unique trail in their efforts to reach the Great Salt Lake. In reality, they took whatever was the fastest, easiest, most direct route already available. So, in crossing Iowa, they employed rough territorial byways, animal traces, and what could be seen of Native American paths. Their trek through present-day Nebraska and Wyoming followed the mighty Platte River, and much of it overlapped or at least ran parallel to the older Oregon Trail. (To avoid bumping into Missourians or other gentiles with whom they had tussled, the Mormons tended to hug the river's north bank, leaving others to plod the Oregon Trail along the Platte's south side.) West of Wyoming's Fort Bridger—originally a civilian trading post, established by renowned mountain man Jim Bridger, and later controlled by the Mormons as a refitting station for emigrant parties—the followers of Brigham Young picked up the faint track of the ill-fated Donner Party, which, on its way to California in 1846, had opened an important stretch through the Wasatch Mountains and on west to the Great Salt Lake.

Because of such rampant borrowings, some historians unjustly discount the importance of the Mormon Trail. But as Irene Paden notes in *The Wake of the Prairie Schooner*, a third of the travelers to Oregon and California after 1849 went along the Mormons' chosen path—Latter-day Saints and gentiles both.

Despite their extraordinary preparations, the Mormon pioneers couldn't escape all hardships, natural or man-made. Almost every diary they kept—and they kept many—mentions high winds blowing over tents, or pounding rains that soaked food supplies, or mud that clutched hungrily at passing boots and wagon wheels. Consider the words of Patty Sessions in 1846: "Mud aplenty. The worst time we have had yet. . . . Froze our shoes in the tent, [and] many could not lie down without lying in the water."

Pneumonia and scurvy struck hard at Winter Quarters (now Florence, Nebraska, an Omaha suburb), where the Mormons waited out the cruel winter of 1846–47; seven hundred Latter-day Saints died on the prairies that year, so many that they stacked up, waiting for graves to be dug. Moving through central Nebraska, travelers encountered prairie fires, either started by lightning or by Sioux hunters trying to stampede buffalo. Rattlesnakes, venomous spiders, fleas, and lice were daily problems. Women's skirts got

Defying the Odds

Estimates of the total number of people who died along the Mormon Trail between 1846 and 1869 vary dramatically, from some thirty-seven hundred to more than six thousand. But it's surprising that the figure isn't much higher.

Nineteenth-century pioneers were generally young and healthy, primarily males with farming backgrounds who could handle the ceaseless rigors of cross-country travel. Women made the journey in much smaller numbers, and even fewer elderly or handicapped people trekked over the Oregon or California trails.

Mormon emigrants, however, were a much more heterogeneous bunch. Multi-generational families took to the trail, with all of their friends and neighbors, as well as the sick, the lame, and the mentally infirm. In *The Gathering of Zion: The Story of the Mormon Trail*, Wallace Stegner describes one camp of Latter-day Saints in 1856 as looking "more like the population of the poor farm on a picnic than like pioneers about to cross the plains." In the trail's later years, when more and more European converts joined the exodus, companies were heavy with teachers, bookbinders, doll makers, and undernourished youngsters, people ill-fit to survive disease or extremes of weather.

Was it the extraordinary organization of those early Mormons or their faith that protected them on their way? Probably a little of both.

To Hell in a Handcart

Easily the worst single disaster on the Mormon Trail occurred in the late fall of 1856.

Some forty-four hundred European converts, sponsored by the church's Perpetual Emigration Fund, had been brought to New York and carried by train to Iowa City, Iowa. Under normal circumstances, they would have been outfitted there with large wagons and animal teams. But a grasshopper plague in Utah had reduced the church's available moneys, leaving only enough to buy these pilgrims light wooden handcarts in which to transport their food and possessions. They would have to *walk* all the way to Salt Lake City—nearly thirteen hundred miles.

The first three companies made it to the Great Salt Lake without major incident. But the last three—including more than a thousand people—got trapped on Wyoming's high plains by winter weather. "Our old and infirm people began to droop," wrote John Chislett, a company captain, "and they no sooner lost spirit and courage than death's stamp could be traced upon their features. Life went out as smoothly as a lamp ceases to burn when the oil is gone. At first the deaths occurred slowly and irregularly, but in a few days at more frequent intervals, until we soon thought it unusual to leave a campground without burying one or more persons."

Food ran perilously low. People starved. A young girl awakened one night in screaming pain, only to realize that a hungry man had dragged her far away from her family's encampment—and was chewing off her fingers while she slept! Adults rescued the young girl, but the would-be cannibal, carried off into the snow, had perished by morning.

Once he realized the peril in which these people found themselves, Brigham Young sent rescue teams east from Salt Lake City to help. But it was too late for many of the converts. While no accurate count is available, estimates are that more than two hundred people died on the trail that winter. Young and his fellow church leaders were held to blame, but Brother Brigham would have none of it. "If any man, or woman, complains of me or of my Counselors, in regard to the lateness of some of this season's immigration," he bellowed, "let the Curse of God be on them and blast their substance with mildew and destruction, until their names are forgotten from the earth."

caught on the wagons and dragged their wearers beneath the wheels. Children were gored by oxen. Measles, cholera, and the rigors of childbirth all took their toll on the faithful.

Still, the trail wasn't without its pleasures and its never-to-be-forgotten wonders. Buffalo were so plentiful on the Great Plains in those years—ten thousand or more might be found in a single herd—that when they stampeded, mused Wilford Woodruff, who later served as the Mormon Church's sixth president, it seemed "the face of the earth was alive & moving like the waves of the sea." Kids tried to make pets out of prairie dogs, and they poked at giant anthills, looking for "beads that had been lost by Indians and collected by these indefatigable little workers," wrote ten-year-old Mary Jane Mount in 1847.

Since so much of their route before the Rocky Mountains was across a flat landscape, travelers were wont to scale any especially lofty point along the way, such as the Ancient Bluff Ruins or Scotts Bluff, in western Nebraska. When they reached Wyoming's Sweetwater River and the granite outcropping of Independence Rock, the Mormons climbed it, danced atop it, and, like many before them, scratched their names in its face. So accustomed were these folks to the rhythms of civilization, that the very emptiness held a mysterious allure. Pioneer John Lingren wrote in 1863:

> There was a wild weird romance about the country like some dream, some imaginary scene materialized. During the evening, sounds of music from different parts of the camp seem strangely harmonious with the almost deathlike silence of these uninhabited regions.

THE ROAD TO ZION

ON JULY 31, 1846, after a voyage that had taken it around South America and out to the Sandwich Islands (Hawaii), the *Brooklyn* and its load of Mormons finally sailed into San Francisco Bay. As he approached the hamlet there, Sam Brannan stared in disbelief, for rather than a Mexican flag whipping in the wind above the central plaza, he spied an American flag. The very gentiles he had come so far to escape had somehow preceded him to this western frontier!

As one story has it, Brannan exclaimed in disgust, "There's that damned rag again."

What had happened was this: In the six months that the *Brooklyn* was at sea, the United States had provoked a war with Mexico, hoping to win control of California and the territory that would become Arizona, New Mexico, Nevada, and Utah. Captain John B. Montgomery and his sloop-of-war, the *Portsmouth*, had arrived in the Bay Area only twenty-two days before the *Brooklyn* to officially claim the area on behalf of President James K. Polk. Any thoughts Brannan had of establishing a Mormon empire in Northern California were now out the window.

Another year passed before Brigham Young made it to the valley of the Great Salt Lake. Advance parties had scouted the area and been less than impressed. One woman scoffed at the notion that this barren plain hemmed in by the Wasatch Mountains might host their modern Zion: "We have traveled fifteen hundred miles to get here, and I would willingly travel a thousand miles farther to get where it looked as though a white man could live."

Young brushed aside any suggestions—including those from Brannan, who had ventured east to intercept the party—that the Mormons continue past the lake and on to more fertile California. "God has made the choice, not Brigham Young," he declared. As for Brannan's choice? He would return to San Francisco and find his passion in capitalism, not the church, growing rich as a newspaper publisher and real-estate magnate.

And so, on July 24, 1847, Young, sick with mountain tick fever, landed in the valley and decreed that it would henceforth be their home, the end of the Mormon Trail. The next night, he shared his vision of the Mormon future:

> We do not intend to have any trade or commerce with the gentile world. . . . The Kingdom of God cannot rise independent of the gentile nations until we produce, manufacture, and make every article of use, convenience, or necessity among our own

The driving of the last spike on the transcontinental railroad in 1869 tolled the death knell for the overland trails. Polygamy—practiced but not always admitted by the Saints—was publicly admonished by the Church in 1890, three years before the completion of the magnificent Mormon Temple in Salt Lake City.

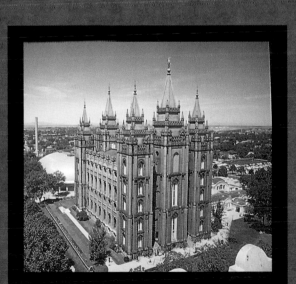

people. . . . I am determined to cut every threat of this kind and live free and independent, untrammeled by any of their detestable customs and practices.

Of course, things wouldn't be quite that easy.

The California gold rush in its first two years attracted a hundred thousand prospectors, many of them following the Mormon Trail. As those men passed through aborning Salt Lake City, they spread rumors of untold wealth located not far to the west, enticing some of the Latter-day Saints to follow—a fact that stirred Young's wrath. ("If you elders of Israel want to go to the gold mines, go and be damned," he cursed.)

Brother Brigham wanted his flock uncorrupted by gentiles, and so he petitioned the U.S. Congress to establish a new provisional state, taking in most of the Southwest. This place would be governed by Mormons and dubbed "Deseret," after the Book of Mormon word for the honeybee, symbol of industriousness. But Congress balked, creating (under Young's governorship) a territory only one-quarter the proposed size and naming it for the local Ute Indians. Even that was too much for many Americans, who were disturbed by the Mormons' linking of church and state, and positively scandalized by the church's openness on the matter of plural marriage—a doctrine that had already given Young twenty-seven wives (including eight of Joseph Smith's widows) and fifty-six children. He would eventually be "sealed" with an additional fifty women.

> "THE MORMONS are the common enemies of mankind and ought to be destroyed."
>
> —A Missouri minister (circa 1836)

Tensions came to a head in the summer of 1857, when President James Buchanan sent twenty-five hundred federal troops west to put down polygamous behaviors. Before his army could reach Utah, though, angry Mormons helped Paiute Indians ambush a wagon train in which rode some Arkansas horsemen who had made threats against Young and his followers. In less than half an hour, 120 people were killed. Buchanan called off his invasion, but insisted that

Young resign his post as governor and permit federal troops to be stationed near Salt Lake City, where they could ensure against any more violence. Until he died forty years later—with the name of Joseph Smith on his lips—Brigham Young denied any complicity in the massacre.

As to the cross-country trail that Young had helped create, it remained busy for two decades. The Pony Express and Overland Stage used it. Some seventy thousand Mormons are said to have crossed it. And that doesn't include those who traveled east to pick up supplies, do repairs on the road, or lead new companies to Utah. Not until the first transcontinental railroad was completed in 1869, dedicated with a spike-driving ceremony at Promontory Point, seventy miles northwest of Salt Lake City, did the Mormon Trail fall quiet, the bugles that for so long had stirred its travelers silenced forever.

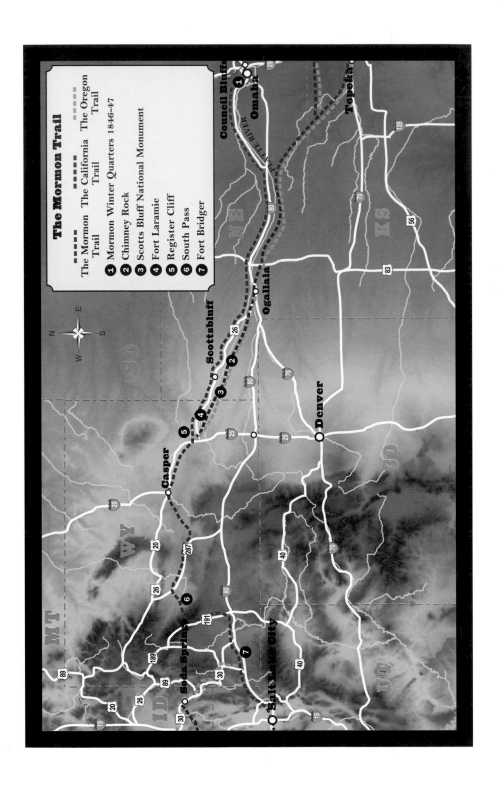

The Mormon Trail Today

Faith paved the way for the first Mormons involved in what historian Hubert Howe Bancroft called "a migration without parallel in the world's history." Today, much of the Mormon Trail is paved with asphalt. To retrace the route, follow U.S. 30 west from Council Bluffs, Iowa. At Ogallala, Nebraska, pick up U.S. 26 heading west into Wyoming; this meets Interstate 25 and leads to Casper. From there, continue west on Wyoming Route 220 and U.S. 287; cross South Pass on Wyoming Route 28, then follow that to Interstate 80 and continue on I-80 into Utah.

HEADING WEST

Reminders of Mormon settlement in Nauvoo, Illinois, are few, but you can still see **Joseph Smith's home** on the banks of the Mississippi River, as well as the foundations of the temple that Smith's followers built on a hill overlooking the town. (The temple itself was destroyed by arson.)

Council Bluffs, Iowa (known to the Mormons as Kanesville), was a principal staging area for westbound pioneers. It later became a prosperous railroading center. The **Rails West Museum** in Dodge Park honors that industry's contribution to the city. Right across the Mississippi lies Omaha, Nebraska, and the **Winter Quarters Historic Mormon Pioneer Monument and Cemetery**, a tribute to the many Mormons who perished there during the harsh winter of 1846–47. The grounds feature a full-sized pioneer wagon, handcart, and log cabin, as well as the restored **Mormon Mill**, one of the area's oldest structures.

At **Grand Island**, Nebraska, the **Stuhr Museum of the Pioneer Prairie** offers exhibits and films showing what life was like for early emigrants. Its campus also includes a reproduced 1860s railroad town. Near the western edge of the state, you'll pass **Chimney Rock**, a sandstone spire that rises dramatically from the plains and was a first suggestion to travelers that they would soon encounter much more rugged terrain. The Chimney Rock Visitor Center near Bayard houses a fine museum and provides a panoramic view of the landmark. At nearby **Scotts Bluff National Monument,** a visitor center details the history of the westward migration. Also here is the poignant resting place of Rebecca Winter, a fifty-year-old woman who died of cholera in 1852. Of the thousands of Mormons who perished on the plains, she was one of the few whose grave was properly marked.

Fort Laramie, in Wyoming's mountain range of the same name, marked another transition for the Mormons—it was the first and last sign of civilization for many miles, and a point where the Mormon, Oregon, and California trails merged. Several structures, including the barracks, have been restored at the Fort Laramie National Historic Site. Just to the west, in Guernsey, is **Register Cliff,** a petrified notebook of signatures left by pioneers who had survived to this point. But the Saints left behind more than names here; their wagons, forced to go single-file down Mexican Hill, cut wheel ruts in the rock, some five feet deep—and still visible.

At **Casper,** Wyoming, the Mormons built ferries and helped other pioneers cross the North Platte River—for a profit. So popular did this idea become that, eventually, a toll bridge was built. **Historic Trails Expeditions** schedules train tours that depart from Fort Casper and follow the actual Mormon Trail. Before leaving Wyoming, stop at **Fort Bridger.** Located off Interstate 80, this trading post was established in the early 1840s by mountain man Jim Bridger and later served as one of the most important stations along the trail. The Mormons either bought or stole the fort, depending on which account you believe. Some of its buildings are in ruins, but a museum displays Indian artifacts, and staff members perform demonstrations of activities from military and pioneer life.

SALT LAKE CITY

An imposing sixty-foot-tall monument at **"This is the Place" State Park,** in Utah's Emigration Canyon, east of Salt Lake City, commemorates the Saints' scaling of the Wasatch Mountains and their final descent into the new homeland chosen for them by church leader Brigham Young.

The **Salt Lake City Visitor's Center** gives a valuable introduction to Mormon history—helpful in understanding why and how this city grew as it did. **Temple Square** (bound by North Temple, South Temple, West Temple, and Main Streets) is the ten-acre heart and lungs of the town that Young's followers built. The square features several memorials and statues, but the centerpiece is the **Mormon Temple,** a many-spired granite edifice that took forty years to build, being completed in 1893. Although the temple is closed to non-Mormons, the neighboring **Tabernacle** invites the general public in to hear its famed choir and its frequent organ recitals. Through demonstrations, films, and artwork from around the world, the **Museum of Church History and Art** details Mormonism's growth from 1820. **Beehive House,** Brigham Young's white-columned residence, has been beautifully restored and contains period furnishings.

To learn more about the Mormon Trail, call the Iowa Convention and Visitor's Bureau, 712-325-1000; Nebraska's Stuhr Museum, 308-385-5316; Wyoming's Fort Laramie National Historic Site, 307-837-2221, and Fort Bridger, 307-782-3842 or 307-777 7014; and the Salt Lake City Visitor's Center, 801-240-2534. —*Ellen L. Boyer*

The
California Trail

O NLY IN RETROSPECT DO some things seem obvious, and historical events that at the time weren't recognized as significant take their place as markers for the starts or ends of eras. It's clear, now, that the early 1840s were such a time.

The North American fur trade was in a state of decline. After spending more than three decades trapping beavers on every river and rivulet of the West—all to supply the European and American beau monde with the pelts needed to create their fashionable felt hats—mountain men like Jim Bridger, Jim Beckwourth, and Joe Meek suddenly realized that they had done their often-perilous jobs too well: The beavers were pretty much gone, and the market price for those that remained had tumbled.

Driven by a lust for land, gold, or simply adventure, emigrants in the mid-1800s crossed the continent to make California an important new part of the United States.

By 1843 Bridger, ever the pragmatist, had all but forsaken the hunter's life for a modest log fort he raised on Black's Fork of the Green River, in what is today southwestern Wyoming. There he waited. And waited. And waited some more. The erstwhile Saint Louis blacksmith and discoverer of the Great Salt Lake (upon tasting it, Bridger had concluded—wrongly—that it must connect with the Pacific Ocean) fully expected a flood of California- and Oregon-bound wagon trains, all of them needing the provisions with which

THE EMIGRANT'S GUIDE TO THE GOLD MINES.

THREE WEEKS

IN THE

GOLD MINES,

OR

ADVENTURES WITH THE GOLD DIGGERS OF CALIFORNIA

In August, 1848.

TOGETHER WITH

ADVICE TO EMIGRANTS,

WITH FULL INSTRUCTIONS UPON THE BEST METHOD OF GETTING
THERE, LIVING, EXPENSES, ETC., ETC., AND A

COMPLETE DESCRIPTION OF THE COUNTRY,

With a Map and Illustrations.

Y HENRY I. SIMPSON,
OF THE NEW YORK VOLUNTEERS.

NEW YORK:
JOYCE AND CO., 40 ANN STREET.
1848.

Lust for gold blinded many a California emigrant into believing what they read in guidebooks—some of which were long on enthusiasm and promises, but short on practical experience.

he had stocked his outpost. Some of Bridger's former colleagues thought him crazy for becoming essentially a shopkeeper. But Bridger saw then what would later become clear to many others: The days of the scruffy mountain men were coming to a close, and the age of the overland emigrant was just beginning.

In a way, it was adventurers like Bridger who were responsible for the whole cross-country movement. They had explored the West and told others of its copious wonders. Now, people wanted to ogle for themselves those Brobdingnagian peaks and spacious valleys about which they had heard. These new seekers felt no compunction in leaving wherever they had been living. A great many of the folks who eventually went to California and Oregon had moved at least once before in their lives; moving had in fact, become essential behavior in a nation bent on stretching from sea to shining sea. A trek to the West Coast was merely another leap in the hop-scotching migration that had already scattered Americans from the East Coast down into the fecund Mississippi Valley and on to the parched wilds of Texas and New Mexico.

Travelers over the California Trail had almost the same adventurous spirit as Bridger and his mountain men. However, they were frequently less able to cope with the hazards that the West threw in their paths—river fordings, desert crossings, and, of course, the conquering of California's intimidating Sierra Nevada. Especially in the trail's formative years, this unpreparedness could have dire consequences. Perhaps it was thirteen-year-old Virginia Reed, a survivor of the Donner Party, who offered the sagest and certainly the most poignant advice to anyone else anxious to head for California: "Hurry as fast as you can and don't take no cut-offs."

FOOLS RUSH IN

THERE WAS A CHARMING, if worrisome, naïveté about the first overland party of emigrants that departed the Midwest for California in 1841. About five hundred Missourians had signed on in the previous year to participate in this expedition, among them John Bidwell, an itinerant schoolteacher in his early twenties. The number willing to make the journey was especially amazing, since, as Bidwell readily conceded, "Our ignorance of the route was complete. We knew that California lay west, and that was the extent of our knowledge."

Arrangements had been made for everyone to gather on May 19, 1841, at a point on the Santa Fe Trail approximately twenty miles west of Independence, Missouri. Yet, when Bidwell arrived, there was only one other wagon on hand. During the winter, it seems, newspapers had carried word of an American being tossed into a California jail for simply suggesting the United States might someday take possession of that Mexican-held territory. Most of the would-be pioneers weren't excited by the prospect of incarceration for sharing that selfsame view and promptly canceled out. Bidwell wasn't discouraged, however, and within a few days he had recruited new wagons and some thirty-five prospective travelers— each of them every bit as clueless as he was about what lay ahead.

Fortunately, they happened to encounter one of Jim Bridger's numerous old mountain buddies, Thomas Fitzpatrick, a slender and intelligent Irishman known to the Cheyenne as "Broken Hand," owing to a rifle explosion that had taken three of his fingers. Fitzpatrick had been hired to lead a trinity of Jesuit missionaries— chief among them, Father Pierre Jean De Smet—all the way to Oregon Country. Since the California Trail and Oregon Trail kept to the same course for roughly twelve hundred miles, until a fork west of South Pass in the Rocky Mountains, Fitzpatrick agreed to shepherd Bidwell's contingent that far, as well.

Early on the Missourians elected an expedition captain—not Bidwell or even another congenial young member of their group who called himself Talbot H. Green but, strangely, John Bartleson, a disagreeable sort whose name would forever be attached to this party. And they studied Fitzpatrick as he herded them through each leg of the journey and found them suitable campsites every evening, hoping to learn how they might carry on once he and the missionaries had split from them. They learned some valuable lessons, as along the way they broke trail down stream banks, fired into buffalo herds for food, and saw one of their companions caught by a mischievous band of Cheyenne, who made off with the man's mule, his weapons, and even the clothes from his back.

The combined parties picked up more members as they rolled west (bringing their total number to more than seventy). They made swift pace, passing Fort Laramie (Wyoming) and continuing some 560 miles more to Soda Springs (Idaho) on the Bear River. There, Father De Smet's unit turned north, following the main trail for Oregon. A large part of the Bartleson Party—including most of the families—went with them, afraid to lose Fitzpatrick's skilled guidance, leaving Bidwell and thirty-four others in nine wagons to struggle toward California.

And struggle they did, looping north around the Great Salt Lake and blundering through what is now dry, northern Nevada. Their food stores ran dangerously low, and game was at an absolute premium. Finally abandoning their wagons as a useless drag on their progress, the Bartleson Party continued on foot, the only mother in the bunch clutching her year-old babe to her breast. They slaughtered their oxen one by one and bargained with local Native Americans for any kind of sustenance (in one case, a gummy concoction that turned out to be mashed insects). They hugged the Humboldt River as it dove south, then continued wandering south farther than most later companies would, climbing the Sierra at Sonora Pass. After being reduced to munching on boiled acorns and mule meat, they made it to the San Joaquin Valley. There they found relief at a ranch owned by John Marsh, a Harvard grad and undertrained practitioner of medicine, whose glowing reports about California's life and climate had found their way into eastern newspapers, to be devoured by Bidwell and others. It had taken them nearly seven months to travel almost two thousand miles.

Because they had been forced to leave their vehicles behind, the Bartleson Party was, strictly speaking, not the first wagon train of California-bound emigrants to reach their destination. Still, they were "in many ways outstanding," as George R. Stewart wrote in *The California Trail: An Epic with Many Heroes*, the foremost history of this transcontinental route: "In its concentration of vigor, toughness, and ability, we can believe that no other company—indeed, few chance-gathered groups of Americans ever assembled—could surpass it."

Several of these pioneers would go on to prominence, or at least prosperity. Talbot Green, for instance, became a leading merchant in San Francisco and had a major street named in his honor. He was a popular candidate for mayor in 1851—at which time someone recognized him as Paul Geddes, a bank clerk who had embezzled funds and deserted a wife and child back east. (The affable Mr. Geddes/Green subsequently left the Bay Area, promising to disprove the charge—he never did, and he never returned.) In the meantime, John Bidwell had drifted to the Sacramento Valley, where he worked as chief clerk for none other than John Augustus Sutter—the soon-to-be father of California's golden Mother Lode.

Like so many others who created a comfortable existence for themselves in nineteenth-century California, Sutter was a fugitive from justice when he sailed into San Francisco Bay in 1839. He had left behind a stack of bad debts in his native Switzerland, resulting from a dry-goods-and-drapery enterprise gone terribly wrong. (He had also left behind a domineering wife and five children.) Warrants in Europe called for his prompt arrest.

> "IT IS SAID THAT during the California gold rush, travelers coming to the fork in the Oregon Trail had to choose between the road to California, marked by a pile of glittering quartz, and a road with a sign reading 'To Oregon.' Those who could read came to Oregon."
>
> —DICK PINTARICH,
> *Great Moments in Oregon History*

Still, Sutter can't be deemed a thorough scoundrel. In fact, according to historian Hubert Howe Bancroft, he was "an inborn gentleman." And he apparently had sufficient savoir faire to talk Pio Pico, the Mexican governor of California, into granting him close to fifty thousand acres of land in two sections northeast of present-day San Francisco: one along the Feather River and another near the confluence of the Sacramento and American Rivers. High above the American, Sutter built an adobe fortress and founded an agrarian colony—Nueva Helvetia (New Switzerland)—which he hoped would attract other Swiss immigrants to the West. One of Bidwell's initial responsibilities as Sutter's clerk was to arrange for the contents of an old Russian installation on California's north coast to be moved to Sutter's Fort. Among the goods were a handful of French cannons with which Sutter planned to protect his colony from attack by Indians or Mexicans.

Sutter's fellow countrymen didn't exactly storm into the Sacramento Valley. However, his fort and the supplies it sold did begin to draw another sort of crowd: those hardy, reckless souls who ventured to California in the wake of the Bartleson Party.

A GREAT THOROUGHFARE

M OST OF THE AMERICANS WHO trooped across the continent between 1842 and 1844 headed toward Oregon Country, not California. The dispute between Great Britain and the United States for ultimate control of Oregon seemed likely to be resolved in favor of the Americans and the land claims made by American colonists. There was less confidence in Washington's ability to end the centuries-old hold over California that Mexico had inherited from the Spanish Empire. Besides, amateur promoters such as minister/lecturer Jason Lee and Hall Jackson Kelley, a former New England textile mill owner who had been obsessed with Oregon ever since reading *The Journals of Lewis and Clark*, had been touting the northwest territory to both the public and Congress since the early 1830s. By 1844, Boston's *Daily Evening Transcript* could report, "Hundreds are already prepared to start [for Oregon] in the spring. . . . The Oregon fever has broken out, and is now raging like any other contagion." No wonder the westward course became best known as the Oregon Trail.

The southbound cut-off from that main route to California was straightened and improved by various parties in 1842 and 1843. Not until 1844, however, did a migrating group make it over the Sierra without losing all of its wagons in transit.

Led by Elisha Stevens, a reclusive, taciturn blacksmith, and

For a brief time in the 1860s, Pony Express riders followed the California Trail, carrying mail across the country. But for most of its life, the trail saw wave after wave of ox- and mule-pulled prairie schooners.

guided part of the way by yet another mountain man, Caleb Greenwood, this company—a mix of grandparents, families, and young men—set off from the Missouri River in the middle of May. At Greenwood's behest, they took a rough but only moderately risky shortcut west of South Pass, saving themselves eighty-five miles. They pulled up to Fort Hall, northwest of Soda Springs on the Snake River, in mid-August. Two months later, and with some assistance from an amicable native called Truckee, they reached a western Nevada wasteland that the Bartleson Party had conve-

Aid for the Traveler

Some guidebooks for the emigrant were actually based on solid experience. In 1859, U.S. Army Captain Randolph B. Marcy published *The Prairie Traveler*. Having spent a quarter-century on America's western frontier, Marcy set down some words of wisdom for pioneer travelers, including the following:

What to wear: "Cotton or linen fabrics do not sufficiently protect the body against the direct rays of the sun at midday, nor against rains or sudden changes of temperature. Wool, being a non-conductor, is the best material for this mode of locomotion, and should always be adopted for the plains. The coat should be short and stout, the shirt of red or blue flannel, such as can be found in almost all the shops on the frontier: This, in warm weather, answers for an outside garment. The pants should be of thick and soft material, and it is well to have them reenforced on the inside, where they come in contact with the saddle, with soft buckskin, which makes them more durable and comfortable. Woolen socks and stout boots, coming up well at the knees, and made large, so as to admit the pants, will be found the best for horsemen, and they guard against rattlesnake bites."

Makeshift tobacco: "In passing over the Rocky Mountains during the winter of 1857–8, our supplies of provisions were entirely consumed eighteen days before reaching the first settlements in New Mexico. . . . In this destitute condition we found a substitute for tobacco in the bark of the red willow, which grows upon many of the mountain streams in that vicinity. The outer

niently bypassed three years earlier: the Forty-Mile Desert—a
dreadful day-and-a-half-long wagon crossing that was the
California Trail equivalent of New Mexico's La Jornada del
Muerto.

Here, things commenced to get diccy. Winter was slowly but
surely overtaking the Stevens Party. Snow fell, covering the grass
to such a height that the oxen could not feed upon it, and two of
the beasts starved to death. An advance team of four men and two
women eventually went ahead to bring back help from Sutter's

bark is first removed with a
knife, after which the inner bark
is scraped up into ridges around
the sticks, and held in the fire
until it is thoroughly roasted,
when it is taken off the stick, pul-
verized in the hand, and is ready
for smoking."

Winter footwear: "In traveling through deep snow during
very cold weather in winter, moccasins are preferable to boots or
shoes, as being more pliable, and
allowing a freer circulation of the
blood."

**Finding water in dry coun-
try:** "A supply of drinking water
may be obtained during a shower
from the drippings of a tent, or by
suspending a cloth or blanket by
the four corners and hanging a
small weight to the center, so as
to allow all the rain to run toward
one point, from whence it drops
into a vessel beneath. . . . When

there are heavy dews water may
be collected by spreading out a
blanket with a stick attached to
one end, tying a rope to it, drag-
ging it over the grass, and wring-
ing out the water as it
accumulates."

Vigilant mules: "Mules are
very keenly sensitive to danger,
and, in passing along over the
prairies, they will often detect the
proximity of strangers long before
they are discovered by their riders. Nothing seems to escape their
observation."

Meeting Indians: "On
approaching strangers these people
put their horses at full speed, and
persons not familiar with their
peculiarities and habits might
interpret this as an act of hostil-
ity; but it is their custom with
friends as well as enemies, and
should not occasion groundless
alarm."

Fort, while the main body of pioneers slogged on to what is today Donner Lake, there to plan their next moves.

They chose to consolidate their eleven wagons to five, leaving the balance behind at the lake, together with three young men who would protect the vehicles against Indian larceny. The remaining settlers pushed west. They located a wagon-friendly pass through the steep wall of the Sierra (a gateway that has since come to be known, with some lingering horror, as Donner Pass) and in mid-December dropped down into the Sacramento Valley. There they found their advance band.

Two of the three wagon guards they had left behind joined them weeks later, explaining that, as winter tightened its grip over the region and they grew desperate for food, they had had to surrender the surplus wagons to the natives. And what of the third man, Moses Schallenberger? Alas, they explained, he had grown weak and was left behind for dead.

Imagine everyone's amazement when, in February 1845, Schallenberger was found in the Sierra, looking pretty darn disheveled but still alive!

So, despite the odds against it, the Stevens Party had achieved something remarkable: It had completed its cross-country trek without a total material loss and with not a single human casualty. As this news washed back east, interest in making the journey to California grew—and cast a shadow over Mexico's ability to maintain its control of that vast territory. "We find ourselves threatened by hordes of Yankee emigrants, who have already begun to flock into our country, and whose progress we cannot arrest," Governor Pico fretted to his superiors in Mexico City. "Already have the wagons of that perfidious people scaled the almost inaccessible summits of the Sierra Nevada, crossed the entire continent and penetrated the fruitful valley of the Sacramento. What that astonishing people will next undertake, I cannot say."

Traveling in ranks of ten or twelve for some measure of mutual protection, most of the pioneers' covered wagons, or "prairie schooners," as newspaper wits dubbed them, launched toward California from one of two Missouri towns—Independence or Saint Joseph—forming ragged, canvas-topped caravans across the plains.

The story of the Donner Party ranks as the most amazing in the history of the California Trail, with equal parts of tragedy and triumph. Delayed through Utah by taking a shortcut that wasn't, and trapped by the snows in the Sierra, they lost almost half their number before being rescued.

In the words of one observer, an army captain from Virginia by the name of Philip St. George Cooke, the California Trail in those days was a truly inspiring sight:

> Here was a great thoroughfare—broad and well-worn—the longest and best natural road perhaps in the world. Endless seemed the procession of wagons; mostly very light, and laden only with children and provisions, and the most necessary articles for families; and drawn generally by two yokes of oxen; some three hundred wagons or families, they said, were in advance.

The wagons usually started rolling immediately after the first

Ships of the Prairie

"As the long rifle and the log cabin stand for the settling of the first frontier across the Alleghenies, the sturdy covered wagon will forever call to mind the winning of the West."
— George R. Stewart,
American Heritage

It's an image born in fact and burnished by fiction: Lines of covered wagons wobbling across North America during the nineteenth century, their occupants driven by curiosity, necessity, or mere restlessness to find a new life west of the Rocky Mountains.

But contrary to some Hollywood depictions, the wagons that carried emigrants to California, Oregon, and elsewhere were not the huge, lumbering Conestoga type—recognizable by their boat-shaped beds and sway-backed covers—that had borne earlier generations through New England and down the busy Santa Fe Trail. Instead, the wagons of the westward migration were smaller and lighter, requiring fewer animals to pull the ton or less in cargo that they held.

Each wagon consisted of three parts: an oblong wooden box of a body, nine or ten feet in length and about four feet in width, often with a false floor under which went reserve supplies; a canvas or cloth top (waterproofed with paint or linseed oil) stretched over bows of bent hickory, allowing enough room inside for a man to stand upright; and running gear that included iron tires, yet mostly of May, and with the trail now well blazed, their occupants reckoned to be sunning themselves in "Californy" within six months. Beside them they might carry Lansford W. Hastings's *The Emigrants' Guide to Oregon and California* or some other ostensibly authoritative text, most of them penned by men with greater enthusiasm for starting toward the Pacific frontiers than actual experience in reaching there. These guides tended to overstate the route's safety. Truth was, the Paiute Indians grew increasingly testy and inclined toward violence as settlers streamed down the Humboldt River, through their traditional homeland.

Pioneer diaries also belied the assurances in many guides. Illness and equipment breakdowns were common themes in early

wood axles and tongues. (The latter two were susceptible to breaking along the trail, but pioneers could cut down the nearest tree and fashion replacements.) "Front wheels were smaller than rear wheels, but generally not by much," noted George R. Stewart in *The California Trail: An Epic with Many Heroes.* Too-large wheels up front reduced maneuverability; however, hind wheels of a noticeably smaller diameter made the wagon harder to pull. Finally, a "tar bucket" (containing either tar or resin, combined in equal measure with tallow) swung from the back of the wagon bed, for convenient lubricating of the friction-prone wheels and kingbolt.

Although horses could travel faster than mules or oxen, they required more food and were less able than those other animals to endure constant hauling. As a result, not until late in the century, after trails had been smoothed, did horses haul many wagons. Before that, it was oxen and mules—four or six of which were yoked (in pairs) to every wagon—that did most of the work. Oxen were, by far, cheaper to buy. They were also less liable to be stampeded or stolen by Indians—and beef was a lot tastier than mule meat if the other food stocks ran low.

Wending over the plains, these wagon trains looked like nothing so much as fleets of small, white-sailed ships. Thus their familiar nickname, rarely employed by the emigrants themselves: "prairie schooners."

diaries. As were accidental gunshot wounds. Apparently every chucklehead crossing the prairies saw it as his God-sworn duty to arm himself for extended battle, even when he was wholly unacquainted with the proper use of firearms.

Given the perils, it's curious that this transcontinental migration came to be known in the mid-1850s as a relatively pleasant trip. "Many people," Stewart wrote in *The California Trail*, "at least in retrospect, considered the crossing their equivalent of a Grand Tour, and looked back upon it as pleasurable and exciting. This was particularly true of boys and girls, who felt little sense of responsibility and remained a part of a strongly knit family group."

Not every company, though, made it through unscathed.

A WINTER'S TALE

O N JULY 20, 1846, a wagon train paused west of South Pass, where two years before, the Stevens Party had begun its shortcut to Fort Hall. There, this caravan split: The larger group—commanded by Lillburn Boggs, the former Missouri governor who had called for the elimination of Mormons from his state—headed northwest to Oregon; the smaller contingent of twenty wagons, containing ninety-one people, hied toward California. Among this latter group were a pair of well-to-do farmers from Illinois, brothers George and Jacob Donner, both in their sixties, traveling with their families and as many possessions as they could jam into six wagons. They were joined by their friends, cabinetmaker James F. Reed and his wife, Margaret, who, with their four children, rolled along quite agreeably in a semiluxurious wagon fitted with a sheet-iron stove inside.

Had this emigrant train—named in honor of George Donner, its wagon master—stuck to the familiar California Trail, it would likely not have merited so much as a footnote in our history books. But its members thought they had a superior alternative: a new cut-off that Lansford Hastings himself proclaimed would shave a full two hundred miles from their journey. Heading first

With the discovery of gold at Sutter's Mill on the South Fork of the American River, the flood of emigrants and prospectors to California increased fiftyfold. Wagon trains that might have numbered a dozen prairie schooners now stretched on for miles.

THE "PRAIRIE SCHOONER."

to Fort Bridger, they planned to skirt the Great Salt Lake on the south and then continue west until they ran into the old Fort Hall trail on the Humboldt River. Sounded easy. Except that this shortcut looked far better on a map than it did on the ground.

Having to cut a thirty-six-mile wagon path over Utah's densely thicketed Wasatch Mountains was exhausting work enough, but then having to trudge across the waterless, eighty-mile-wide Great Salt Lake Desert almost proved the Donner Party's undoing. Most of the oxen were lost, and the wagons they pulled had to be left behind. When these emigrants finally rejoined the California Trail in eastern Nevada, they were three weeks behind schedule and snow had begun to fall. Fear and dis-illusionment set in. Petty quarrels became frequent. During a dis-agreement over the order in which wagons should proceed up a sandy hill, James Reed knifed another man. He claimed it was self-defense, but Reed's fellow travelers—many of whom consid-ered him arrogant and probably would have lynched him on the spot—banished Reed from the group. He continued to California on his own, while his family stayed with the Donner company.

The story of America's westward migration contains few chapters so tragic, so terrifying, or so revealing of man's instinc-tive resolve to live than that of the Donners, the Reeds, and the other clans trapped during the winter of 1846–47 at the same lake the Stevens Party had reconnoitered two years earlier. Unable in several attempts to cross the snowbound Sierra pass later named in their memory, members of the Donner Party tried to wait out the cold, building cabins, watching their comrades perish of mal-nutrition or a paucity of hope, and eating whatever they could find. ("[W]e had to kill little Cash the dog & eat him, . . . " Virginia Reed wrote in a letter to a cousin after her rescue. "We ate his entrails and feet & hide & evry thing about him.") As con-ditions worsened, panic breached the walls of human decency, and some turned to cannibalism, repulsing even themselves in that last desperate act of survival.

Relief parties, one led by the banished James Reed, did not arrive at Donner Lake until February 1847. What members of the wagon train remained alive couldn't believe their eyes. "Are you men from California," one half-starved woman asked her rescuers, "or do you come from Heaven?" Of the ninety-one people in the Donner Party, only forty-nine reached their destination.

Hearing of the Donner nightmare and worried also that the ongoing Mexican War might engulf all of California, many wagons heading west in 1847 chose to steer for Oregon, instead. Still more followed Brigham Young to the future site of Salt Lake City.

Yet this eclipsing of California would not last long.

THE TRAIL TO EL DORADO

JAMES W. MARSHALL, a carpenter charged with supervising the construction of a sawmill for John Sutter on the South Fork of the American River (near the present-day town of Coloma), went to inspect that mill's progress on January 24, 1848. While assessing the depth of its tailrace (a ditch that diverted water to power the mill wheel and then returned it to the river), something caught his eye. It was "shining in the bottom of the ditch, . . ." Marshall recalled later. "I reached my hand down and picked it up; it made my heart thump, for I was certain it was gold."

Sutter tried initially to keep this discovery hush-hush, believing that the development of a town around his fort and the future of his other commercial enterprises in the Sacramento Valley would be set back severely by the distraction of easy wealth nearby. But news of Marshall's find leaked out, setting off a gold rush the likes of which had never been seen before. "The whole country from San Francisco to Los Angeles and from the seashore to the base of the Sierra Nevada," San Francisco's weekly *Californian* exclaimed in May 1848, "resounds to the sordid cry of gold, gold! GOLD!, while the field is left half planted, the house half built and everything neglected but the manufacture of shovels and pick-axes."

In 1849 alone, almost eight hundred ships departed New York's harbor, bound for the Golden Gate. By 1851, a hundred thousand forty-niners, as the gold-seekers were called, had braved the California Trail to take their shot at panning the streams around Sutter's Fort.

According to some diarists, caravans that had been only a few wagons long before the gold rush now extended to six miles in length. "In a single year," George Stewart notes, "the numbers so increased that for *one* person who traveled the trail to California in '48, *fifty* traveled it in '49."

Most of these folks were no better off after the gold rush than they had been before. And in one of the supreme ironies of American history, even Sutter—on whose land the whole frenzy had begun—lost out. Choosing to concentrate on other business rather than participate in the excitement, he again piled up a mountain of bad debts. Years afterward, he tried to petition Congress for fifty thousand dollars to redress the damage that thieves and trespassers had done to his domain. His cause won high-profile endorsements, but Sutter died in 1880, before Congress was willing to open its purse on his behalf.

Trail Use and Abuse

At no previous time was the California/Oregon/Mormon Trail in such heavy use as after news broke of gold being discovered at Sutter's Mill. In July 1849, John D. Lee, a Mormon and "spiritual son" of Brigham Young, set off east from Salt Lake City against the tide of forty-niners. It didn't take him long to realize that the trail was no longer the peaceful, pristine path it had once been:

[T]he road was so lined with wagons . . . that one would be scarcely ever out of sight of some train. Dust very disagreeable but not to compare with the stench from dead carcasses which lie along the road, having died from fatigue and hunger. Destruction of property along the road was beyond description, consisting of wagons, harness, tools of every description, provisions, clothings, stoves, cooking vessels, powder, lead & almost everything, etc. that could be mentioned.

Very frequently some 20 or 30 persons would surround [my] wagon and plead for a moment's instructions, some of them with consternation depicted on their countenances, their teams worn out, women & children on foot & some packing their provision[s], trying to reach some point of refuge.

(Geoffrey C. Ward, *The West: An Illustrated History*, 1996, quoting John D. Lee)

Luckier was young John Bidwell, who had gone west with that first overland party in 1841. He struck it rich during the rush and put his money to good use, buying a twenty-six-thousand-acre ranch in northern California and founding the town of Chico there. Bidwell went on to run (unsuccessfully) for president in 1892 on the Prohibition Party ticket. He died eight years later.

If the California Trail and the gold rush did not lead every emigrant to riches, however, they did accomplish something greater. In little more than a decade, they stretched the grasp of the still-young United States. American pioneers, who had not pressed much past the Mississippi River since Daniel Boone breached the Cumberland Gap, had now in tremendous strides conquered the Rockies and the Sierra Nevada to win a place for themselves at the farthest edge of the continent.

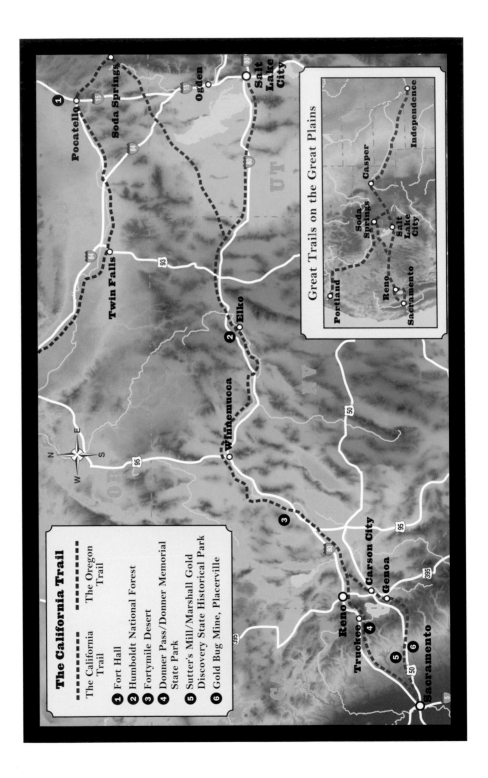

The California Trail

- - - - The California Trail
- - - - The Oregon Trail

1 Fort Hall
2 Humboldt National Forest
3 Fortymile Desert
4 Donner Pass/Donner Memorial State Park
5 Sutter's Mill/Marshall Gold Discovery State Historical Park
6 Gold Bug Mine, Placerville

Great Trails on the Great Plains

The California Trail Today

The California Trail, for the most part, follows the same course as that of the Oregon Trail, and it either parallels or overlaps the Mormon Trail. From beginning points in Missouri and Iowa, they head west, not diverging until almost beyond Wyoming. To follow the California Trail today, begin at Salt Lake City and continue west on Interstate 80 through the state of Nevada, over California's Sierra Nevada, and down the foothills to Sacramento.

NEVADA

The trail comes into its own at the cattle town of **Elko,** where the **Northeastern Nevada Museum** (1515 Idaho Street) gives life and depth to history in a series of exhibits focusing on Native Americans and the mining industry. Also featured are an 1860 Pony Express cabin and other remnants of pioneer life. If you have a hankering for cowboy culture, visit the **Western Folklife Center** (501 Railroad Street), housed in Elko's restored Pioneer Hotel, or stop by the **J. M. Capriola Company,** which continues its tradition of making saddles by hand. One specimen on display dates back to 1900.

The **Humboldt National Forest** forms a green crescent of two million acres around Elko and includes the **Lamoille Canyon Scenic Area,** with its twelve miles of hiking trails and spectacular overlooks. Follow I-80 west for two hundred miles along the **Humboldt River Valley,** then pass over the legendary **Fortymile Desert**, the bane of many a pioneer's travels. **Ragtown Crossing,** at the Carson River, marks the end of the desert. Near there, in the tiny town of Fallon, drop in at the **Churchill County Museum and Archives** (1050 South Maine Street) to look over some of the many artifacts that were left in the desert by thirsty cross-country trekkers of the nineteenth century.

Carson City, some 250 miles west of Elko, started out as a silver-mining town; now it's Nevada's capital and home to the **Nevada State Museum** (600 North Carson Street). Once a U.S. Mint used to coin silver dollars, the museum now features exhibits of currency and pioneer memorabilia, and a replica of an old ghost town. If you prefer locomotives to lucre, don't miss the **Nevada State Railroad Museum** (2180 South Carson Street), which showcases components of the Virginia and Truckee Railroad line. Or get a feel for the area's native heritage at the **Stewart Indian Museum** (5366 Snyder Avenue), with its plentiful rugs, jewelry, and artwork.

Just outside of Carson City, **Genoa** was the first permanent settlement in Nevada, established in 1849 by one of Brigham Young's traders. Its **Mormon Station Historic State Park** (1060 Mallory Way) is a restored trading post, a place where weary west-bound travelers once rested and dabbled in commerce.

CALIFORNIA

Crossing the Sierra Nevada takes almost no effort today, but **Donner State Memorial Park,** just two miles west of the California border town of Truckee, is a stark reminder of how grueling this crossing was in the nineteenth century. The park covers 353 acres around where members of the ill-fated Donner Party made their stand during the harsh winter of 1846–47. The park's **Emigrant Trail Museum** details Truckee's railroad and immigrant history.

Continue west along I-80 about fifty miles and turn south to **Coloma,** where **Marshall Gold Discovery State Historical Park** (on Route 49) commemorates James W. Marshall's finding of gold at Sutter's Mill in 1848. The park's 270-plus acres encompass Marshall's 1860 cabin, a statue of Marshall pointing to where he first saw the traces of yellow wealth, and a replica of Sutter's Mill. In Placerville, not far away, take a tour of the restored **Gold Bug Mine.** The **El Dorado County Historical Museum** (100 Placerville Drive) offers relics from the Miwok, Maida, and Washoe Indian cultures, and other glimpses of what life was like in Northern California in pre–gold rush times.

Sacramento, where the California Trail ends, was baptized as the state's capital in 1854, but the town grew from a fort that John

Sutter built in the early 1840s. **Sutter's Fort State Historic Park** (2701 L Street) details that Swiss visionary's settlement with gold-rush relics and dioramas of mid-nineteenth-century Sacramento life. At Second and I Streets in Old Sacramento, the **California State Railroad Museum** (featuring, among other things, twenty-one restored locomotives) tells how emigration was made much simpler by the completion in 1869 of America's first transcontinental railroad. Across from the museum stands the **Central Pacific Passenger Station,** the first California terminal of that cross-country railway system.

For more information about the Nevada portion of the California Trail, contact Elko's Northeastern Nevada Museum, 702-738-3418, or the Nevada State Museum, 702-687-4810, in Carson City. Sutter's Fort State Historic Park, 916-445-4422, in Sacramento, can fill you in on facts and sites relevant to the California gold rush. —*Ellen L. Boyer*

California's Mission Trail

Sonoma • San Francisco • San Jose • Carmel • San Miguel • Los Angeles • San Diego

CALIFORNIA MISSION TRAIL

PACIFIC OCEAN

I MAGINE A FAR-OFF LAND, an island rich in pearls and gold, inhabited by black, cave-dwelling amazons—skilled warriors ruled by a valiant pagan queen named Calafía. As early as 1510, such a place had been imagined and written of in *Las Sergas de Esplandían (The Exploits of Esplandían)*, a popular novel of chivalry and romance by Garcia Ordoñez de Montalvo. Described as lying "on the right hand of the Indies" this golden isle came to represent a promised land. Its name: California. By 1542, when Portuguese-born navigator Juan Rodríguez Cabrillo sailed north from New Spain (Mexico) to "discover" California on Spain's behalf, the name was in common enough usage that Cabrillo employed it in his journal.

To tame the frontier of the New World, Spanish padres created a chain of missions that transformed the native culture and still stand as remnants of European empire.

More than two hundred years would pass, however, before the Spanish Crown actively pressed a claim to this new territory with the establishment of the California missions.

During those two centuries, Spain's interest in what was then known as Alta (or Upper) California waned, especially in the late 1500s, after the expeditions of Francisco Vásquez de Coronado and Juan de Oñate had found there were no prosperous (and conquerable) native empires like that of the Aztecs north of New Spain. After 1602, when Sebastián Vizcaíno sailed north from Acapulco to

Mission San Diego de Alcalá, established in 1769, marked the start of the Franciscan mission chain north of New Spain (Mexico)—and the first push by Spain into Alta California. The expedition led by Gaspar de Portolá and Father Junípero Serra began a half-century of mission foundings.

locate new harbors in Alta California, Madrid turned its attention toward colonies in the Caribbean and Central and South America. Catholic clergymen begged for funds to erect missions at San Diego and Monterey, but their words fell on deaf ears. In the absence of any threat to their sovereignty over the area, administrators in both Old and New Spain were content to leave Alta California unguarded and undeveloped for another century and a half.

All this changed in the late 1760s, when Spain's King Charles (or Carlos) III heard about Russian fur traders migrating down the west coast of North America from their settlements in Alaska, hunting for precious seal pelts. Like his predecessors, Charles had long been satisfied with a hands-off policy toward Alta California. His only previous decision affecting the area had come in 1767, when he ordered the expulsion of Jesuit missionaries from Baja (or Lower) California, convinced that they were withholding from his treasury the storied gold of the Californias. In their place he installed the Franciscans, a group he considered less powerful and much less prone toward duplicity, but which could advance Spain's missionary agenda in the New World with equal zeal.

Russian encroachment struck Charles as no less a threat to his influence in the New World than untrustworthy missionaries. It didn't matter that Charles had barely noticed the territory before: Alta California was part of his domain, and he wasn't about to let a bunch of seal trappers grab it.

So in 1769 Charles made his second important decision about the region. He ordered his personal agent in New Spain, Visitador-general José de Gálvez, to reinforce the Crown's authority north of Baja. An ambitious gent, Gálvez was ruthlessly loyal to his king, quick to flog, imprison, hang, or behead anyone who disputed Charles's orders. He was, in the words of one historian, "a raving lunatic," so unstable that he had to be physically restrained on a regular basis. Yet his skills and energy as an administrator set Gálvez apart from many leaders in New Spain, and for that reason Charles ignored his, well, less-attractive side.

Gálvez responded to the Russian "menace" with characteristic speed and pragmatism. He reasoned that while he could chase the

Russians off with a display of military superiority, Spain could make an enduring claim on Alta California by establishing missions there, as it had been doing on the Baja Peninsula since the 1690s. Gálvez didn't care one whit about saving the souls of "heathens," but he knew that missions had been an important tool in expanding the Spanish empire.

By 1531, Spain already held dominion over more of the globe than the British would ever rule. But there simply weren't enough natural-born Spaniards to secure the realm. The solution? Set up missions, where priests, protected by soldiers, would convert native inhabitants into third-class citizens, thereby allowing Spain to declare that even its most remote colonies were populated by its subjects. Gálvez intended to repeat this tactic north of Baja, erecting a series of self-supporting missions, a day's horse ride apart, and each accompanied by a *presidio*, or garrison, to guard against foreign invaders.

Gálvez decided on a two-pronged approach, mounting expeditions to go by land and sea. His pathfinders would head initially for San Diego. From there, they would push on to fortify Monterey.

The Decline of the Missions

Ever since the independence of Mexico, the [California] missions have been going down; until, at last, a law was passed, stripping them of all their possessions, and confining the priests to their spiritual duties; and at the same time declaring all the Indians free and independent *Rancheros*. The change in the condition of the Indians was, as may be supposed, only nominal: They are virtually slaves, as much as they ever were. But in the missions, the change was complete. The priests have no power, except in their religious character and the great possessions of the missions are given over to be preyed upon by the harpies of the civil power, who are sent there in the capacity of the *administradores*, to settle up the concerns; and who usually end, in a few years, by making themselves fortunes, and leaving their stewardships worse than they found them.

(Richard Henry Dana, *Two Years Before the Mast*, 1842)

Father Serra first cele-
brated Mass in the
Monterey area in 1770.
It was here that he con-
secrated the second mis-
sion (and his future
headquarters), Mission
San Carlos Borromeo,
thought by many to be
the most beautiful of the
missions.

The overland contingent would be charged also with creating a primitive coastal highway—California's own El Camino Real (or Royal Road)—for later use by Spanish forces and mission builders.

Gálvez named two men to take responsibility for this endeavor's outcome, men whose talents he hoped would prove complementary. Gaspar de Portolá, the recently installed governor of Baja California, would command the overall project. In charge of mission development would be Father Junípero Serra.

THE SWORD AND THE STAFF

Two more different individuals might have been hard to find. Captain Portolá was an outspoken, middle-aged career officer in the Catalan Dragoons, a beribboned veteran of campaigns in Portugal and Italy who relished the chance to escape the tedium of the governor's post and head the first overland party of whites into Alta California.

Serra had led a much harder, less public life. Born Juan Miguel José Serra on the Spanish island of Mallorca, he had learned early from his farming parents to respect and love the Catholic Church. By the time he was fifteen, Serra was prepared to begin the rigorous training necessary to join the Franciscan order. Three years later, in September 1731, he donned the gray robes and sandals of the order and took vows of poverty, chastity, and obedience. He also adopted the name "Junípero," in honor of a good-humored and magnanimous companion to Saint Francis. After teaching at a Spanish convent, in 1749 he began his New World adventure as a missionary in northern New Spain.

Serra's close friend and biographer, Father Francisco Palóu, described him as intensely serious, "so that exteriorly he appeared to be austere and almost unapproachable. But as soon as one talked and dealt with him, one had to change his opinion and consider him gentle, amiable, and attractive, for he won the hearts of all." A short man (barely five feet, two inches tall), Serra had been sickly as a child and remained frail into adulthood. He suffered from terrible nearsightedness and neglected his own need for sleep. He was handicapped by an ulcerated leg (said to have been the result of an untreated spider bite) and had a pious tendency toward self-flagellation, which he excused as his way of atoning for the sins of others. Yet Serra could almost always find the strength to walk or ride great distances to spread the gospel. He was entering the twilight of his life—fifty-five years old—when Gálvez called on him to go to Alta California, but Serra was more than willing to give up heading the Baja missions to join what he called this "sacred expedition."

Accursed expedition was more like it.

Portolá broke his force into four parties: two going by sea to San Diego, two by land. The initial contingent sailed from La Paz, on the eastern coast of Baja, aboard the packet *San Carlos* on January 7, 1769. A second ship, the *San Antonio*, departed a month later; however, poor maps and vigorous headwinds conspired to drive the *San Carlos* far north of her destination, and the *San Antonio* actually reached San Diego seventeen days ahead of her sister. A worse fate befell the supply ship *San José*, which was to meet the other two in San Diego. After a troubled start, the *San José* was compelled to return to port. It set sail again in the spring of 1770, loaded down with much-needed food and trading goods, and was never heard from again.

The land-based expeditions, traveling north through Baja, experienced their own miseries. Led by Captain Fernando Javier Rivera, the advance unit—25 cavalrymen, 50 Christianized natives from New Spain, and a pack train 180 mules strong—found the going "sterile, arid, lacking grass and water, and abounding in stones and thorns," according to Father Juan Crespí, a subordinate of Serra's and diarist for that group. By the time Rivera's detachment reached San Diego, some two-thirds of the natives had died or fled, and everyone left had been reduced to consuming a single cup of chocolate and one tortilla a day ("without any seasoning or sauce," Crespí complained).

The second overland party, under Portolá and Serra, tried to keep up its strength by demanding supplies at mission settlements along the way. Even so, they ran short of food during the two-month trip, and many of the natives who didn't perish deserted. Portolá, Serra, and the remaining contingent straggled into San Diego on July 1, 1769, to find that of the 219 people who had left Baja in the four parties, only half had arrived. And they were starving or sick or both. Portolá quickly sent the *San Antonio* back to Mexico for provisions for the colony, but on that ill-fated voyage, all but two of the crew perished.

The former dragoon then gathered about sixty men—"skeletons who had been spared scurvy, hunger, and thirst," as he described them—and continued to blaze a trail north along the coast. Portolá's persistence can only be explained as heroic or insane devotion to duty. He didn't know the worst was still to come.

Plagued by sickness and repeated wrong turns, Portolá's force reached Monterey Bay on September 30 without sighting any Russians. Unfortunately, Portolá didn't recognize where they were; he remarks in his diary that he had "found nothing." He may have been expecting a neatly closed and easily fortified bay, or just something more awe-inspiring, considering the glowing reports he had read of it. (A "port sheltered by winds. . . ," one mariner had called Monterey Bay, "a harbor that is all that can be desired.")

Thinking his goal still before him, Portolá pressed on, until in November 1769, he and his men stumbled upon San Francisco Bay—the huge, magnificent harbor that Cabrillo, Sir Francis Drake, and other ocean explorers had failed to discover. But Portolá was disappointed, for he had not completed the assignment given him by Gálvez. He turned back, and six weeks later— after his party had slaughtered most of their mules for food—was once more in San Diego, only to be scolded by Serra, who had stayed behind. "You come from Rome," the padre complained in metaphor, "and you did not see the pope!" (Fortunately for Portolá's reputation, he recognized he had reached Monterey Bay on his second overland attempt, a year later.)

Serra felt he had done a better job of satisfying his obligations. For on July 16, 1769, shortly after Portolá had left for Monterey, the Franciscan climbed to the top of a hill overlooking San Diego Bay and there raised a cross to mark the first mission in Alta California. It would be dedicated to Saint Didacus of

Alcalá, a Franciscan friar who had been canonized in 1588. The natives who watched this ceremony could have been excused for their confusion. They had never seen men ride atop animals or travel the seas in "floating buildings." They didn't know then how completely these odd white interlopers would change their lives.

FATHER SERRA'S LEGACY

O N JUNE 3, 1770, LESS than a year after he founded the San Diego mission, Junípero Serra, having sailed into Monterey Bay aboard the *San Antonio*, strode up the beach to consecrate the second in the chain, Mission San Carlos Borromeo. (It would soon be moved to nearby Carmel.) Following that, the pace of mission establishment along El Camino Real was steady, if not speedy. Over the next fourteen years, Serra and his followers would found seven more missions, including San Antonio de Padua (1771), San Luis Obispo de Tolosa (1772), San Juan Capistrano and San Francisco de Asís (both in 1776), and San Buenaventura (1782).

One summer day, however, cannon fire ripped through the peace that had been so familiar around Monterey Bay, the periodic blasts from a bark offshore being answered by a volley from guns that protected Monterey's presidio. Church bells added to the general tumult, their slow, sonorous peals signaling some event of great import. Men and women streamed down into the valley, all headed toward a small adobe chapel at Mission San Carlos, which stood upon a windy coastal slope.

It was late August 1784, and Father Serra, the man who had devoted more than a decade of his life to making the Carmel mission a symbol of religious salvation in Spanish California, and who had labored even longer to establish a chain of missions along that territory's coastline, was dead at seventy-one.

Records indicate that Serra, who just the year before had made an astonishing five-hundred-mile *walking* tour of his missions, was noticeably weaker in his last month. Sick with tuberculosis, he had rallied somewhat near the end for singing and praying, but the ravages of the disease could not long be denied. So he began making preparations. It's said that Serra parceled out cloth he had to the natives who lived in the mission's shadow and even gave an old woman among them half of the blanket that covered his bed of boards in his small room. In the two centuries since, Serra's

The Mission Chain

Father Junípero Serra and his successors established twenty-one Franciscan missions in California in little more than half a century. They are, in order of the dates they were founded:

1. San Diego de Alcalá—July 16, 1769
2. San Carlos Borromeo de Carmelo—June 3, 1770
3. San Antonio de Padua—July 14, 1771
4. San Gabriel Arcángel—Sept 8, 1771
5. San Luis Obispo de Tolosa—Sept 1, 1772
6. San Francisco de Asís—June 29, 1776
7. San Juan Capistrano—Nov 1, 1776
8. Santa Clara de Asís—Jan 12, 1777
9. San Buenaventura—March 31, 1782
10. Santa Bárbara Virgen y Mártir—Dec 4, 1786
11. La Purísima Concepción de Maria Santísima—Dec 8, 1787
12. Santa Cruz—Aug 28, 1791
13. Nuestra Señora de la Soledad—Oct 9, 1791
14. San José de Guadalupe—June 11, 1797
15. San Juan Bautista—June 24, 1797
16. San Miguel Arcángel—July 25, 1797
17. San Fernando Rey de España—Sept 8, 1797
18. San Luis Rey de Francia—June 13, 1798
19. Santa Inés Virgen y Mártir—Sept 17, 1804
20. San Rafael Arcángel—Dec 14, 1817
21. San Francisco Solano—July 4, 1823

Mission life took many forms: religious instruction, as at Mission San Juan Bautista; the mix of military, civilian, and native cultures, as at Mission San Francisco de Asis; and the working of the land by native neophytes, as at Mission San Francisco Solano.

campaign to convert California natives to Christianity has come under attack, but in the late summer of 1784, no such remonstrances were heard. At the news of the cleric's passing, wrote Father Palóu, "the whole town [of Monterey] assembled, weeping over the death of their beloved father. . . . So great was the crowd of people, including Indians and soldiers and sailors, that it was necessary to close the door [of the church]." And when the padre was laid to rest in the mission church, near the altar, Palóu noted it was "as if some general was being buried."

A sad moment, but one also pregnant with possibility. For if Serra's death closed the first chapter in California's mission history, it opened the next. The work he began would continue over the following five decades, until twenty-one missions stretched from San Diego to Sonoma, strengthening Spain's hold on California—but also attracting attention from England, France, and the United States, which came to covet the bounty of that territory.

LIFE WITHIN THE WALLS

BOTH THE FRANCISCANS and the politicians in Mexico City recognized that the more missions that existed, the easier it might be to tame the California frontier and "civilize" its hundred thousand or so natives. The successors to Father Serra added a dozen missions to the chain by 1823, showing that Spain's trust in the Franciscan order was well placed. But establishing a strong mission system was more easily proposed than accomplished. Neither the padres nor the soldiers posted as their protectors were exemplary agents of colonization. Barely able to support themselves off the surrounding land, they had little hope of cultivating the crops and raising the herds required by expansion-directed settlements.

Enlisting the aid of natives was obvious, but it took some doing. Local chiefs were wooed with trinkets and food, and any of their people who volunteered to join the mission were taught enough Spanish that they could recite religious doctrine and were baptized into the Catholic Church. (Some eighty-eight thousand Indians were converted during the six and one-half decades of missionary work in California.) Once they became part of the community, natives were not free to go; runaways were pursued and returned to the Spaniards. Their behavior was severely restricted. Vices such as gambling were officially forbidden, though never expunged, and the priests were ever-vigilant against recreational carnal contact between the sexes. (It didn't help that many of the soldiers sent to the missions considered it sport to chase after native girls!)

The mission compounds were fairly consistent in design. Most were built in a quadrangle, with bedrooms for the padres, quarters set aside for soldiers and natives, plus a kitchen, sitting room, library, infirmary, guest rooms, and frequently a music room. In the northeast corner of the grounds stood the church, with a cemetery adjacent to the mission and preferably near the chapel. Adobe (dried mud) bricks and thatched roofs marked the construction of the early missions. As time passed, however, the architecture showed more of a Mediterranean flair, wonderfully superfluous in archways and red-tile roofs.

The Church generally assigned priests in pairs to the missions, with one named as the superior. In theory, these men would strictly divide the spiritual and temporal responsibilities of the mission, yet more often than not they shared these tasks. The most important thing they shared, though, was companionship. Loneliness was a plague upon mission priests.

Missionaries spent many hours trying to teach the converts, or "neophytes," European farming techniques, as well as furniture making, blacksmithing, sewing, tailoring, and playing string and wind instruments. At Mission San Gabriel, they even introduced converts to the cultivation of wine grapes, creating a stock—the *vina madre*, or mother vine—that would provide cuttings to many of California's earliest vineyards.

As one might expect, historians are sharply divided over whether this mandatory service should be damned as slavery or excused as flawed benevolence, no more egregious a violation than was common elsewhere in the world at the time. So far, neither viewpoint is universally accepted. No matter how much pleasure they took in seeing neophytes learn, the Franciscans rarely

Mission Santa Barbara: The Franciscans assigned priests in pairs to the missions, as much to stave off loneliness as to share the burdens of responsibility.

approached them as equals.

Natives living at the missions were told they would one day be given ownership of the buildings and lands. Tradition and Spanish edicts held that such missions should exist only for a decade; by then, natives were expected to be capable of living under civil laws and operating their own *pueblo*, or town.

Those guidelines worked well in Central America and Peru, where the natives had developed an advanced culture before the advent of white men. In California, however, tribes were comparatively more primitive, and European opinion of their educability was not optimistic. George Vancouver, a British sea captain who made three visits to California in the late eighteenth century, called natives there "a race of the most miserable beings possessing the faculties of human reason" and "too stupid and indolent to benefit much from the efforts made in their behalf." Despite Spanish promises, California natives never did gain control of the missions they maintained and had often helped build.

Pablo Tac, a Luiseño Indian born in 1822 at the mission in San Luis Rey, wrote poignantly of life at those early religious institutions. In this passage from an 1835 manuscript he describes the well-tended gardens, a feature that, for the Spaniards at least, became a source of pride at many missions:

> The garden is extensive, full of fruit trees, pears, apples, or *perones*, as the Mexicans say, peaches, quinces, pears, sweet pomegranates, watermelons, melons, vegetables, cabbages, lettuces, radishes, mints, parsley, and others which I don't remember. The pears, apples, peaches, quinces, pomegranates, watermelons, and melons are for the neophytes, the others that remain, for the missionary. . . . None of the neophytes can go to the garden or enter to gather the fruit. But if he wants some he asks the missionary who immediately will give him what he wants, for the missionary is their father.

Tac didn't question the class system that forbade him, regardless of his education, from picking fruit just because he was a native. Other neophytes were less content over their harsh treatment. Insurrections were few, but the 1775 rebellion at Mission San Diego, during which a priest was killed, and the burning of the mission at Santa Inés in

Life at the San Diego Mission

Kentucky adventurer James Ohio Pattie came to California in 1828, bearing what he claimed was a rare serum that would prevent mission natives from contracting smallpox—the great decimator of American Indians. Civil authorities in California gave him permission to inoculate natives at the missions there. His observations of life at Mission San Diego de Alcalá were first published in 1831:

This is said to be the largest, most flourishing, and every way the most important mission on the coast. For its consumption fifty beeves [cows] are killed weekly. The hides and tallow are sold to ships for goods, and other articles for the use of the Indians, who are better dressed in general, than the Spaniards. All the income of the mission is placed in the hands of the priests, who give out clothing and food, according as it is required. They are also self-constituted guardians of the female part of the mission, shutting up under lock and key, one hour after supper, all those, whose husbands are absent, and all young women and girls above nine years of age.

During the day, they are entrusted to the care of the matrons. Notwithstanding this, all the precautions taken by the vigilant fathers of the church are found insufficient. . . .

The priests appoint officers to superintend the natives, while they are at work, from among themselves. They are called *alcaldes*, and are very rigid in exacting the performance of the alloted tasks, applying the rod to those who fall short of the portion of labor assigned them. They are taught in the different trades; some of them being blacksmiths, others carpenters and shoe-makers. Those trained to the knowledge of music, both vocal and instrumental, are intended for the service of the church. The women and girls sew, knit, and spin wool upon a large wheel, which is woven into blankets by the men. The *alcaldes*, after finishing the business of the day, give an account of it to the priest, and then kiss his hand, before they withdraw to their wigwams, to pass the night.

(James O. Pattie, *The Personal Narrative of James O. Pattie*, 1831)

1824—sparked by the flogging of a native and which caused the death of two Indians—showed that California's native population had not succumbed completely to the Spanish rules of civilization.

THE SACRED AND THE SECULAR

VIOLENCE IN NEW SPAIN, though, rather than in Alta California, was what brought an end to the mission dreams of José de Gálvez and Junípero Serra. The Spanish empire was in decline even as Serra was establishing his chain of religious outposts, its authority challenged both

Saving Grace

Considering the despoliation that came from Mexico's decision in the 1830s to secularize the California missions, it is amazing that those historic structures still exist to be appreciated.

Mexican authorities divided the missions' extensive acreage between the Native Americans, who had for so long cultivated those lands, and civil administrators, who were charged with maintaining their portion for religious purposes. But without the discipline they had received from the Franciscan padres, many of the natives refused to work, and a good number sold their shares for the price of liquor. Meanwhile, corrupt administrators stole much of the land that they held in trust, and most of the rest was sold to raise defense funds for Mexico. (Of the twenty-one missions, only the one at Santa Barbara remained continuously in the hands of the Franciscan order.) In just a few years, California's mission system had collapsed. The buildings fell into ruin and were often preyed upon by thieves.

The acquisition of California by the United States in 1846 may have prevented the complete destruction of the missions. Sales to private buyers were invalidated, and years later, by presidential proclamation, the government returned control of mission property for religious use to the Catholic Church. However, decades passed before there was money and will enough to do anything but stabilize the missions in their decrepitude.

Some priests were early advocates of restoration. Father Angelo Casanova, for instance, began the resurrection of Carmel's Mission San Carlos from its own colonies and from rivals such as England and the Netherlands. It was no longer in a position to subdue the separatist forces mounting in Mexico.

In late 1810, rebels in New Spain began demonstrating for independence from Madrid; by 1821, the split was complete. Throughout those eleven years, the Alta California missions found their lines of supply and command with Mexico City erratic, at best. Infusions of government capital dried up. Only one more mission— San Francisco de Solano (1823), in Sonoma—came into being after Mexican independence. The Franciscans slowly realized that unless their missions were self-sufficient, they would not last. But even their struggles to save the system were for naught, because in 1833,

Borromeo in 1882 with a dramatic ceremony during which the coffins of Father Junípero Serra and four other priests were unearthed from beneath the mission's floor, then reburied. Two years later, enough work had been done on San Carlos to permit its rededication.

Laymen, too, were instrumental in saving these compounds. In the late 1880s, Southern Californians formed the Association for the Preservation of the Missions (which later became the Landmarks Club). They leased Mission San Juan Capistrano in 1896 and began to restore it, then turned their attention and largesse to the buildings at San Fernando, San Diego, and San Luis Rey.

Preservation sentiments became even stronger after 1900. Northern Californians formed the California Historic Landmarks League, which in 1903 purchased Sonoma's disintegrating Mission San Francisco Solano and set about to repair it. Money from the Native Sons of the Golden West and other philanthropic groups followed, as did government support. Under President Franklin Roosevelt, a company of the Civilian Conservation Corps even made tens of thousands of new adobe bricks needed to rebuild Mission La Purísima Concepción.

As the mission buildings have been returned to health, so, too, have a great number of artifacts (taken out of the churches by the faithful) been returned to their rightful homes. Today, private, public, and church funds continue to be funneled toward the restoration and conservation of these religious and cultural landmarks.

the Mexican republic forced the Church to break up its mission holdings, a process known as "secularization."

Over the next fifteen years, mission property was put into private hands, most of the land going to prominent ranch owners, rather than the poor individuals who had so long labored on the missions' behalf. Natives who had depended on these institutions were cut adrift. Some went to work at the large Mexican ranchos; others sought the continued care of parish priests. The missions themselves began to decline. San Francisco's Mission Dolores, for instance, served for a quarter-century after secularization as a dance hall and tavern, and fights between bulls and bears were sometimes staged on its grounds. (Not until 1859 was it restored as a Catholic church.) Other missions fell to ruins and the assaults of vandals.

Thoughts that the rancho system might continue colonization where the mission system left off were dashed quickly in 1848, when James W. Marshall, a carpenter at John Sutter's sawmill on the South Fork of the American River, discovered gold there. The find set off a rush of men after wealth that would be unrivaled until the Klondike Stampede half a century later. The final blow came with the signing of the Treaty of Guadalupe Hidalgo in 1848, which gave the territory of California to the United States. In two years, it entered the union as the thirty-first state. How ironic that Spain, which had held California for three centuries, lost it just before the legends of golden riches proved true!

The Mission Trail Today

Strung out for 650 miles along California's rugged coastline, the twenty-one Franciscan missions recall a fifty-four-year period of spiritual dedication and cultural invasion. Composed of adobe brick and built with Indian labor, these often exquisite structures were more than merely places of worship; they were important tools in golden-age Spain's campaign to bring the New World to heel. Now restored or, in some cases, reconstructed, these missions—most of them easily accessible from U.S. Route 101—offer a seductive glimpse into California's long and distinctive past. Beginning with the oldest mission and heading north, six of the most popular missions are:

SAN DIEGO DE ALCALÁ

Founded in 1769 "to fulfill the will of God," **San Diego de Alcalá** was the first of nine missions established under Father Junípero Serra. It also housed the first church in California. Originally situated on Presidio Hill, above what is now San Diego's Old Town area, the mission was moved to its present location in 1774, after a deadly skirmish between Native Americans and soldiers. Burned by natives just one year later, the mission was rebuilt in 1780, only to be destroyed by an earthquake in 1803 and reconstructed ten years later. An extensive restoration in 1931 resulted in the mission complex as it is seen today, complete with its impressive bell tower.

Walls inside the church at Mission San Diego remain barren, void of extravagant decor, just as they were when the church was first built. Visitors can attend mass in the church, stroll through a garden courtyard, browse over historic artifacts in a small museum, and study a reconstruction of Father Serra's living quarters. 10818 San Diego Mission Road, San Diego, California 92108; 619-281-8449.

The **Junípero Serra Museum,** located six miles away in Presidio Park—almost on the original site of San Diego de

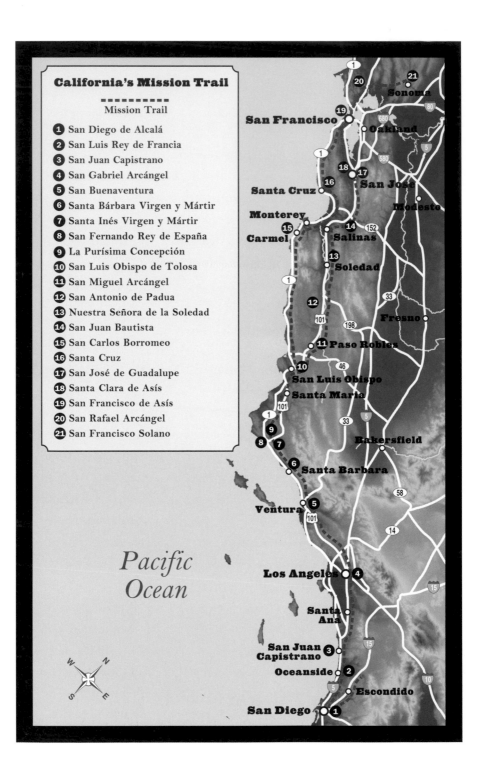

California's Mission Trail

---------- Mission Trail

1. San Diego de Alcalá
2. San Luis Rey de Francia
3. San Juan Capistrano
4. San Gabriel Arcángel
5. San Buenaventura
6. Santa Bárbara Virgen y Mártir
7. Santa Inés Virgen y Mártir
8. San Fernando Rey de España
9. La Purísima Concepción
10. San Luis Obispo de Tolosa
11. San Miguel Arcángel
12. San Antonio de Padua
13. Nuestra Señora de la Soledad
14. San Juan Bautista
15. San Carlos Borromeo
16. Santa Cruz
17. San José de Guadalupe
18. Santa Clara de Asís
19. San Francisco de Asís
20. San Rafael Arcángel
21. San Francisco Solano

Pacific Ocean

Sonoma
San Francisco
Oakland
San José
Modesto
Santa Cruz
Monterey
Carmel
Salinas
Soledad
Fresno
Paso Robles
San Luis Obispo
Santa Maria
Bakersfield
Santa Barbara
Ventura
Los Angeles
Santa Ana
San Juan Capistrano
Oceanside
Escondido
San Diego

Alcalá—tells the story of mission interaction with local Indians and details life in early San Diego. 619-297-3258.

SAN LUIS REY DE FRANCIA

Located near the town of Oceanside, **San Luis Rey de Francia**—eighteenth among the California missions—flourished from its founding in 1798, becoming the largest and most populous of the Franciscan institutions. But after secularization in the 1830s, it was used for other purposes (including as housing for U.S. Army troops) and later largely fell into ruin. A church dedicated in 1815 has been restored, but the rest of the mission is a reconstruction, begun after the complex's rededication in 1893. A museum documents the "salvation" of the Luiseño Indians, and contains artifacts from the mission's founding and the largest collection of religious vestments in the West. 4050 Mission Avenue, San Luis Rey, California 92068; 619-757-3651.

SAN GABRIEL ARCÁNGEL

Stunningly reminiscent of the Catedral de Granada, in Spain's southern province of Andalucía, the mission church at **San Gabriel Arcángel** lies just nine miles east of downtown Los Angeles, in the city of San Gabriel. California's fourth mission, it was founded in 1771, then relocated to its present site in 1775. Construction of the church began in 1791, and it still stands, reinforced now to protect against earthquake damage. Visitors to the mission can wander the ruins of blacksmith shops and kitchen facilities; tour the site's famous winery, which has been preserved as a museum; and stroll through remnants of olive, pear, and orange orchards. San Gabriel's church altar is one of the few originals remaining in the Franciscan chain, and this is the only mission that contains authentic Indian paintings: a set depicting the stations of the cross. 537 West Mission Drive, San Gabriel, California 91776; 818-457-3048.

SAN CARLOS BORROMEO DE CARMELO

The romantic splendor of the second Franciscan mission is set against a background of mountain and sea in the coastal town of Carmel. Just to the north is Monterey, where Father Serra originally founded **San Carlos Borromeo** in 1770. (He moved the mission to Carmel a year later, looking for better farmland and greater distance from the raucous Monterey presidio.) This splendidly landscaped mission served as headquarters of the mission system for thirty-three years, and Serra is buried in the sanctuary of its church. An extensive library and three museums thoroughly detail the mission's history; San Carlos Borromeo also retains the original silver altar furnishings. 3080 Rio Road, Carmel, California 93921; 408-624-3600.

Nearby Monterey is a historical gem. Sites such as the **Custom House,** the **Old Whaling Station,** and **California's first theater** document the area's early commerce and entertainment.

San Juan Bautista

Just a thirty-minute drive north of Carmel sits the town of **San Juan Bautista,** site of the fifteenth mission in the chain. Founded in 1797, the mission contains a colorful altar and reredos that were painted in 1818 by Thomas Doak, a sailor and California's first American settler, who did the painting in exchange for meals. The first Saturday of each month is **Living History Day,** when the mission's history is reenacted with singing and dancing and costumes. Vivid artifacts of the priests' lifestyle are well preserved at the site. An adjacent plaza opens onto a variety of other historical homes and commercial structures, and a trace of the original **El Camino Real** lies just beyond the mission's graveyard. Second and Mariposa Streets, San Juan Bautista 95045; 408-623-4528.

San Francisco de Asís

Captain Juan Bautista de Anza, a descendent of Sonoran soldiers recognized for his pathfinder abilities, arrived at the present site of San Francisco in March 1776. After marking a spot (now occupied by historic **Fort Point,** in the shadow of the Golden Gate Bridge) where he thought a presidio should be built, de Anza and his party went looking for a location for the sixth California mission. They found a sheltered space on a sluggish lagoon several miles to the southeast. Since it was the Friday preceding Palm Sunday of that year—a day known to Catholics as the Friday of Sorrows—de Anza called the place Laguna de Nuestra Señora de los Dolores, or the Lake of Our Lady of Sorrows. It was there that **Mission San Francisco de Asís**—better known as **Mission Dolores**—was built.

This mission has been well preserved. A wooden altar, imported from Mexico in 1780, stands in the church; above it, the original ceiling paint remains unscathed. Next to the church, blossoms of poppies, birds-of-paradise, and exotic bougainvillea enliven the mission cemetery, where visitors can find the graves of some noteworthy pioneers, including Don Luis Antonio Arguello, first governor of Alta California under Mexican rule, and Charles Cora, a gambler who was hanged in 1856, during the city's vigilante period. 3321 Sixteenth Street, San Francisco, California 94114; 415-621-8203.

—Ellen L. Boyer

The Klondike Gold Rush Trail

A T ANOTHER TIME, in another place, the captain might have thought his ship was being overtaken by pirates come to filch the fortune from its hold. But the anxious, red-faced men who tumbled across the moonlit railings of the S.S. *Portland* as it passed Washington's Cape Flattery and churned toward Seattle on July 17, 1897, sought a very different sort of riches. They were newspaper reporters sent to plunder the sixty-eight prospectors on board of whatever information they had regarding the discovery of gold on tributaries of northwestern Canada's Klondike River.

The dream of endless riches lured hordes of adventurers to Canada's north country. But most of them found more pain, frustration, and hardship—and far less gold—than they had ever imagined.

Only two days before, a second steamer out of Alaska, the *Excelsior*, had docked at San Francisco, its scruffy, sunburned passengers stumbling down the gangplank with leather saddlebags, carpet valises, and fruit jars, all full of gold dust and nuggets from the Klondike fields. Among the miners was a former YMCA physical-training instructor, Thomas Lippy, of Seattle. The normally levelheaded Lippy had left the Pacific Northwest a year earlier with borrowed money and the vague hope of "making it" in the northland. Now, he had returned to the States "a veritable Monte Cristo," as one account put it, sharing with his wife,

The Klondike Fever Queen Leaving Seattle

Wilse
N°278

Thousands of would-be prospectors packed the Seattle waterfront, hoping to board ships like the Klondike Fever Queen, to carry them to riches. The Pioneer Building was a new landmark in Seattle's original downtown when gold-rush fever hit in 1897.

Salome, a grip that contained in excess of two hundred pounds of gold, valued at more than $51,000. Another Scattleite, laundryman Fred Price, stood nearby but enjoyed considerably less attention, his five thousand dollars in gold making him a relatively "poor" Klondiker.

Word traveled fast. And far. Within hours of the *Excelsior's* landing, hyperbole about the subarctic mother lode washed over nearly every corner of San Francisco, and before the day was out, telegraph wires sped the prospectors' amazing tales clear across the continent. Not since the California gold rush of 1849 had the West Coast generated such widespread excitement. Demands for more and juicier news copy incited a feeding frenzy. Like their shipmates, the Lippys could not enjoy their visit to the city by the Golden Gate, for whenever they strolled from their suite at the Palace Hotel, packs of journalists descended upon them, determined to capture their every comment. After a few days, the couple fled in disgust to Portland, Oregon.

Stories of mineral wealth from the Far North had been heard before. Alaska's first significant gold deposits were stumbled upon in 1880, and ever since, men had roamed that territory and Canada's neighboring Yukon, panning streams and digging and praying they would be rewarded handsomely for their labors.

Yet when rumors of mammoth deposits in the Klondike began circulating during the late 1890s, they were at first widely dismissed as fantasy. Even a veteran dogsled driver who mushed from the Yukon to Juneau, Alaska, in June 1897, wearing nuggets as buttons on his coat and announcing big strikes, failed to convince many folks. Soon after that, however, the *Excelsior* appeared, and figment became fact. Suddenly, the cry "Klondike or Bust!" was on everyone's lips, though few people knew where the Klondike was and fewer still were sure how to spell its name. ("Clondyke," "Klondyke," and "Klondike" were used interchangeably in early press reports.)

Seattle was already heady with gold fever by the time the *Portland's* running lights were spied off the coast of Vancouver Island. So eager were editors of the *Post-Intelligencer* to feed their readers' appetites for Klondike tidings, that they didn't wait until the ship reached the city. Instead, they chartered a tug at Port Townsend and dispatched their top reporters to intercept the treasure ship as it swung abreast of Port Angeles at 2 a.m. on July 17. Six hours later, when the *Portland* finally nosed into Schwabacher's Wharf (in the vicinity of present-day Pier 57), prospectors waving from its deck and banners flying from its masts, the *P-I* was already peddling the first of three extra editions to the five thousand envious Seattleites who had come to the waterfront to watch.

"Gold! Gold! Gold! Gold!" trumpeted the headlines. "Stacks of Yellow Metal!" It all seemed too good to be true. But the daring men who debarked from the *Portland* that day left little doubt that the Klondike provided what one Seattle editorialist termed "'the open sesame' to a dreamland of wealth."

"They all have gold," wrote one reporter, "and it is piled about the staterooms like so much valueless hand baggage." According to the *P-I*, the ship carried a total of "a ton of gold." For the newspaper, this was a rare—and unintended—understatement. The

Bitter Bierce

Even at the very height of the Klondike madness, not everyone could be convinced to drop everything and head for the gold fields. Ambrose Bierce (1842–?1914), the *San Francisco Examiner*'s foremost columnist and curmudgeon, saw nothing earth-shaking about the rush for riches. Nor did he see the prospectors as having much impact on the north country. "The California gold hunter," Bierce wrote, "did good by accident and crowed to find it fame. But the blue-nosed mosquito-slapper of Greater Dawson, what is he for? Is he going to lay broad and deep the foundations of Empire [tor Great Britain]? Will he bear the banner of progress into that paleocrystic waste? Will he clear the way for even a dogsled civilization and a reindeer religion? Nothing will come of him. He is a word in the wind, a brother to the fog. At the scene of his activity no memory of him will remain. The gravel that he thawed and sifted will freeze again. In the shanty that he builded, the she-wolf will rear her poddy litter, and from its eaves the moose will crop the esculent icicle unafraid. The snows will close over his trail and all be as before."

Portland actually held closer to two tons, making it literally a million-dollar ship. Regardless, "ton of gold" became the catchphrase that fired the imagination of people around the globe, enticing every thrill-seeker, every avaricious soul, and every ne'er-do-well hoping for a better life to join North America's last great frontier adventure: the Klondike Stampede.

For three years, that daunting, dangerous, and frequently disappointing gold rush dramatically expanded interest in the Alaska and Yukon territories. It put lowly, remote Dawson City—the Yukon town nearest to the gold fields—prominently on the map, and ended an economic depression that had kept a stranglehold on North America and Europe throughout the mid-1890s. And, of course, it wrought tremendous changes upon adolescent Seattle.

No American port or railhead was closer than Seattle to Alaska and the principal overland trails that led to the Klondike. As a result, the city became the embarkation point and outfitter for nearly every would-be Croesus. In the month following the *Portland's* arrival at Elliott Bay, fifteen hundred people sailed north from the city, and nine fully booked ships crowded the harbor, waiting to follow them. Mining schools and new hostelries opened to serve the lucre-hunting hordes who funneled through town. Shipyards bustled with construction of ocean- and river-going craft.

As the *New York Herald* remarked, "Seattle has gone stark, staring mad on gold."

AN INSULT REPAID

HAD GEORGE WASHINGTON Carmack and his two Native American friends known what would come from their locating gold on a branch of the Klondike River, they might have covered over the precious metal and never breathed a syllable about it.

Carmack was much content with his life in the northern wilderness. Although born in Northern California, the son of a forty-niner, Carmack had become more and more like the natives he encountered since his move to the North in 1885 and his employment as a trail packer. He learned their rituals and dialects, wed the daughter of a Tagish tribal chief, and dreamed of being a chief himself someday. He built a home for his family on the Yukon River—the mighty two-thousand-mile-long waterway that drains north and west from Alaska's Coast Mountains to the Bering Sea—and there he read, composed poetry when it suited his mood, and played an organ to the howling accompaniment of wolves.

Probably the last thing he wanted was a storm of outsiders destroying the tranquility of his Yukon Eden. But that's exactly what he got after the summer of 1896.

Carmack, his wife, Kate, and their daughter, together with Kate's brother Keish (known to whites as Skookum Jim) and another native, Tagish Charley (sometimes called Dawson Charley), were fishing for salmon at the confluence of the Yukon and Klondike Rivers when into their midst paddled Robert Henderson. A seasoned prospector, originally from Canada's Atlantic provinces, Henderson had spent the better part of that year tapping a small vein of riches on the aptly named Gold Bottom Creek, several days' travel southeast of the mouth of the Klondike. In need of supplies, he had boated to the nearest trading post, at a place called Fortymile, and was then returning to his claim.

Like many gold hunters, Henderson tended to share news of his latest diggings, trusting there would be enough "color" (gold) to go around and that he would be invited to partake of the next guy's luck. He had told the Fortymilers about Gold Bottom and wanted to be equally generous with Carmack. But, the tale goes, Henderson was something of a racist. He made it clear that while Carmack was welcome on his stream, his native brethren were decidedly *not*.

The insult stuck in George Carmack's craw. By August 1896, it had festered into full-blown hatred. Too bad for Henderson, because on August 16 Carmack, Skookum Jim, and Tagish Charley were exploring a Klondike branch called Rabbit Creek when they happened upon a vein of color squeezed between slabs of bedrock—like cheese in a sandwich, one would later remark. Carmack had never yearned for riches, yet he couldn't resist the opportunity to stake a claim this promising. So he and his friends hied off to the claim recorder's office at Fortymile, telling everyone they met on the way about Rabbit Creek.

Tagish Charley, hauling supplies by sled, was one of the three men who made the original gold find on Rabbit Creek in 1896. In a little more than a year, Skagway was a bustling halfway point to the gold fields, and gold bricks and bags of dust were piling up in Dawson City, to be shipped to Seattle.

It didn't take but another month for most of that stream—redubbed Bonanza Creek—to be parceled out among "sourdoughs" (Yukon old-timers) already living in the area. As newcomers arrived, they turned to the nearby Indian River and to Bear, Hunker, and Eldorado Creeks, all of which, in time, gave up kings' ransoms. Small towns in the Yukon Valley were quickly deserted as miners followed the rainbow to what they believed was the Klondike's pot of gold.

Only one prospector was conspicuously absent from this maiden wave of the stampede: Robert Henderson. Carmack knew Henderson had resumed panning at Gold Bottom, yet his lingering resentment prevented Carmack from telling him of the Bonanza strike. Henderson didn't hear until it was too late.

Fate turned further against Henderson after that. His competitors on Gold Bottom Creek, laboring downstream from where he had been for months, discovered much richer deposits than he ever had. Rather than bury his disappointment and stake a new claim nearer theirs, Henderson moved deeper into the backcountry, hoping to unearth a richer lode. Eventually, sick and bitter over the bounty he had missed, he gave up prospecting, took the mere three thousand dollars he had to show for his years of hard work, and hopped a steamboat for Seattle—only to have his money stolen during the trip.

THE CLARION CALL

I F NOT FOR inclement weather, the Klondike gold rush might have been in full roar by early 1897. But the cold and isolation of the Yukon in winter are the stuff of legend. Waterways freeze solid enough for dogsleds to use them as highways, and men there tended to stop shaving after October 15, because it was too much trouble to melt enough snow for a grooming bowl full of water.

River traffic, which usually carried Yukon and Alaska news to the outside world, was completely shut down by ice shortly after Carmack's discovery. The informal "moccasin telegraph" spread the word throughout the surrounding region, and by January 1897, a

San Francisco of the North

Seattle wasn't the only town remade by the Klondike gold rush.

When news first broke in 1896 of gold being discovered, nearby Dawson City was little more than a ragged tent encampment at the swampy junction of the Yukon and Klondike Rivers, across from a summer camp for the Han Indians. Yet, thanks to the newfound wealth and the prospecting hordes that flowed through town over the next two years, Dawson was transformed into "the San Francisco of the North." Its population swelled as high as forty thousand, making it easily the largest city north of Seattle and west of Winnipeg, Manitoba.

During the stampede, Dawson City was a pretentious mix of hotels and bars, whorehouses, and opera houses. Trail-packers raced their dogsleds down Front Street, the then-flashy riverfront drive, and seemingly endless lines snaked from each of the town's only *two* public outhouses. Almost anything you wanted was available there—usually for a very high price—from moccasins to locally unearthed mammoth tusks, from pink lemonade to Paris gowns.

Status and respect could be bought along with everything else in Dawson City—if your wallet was fat enough. And everyone who came to the Klondike in those days had a scheme for fattening their wallets, whether by mining the ground, mining the miners (as card sharps and confidence men were wont to do), or minding some enterprise that distracted prospectors from their greed. "Arizona Charlie" Meadows followed that last approach. A friend and imitator of frontier showman Buffalo Bill Cody, Meadows cannibalized wood from beached sternwheelers to construct his Palace Grand Theater on King Street, and between singers and vaudevillians he demonstrated his marksmanship—until the night he shot part of his wife's thumb off and she huffily left the act.

Notwithstanding some of the violent imagery of Robert W. Service (whose poems "The Shooting of Dan McGrew" and "The Cremation of Sam McGee" became synonymous with the gold rush), Dawson was a relatively safe place. Credit that to the North-West Mounted Police, who shut down businesses on the Sabbath and forbade the carrying of sidearms, much to the chagrin of gun-happy Americans (who made up 80 percent of the city's populace in 1898). The Mounties made theft rare in town, murder even more uncommon. In fact, they did such a fine job that Dawson banks didn't bother to surround their teller cages with iron bars; they used chicken wire, instead.

At night the Mounties, perhaps more intent on managing the town's wild streak than expunging it, turned benignly neglectful eyes on Front Street, where saloons, gambling parlors, and dance halls reigned. Amid the tinny piano melodies and the din of voices, performers like Kathleen Eloise ("Klondike Kate") Rockwell, a vivacious redheaded singer/dancer from the Northwest, did their best to win men's hearts, while their more salacious sisters—the prostitutes of "Paradise Alley," a row of shacks half a block off Front—competed for the men's pocketbooks. And everywhere, it seemed, some mud-caked miner was celebrating his good luck with whiskey, paying for drinks from a heavy bag of gold dust. The dust was so plentiful and traded so carelessly in the city's heyday that kids hired to clean out one Front Street saloon could often make twenty dollars a night from their sweepings.

But while Seattle continued to boom after the gold rush, Dawson City fell. By 1899, people who had not struck it rich were packing up and leaving in droves. The former Queen City of the Klondike and capital of the Yukon Territory lost 90 percent of its population by 1900. It had withstood floods and devastating fires during the stampede, but it could not survive disinterest. In subsequent decades, individual gold claims were snapped up by large mining concerns with the money and technology necessary to mine ever-deeper deposits. Families moved in to civilize the town, and in 1955 the Yukon government moved out, transferring the provincial capital to Whitehorse.

Today, there are just over two thousand people living in Dawson City. Some of them continue to hunt for gold, but the majority work in the tourist economy. The process to make Dawson a national historical monument was begun in 1959, and since then the Canadian parks service has done an excellent job of restoring or re-creating many significant structures. Despite its lost glory, there remains a boisterousness and optimism about this dirt-street town. Especially come evening, when performers at the reconstructed Palace Grand present the *Gaslight Follies*, a spirited revue reminiscent of what might have been offered in the late 1890s. Sitting in the audience, it doesn't take much to imagine that the past century never happened, that the gold rush never ended—and that Arizona Charlie is going to march onstage any minute and take aim at his wife's thumb all over again.

few thousand veteran prospectors residing as far south as the Pacific Northwest had heard about the gold finds and were preparing to brave the Yukon's frigid temperatures. For the most part, though, this remained an "insiders' rush" until the *Excelsior* and *Portland* reached the West Coast the following summer. After that, no amount of snow and ice could stay the northward flood of humanity.

Robert W. Service, the renowned "Bard of the Klondike," didn't actually reach the Yukon until 1904, well after the excitement had died down. But his poem "The Trail of Ninety-Eight" captured the delirium of that time:

> Gold! We leapt from our benches. Gold! We sprang from our stools.
> Gold! We wheeled in the furrow, fired with the faith of fools.
> Fearless, unfound, unfitted, far from the night and the cold,
> Heard we the clarion summons, followed the master-lure—Gold!

By late July 1897, bank clerks, barbers, ferry pilots, and preachers from all over Seattle had quit their jobs and booked passage to southeast Alaska. There, from the raw hamlets of Skagway and Dyea, two mountain trails—respectively, the White Pass route and the more popular Chilkoot Pass route—led toward the Klondike. The *Seattle Times* lost most of its reporters to "Klondicitis," as the gold madness was being called, and the ranks of the police force were equally decimated. Streetcars stopped running as drivers deserted their posts.

Seattle's mayor, W. D. Wood, himself fell victim. Attending a convention in San Francisco when the rush commenced, Wood didn't even bother to go home. He telegraphed his resignation, raised money to buy a ship in the Bay Area, and was so excited about sailing to Alaska that he forgot to load fifty thousand pounds of his passengers' belongings. He was almost lynched at dockside.

Presently, anything a budding prospector thought he might need could be purchased on the shores of Seattle's Elliott Bay, from heavy mackinaw jackets and fur-seated trousers, to "crystallized eggs," milk tablets, canvas bathtubs, and huge "portable" stoves. Bicycles—some with skis instead of a front wheel—were snapped up by people who had obviously never faced mountains as forbidding as those around the Klondike. Horses that had been steps away

Mining the Gold Rush

Seattle in the early 1890s was anything but a boomtown.

In 1889, thirty of its central business blocks had been leveled during a twelve-hour fire. Four years later, the city was hit by a devastating depression that swept the entire nation.

Seattle desperately needed the Klondike Stampede's fiscal boost. Yet how could it beat out San Francisco and Vancouver, British Columbia, to become the principal jumping-off point to the Far North? After much consideration, the chamber of commerce decided the city needed a press agent.

So it hired Erastus Brainerd.

Connecticut-born and Harvard-educated, Brainerd was volatile, erudite, and more than a tad egotistical. Prior to his reaching Seattle in 1890, he had been an art curator in Boston and an editor at newspapers in Atlanta and Philadelphia. On the rebound from financial failures in managing his own papers, Brainerd signed on to edit the newly combined *Seattle Press-Times* (now the *Seattle Times*). But his concept for the daily was several intellectual rungs above what its readership wanted. He was let go, only to be named as Washington state's land commissioner, a position he held until 1896.

Free publicity from the *Portland*'s "ton of gold" gave Brainerd a major head start in touting his city and its links to Alaska and the Yukon. He followed it up by blitzing newspapers and magazines with advertisements that detailed Seattle's convenient access to the gold fields. He penned stories about the Seattle-Alaska connection for East Coast publications, then turned around and quoted his own phrases from those stories in news releases. He assembled fat packets of photographs showing Alaska and Seattle, and dispatched them to European and South American rulers. (One such folder reached Germany's Kaiser Wilhelm II, who, convinced it was a bomb, refused to open it.)

Just how successful was Brainerd in selling the connection between Seattle and the promise of Klondike wealth? Enough so that he, himself, went north in the spring of 1898. But rather than join the ranks of prospectors, he served in Alaska as a "mining consultant" before returning to Seattle in 1904. As the new editor of the *Post-Intelligencer*, he railed against the vices (gambling, prostitution, drunkenness) that were part of the city's gold-rush legacy. When he died in 1922, his obituaries failed to mention that he had made Seattle "the gateway to the Klondike."

from the glue factory commanded outlandish prices on the docks, and when they were in short supply, reindeer and elk substituted. Told that dogsleds would help speed them to their pots of gold, these fortune hunters fought over the malamutes and mutts being imported into the city on a weekly basis. They even shanghaied household pets. "Somebody stole our dog. . . ," complained young Mattie Harris, whose mother had refused to sell the family canine to a departing argonaut. "The man took him and went on. We couldn't go after him." Only animals that were kept inside could be considered safe from harness.

As the human tide rose in the Yukon, Canada's North-West Mounted Police swept in to maintain order—and to ensure that stampeders were properly equipped. The Mounties absolutely insisted (and double-checked at border crossings on the Chilkoot and White Pass trails) that anyone entering the territory come with a year's stock of food—about 1,150 pounds. Added to the tents, cooking utensils, mining tools, winter attire, and other materiel necessary for an expedition, that meant that each Klondiker had to transport roughly a ton of belongings. No easy task, since a man could reasonably carry only fifty or sixty pounds on his back at a time. He had to either pack his personal mountain of goods atop horses or shuttle it along in portions, cacheing each successive load as he went back several miles for the next, eventually making dozens of trips over the same ground.

Merchants owed a tremendous debt of gratitude to the Mounties' checkpoints. Adventurers coming from distant parts usually waited until they reached Seattle or Vancouver, British Columbia, before loading themselves down with these goods. Seattle stores had to order in so many provisions that the overflow inventory was stacked five or more feet high along some thoroughfares in what was then downtown (today's Pioneer Square Historic District).

Any remaining money the stampeders had before they left Seattle generally went toward entertainments, because they knew they would not see civilization for a while. Billiard halls, saloons, and Turkish baths all did a boomtown trade. So did prominent local brothels, like those owned by Lou Graham and Rae Roberts, where

The hard way and the railway: Set out on the Chilkoot Trail and you had to haul your supplies up the icy "Golden Stairs." Choose the White Pass and you found a route so treacherous it became known as "Dead Horse Trail." In 1900, the White Pass & Yukon Railroad supplanted overland travel.

miners got one last night of warmth to remember in the chilly days to come. Especially in the rush's first year, city streets were crowded and noisy all night, convincing a sober New Yorker named Arthur Dietz that Seattle was "more wicked than Sodom."

LIFE AND DEATH ON THE TRAIL

ESTIMATES ARE that a million people seriously considered joining the Klondike gold rush in its early days. Fully one hundred thousand of them, from all points on the globe, eventually journeyed to Alaska and the Yukon, leaving behind their children, their spouses, their careers for one wild dance in the arms of Lady Luck.

No matter their preparations, they often fell short of anticipating what the Far North might throw their way. Men, women, and children faced blizzards while hiking mountain passes. Thieves took their money; frostbite and food poisoning sapped their strength and optimism; and in some cases, snow slides and floods took their lives. Even the insects conspired to make life just a wee bit more hellish. "The mosquitos are horrible," Jonas B. Houck, a resident of Detroit, wrote to his wife from the Yukon on June 9, 1898. "We wear cheesecloth nets around our heads and neck . . . and they bite through buckskin gloves and also through overalls and woolen socks. In size they are like Michigan mosquitos, but they are ten times as savage and there are millions of them."

Yet even had they known what would befall them, these people would likely have set off for the Klondike anyway. The tug of gold was that powerful.

The routes they took differed. Thousands tried to cross Canada, a tortuous overland trek of almost sixteen hundred miles from Edmonton, Alberta, to Dawson City that few followers completed. Many others, crossing over glaciers from the Gulf of Alaska, perished by falling into crevasses. Well-to-do Klondikers preferred a safer 4,722-mile ship excursion from Seattle to St. Michael, on Alaska's west coast, and then up the Yukon River.

But the majority came first to San Francisco, Seattle, or

Soapy Smith and his band of thugs terrorized prospectors heading out from Skagway on the White Pass Trail. When adventurers set up camp at Lake Lindeman they were still five hundred miles from the gold fields—but the worst was behind them.

Vancouver (many traveling on special "gold-rush cars," provided by America's transcontinental railroads) and then boarded, bought, or did their best to hijack anything that might float them thirteen hundred miles up the Inside Passage to the Chilkoot and White Pass trailheads. Both trails would take them over the Coast Mountains, across the United States–Canada border, and then on to the headwaters of the Yukon River. From there, they could boat all the way to Dawson.

Neither trail was well regarded; one Klondiker who had traveled both quipped, "Whichever way you go, you will wish you had gone the other." However, the White Pass route, which began in Skagway, inspired the most tales—and the most terrors.

Set beside an exquisite glacier-shaded harbor (jammed during

Chilkoot Trail Supplies: One Man, One Year

Photos of a human chain of stampeders trudging up the Chilkoot Pass have come to symbolize the Klondike gold rush. In 1897–98, the North-West Mounted Police set up a border crossing into Canada at the summit of the Chilkoot. They ordered every stampeder to carry a year's worth of supplies. After all, there was no turning back once they were into the Klondike, and commerce was limited, to say the least. As a result, many stampeders struggling up the mountain rampart were bent double under the weight of their packs, which typically contained the following:

McDougall   and   Secord

Klondike Outfit List (clothing & food):

- 2 suits heavy knit underwear
- 6 pairs wool socks
- 1 pair heavy moccasins
- 2 pairs german stockings
- 2 heavy flannel overshirts
- 1 heavy woolen sweater
- 1 pair overalls
- 2 pairs 12-lb. blankets
- 1 waterproof blanket
- 1 dozen bandana handkerchiefs
- 1 stiff brim cowboy hat
- 1 pair hip rubber boots
- 1 pair prospectors' high land boots
- 1 mackinaw, coat, pants, shirt
- 1 pair heavy buck mitts, lined

most of the gold-rush period with vessels that had been abandoned by impatient adventurers), Skagway was a hash of tree stumps and tents and hastily rendered wooden structures, a place attuned to the discordant rhythms of saws, neighing horses, creaking wagons, and men bargaining for goods. California naturalist John Muir likened it to "a nest of ants taken into a strange country and stirred up by a stick." He might have added that Skagway was a hucksters' haven, lorded over by one Jefferson Randolph Smith—better known as "Soapy," thanks to his fondness for a confidence game that involved paper money wrapped around bars of soap. Smith, a mustachioed former Georgian, was a politically savvy crook, mounting a reputable front at the same time that he controlled an extensive network of card sharps, grifters, harlots, spies, and murderers. From

1 pair unlined leather gloves	10 lb. baking powder
1 duck coat, pants, vest	20 lb. salt
6 towels	1 lb. pepper
1 pocket matchbox, buttons, needles and thread, comb, mirror, toothbrush, etc.	2 lb. baking soda
	1/2 lb. mustard
	1/4 lb. vinegar
mosquito netting/1 dunnage bag	2 doz. condensed milk
1 sleeping bag/medicine chest	20 lb. evaporated potatoes
pack saddles, complete horses	5 lb. evaporated onions
flat sleighs	6 tins/4 oz. extract beef
100 lb. navy beans	75 lb. evaporated fruits
150 lb. bacon	4 pkg. yeast cakes
400 lb. flour	20 lb. candles
40 lb. rolled oats	1 pkg. tin matches
20 lb. corn meal	6 cakes borax
10 lb. rice	6 lb. laundry soap
25 lb. sugar	1/2 lb. ground ginger
10 lb. tea	25 lb. hard tack
20 lb. coffee	1 lb. citric acid
	2 bottles jamaica ginger

his arrival in Alaska in 1897, until a vigilante gunned him down a year later, Soapy Smith was "the Uncrowned King of Skagway."

Prospectors who hoped that their march up the White Pass Trail would free them from the Smith gang's predations soon learned that Soapy's cronies were active even there, posing as clerics or gold seekers, all ready to fleece the unsuspecting. Transporting large amounts of cash to Dawson City was near impossible, until bankers caught on to the fact that if they dressed as grubby miners and carried their funds in inconspicuous packs, Soapy's confederates would ignore them in favor of more prosperous-looking marks.

Criminal threats, however, were nothing when compared with the natural dangers of that trail. Surveyed in 1887, the route via White Pass and on to Lake Lindeman stretched for about forty-five miles. It was a reasonably low course, convincing greenhorns that they could tackle it with ease. That was a serious misconception. Switchbacks, deep mudholes, and perilous cliff-side stretches made the trail slow going—and deadly. So narrow was the pass in some places that pack animals had to stand for hours under their crushing loads, waiting for obstacles to be cleared ahead. And when they could move again, their owners pushed them ruthlessly. One stampeder recalled seeing a horse walk off the face of a cliff. "It looked to me . . . like suicide," he said. "I believe a horse will commit suicide, and this is enough to make them."

Journalist (Edwin) Tappan Adney, a special correspondent for *Harper's Weekly* and the *London Chronicle*, who followed the Klondike stampeders over White Pass, took an equally jaundiced view of the trail: "When the sun and rains shall have melted the snow of the Chilkoots, the White Pass Trail will be paved with the bones of horses, and the ravens and foxes will have feasted as never until the white man sought a new way across the great mountain. As many horses as have come in alive, just so many will bleach their bones by the pine-trees and in the gulches—for none will go out." Indeed, few of the three thousand steeds used on the White Pass route in late 1897 survived, inspiring seasoned travelers to nickname it the Dead Horse Trail.

By contrast, the Chilkoot Trail was deemed comparatively free of hazards—aside from the occasional avalanche (one of which killed at least sixty people in 1898)—and blessedly free of con men. It began in Dyea, nine miles north of Skagway on Lynn Canal. Though now only a memory, except for some rotten pier pilings and crooked cemetery markers, Dyea was a thriving community in the 1890s. There, men could complete their provisioning or hire native packers to help carry their supplies.

The biggest plus for the Chilkoot Trail was its length: only thirty-three miles to Lake Bennett, which lay immediately north of Lake Lindeman. In theory, a hiker could shave a whole day off his travel by taking this more direct route through the Coast peaks. However, the summit of Chilkoot Pass rises six hundred feet higher than that of White Pass, and it includes a quarter-mile-long, thirty-five- to forty-five-degree incline that gains about a thousand feet in elevation. During the summer, conquering this slope meant crawling over huge boulders and trying to find footholds in scree. But in winter, it presented a particular torment. Photos show seemingly endless lines of men trudging almost as one up the so-called Golden

The Tragedy of "Dead Horse Trail"

The horses died like mosquitoes in the first frost, and from Skagway to Bennett they rotted in heaps. They died at the rocks, they were poisoned at the summit, and they starved at the lakes; they fell off the trail, what there was of it, and they went through it; in the river they drowned under their loads or were smashed to pieces against the boulders; they snapped their legs in the crevices and broke their backs falling backwards with their packs; in the sloughs they sank from fright or smothered in the slime; and they were disemboweled in the bogs where corduroy logs turned end up in the mud; men shot them, worked them to death and when they were gone, went back to the beach [at Skagway] and bought more. Some did not bother to shoot them, stripping the saddles off and the shoes and leaving them where they fell. Their hearts turned to stone—those that did not break—and they became beasts, the men on the Dead Horse Trail.

(Jack London, from the short story "Which Make Men Remember")

Stairs: as many as fifteen hundred ice steps carved into the ascent's steepest portion. The men responsible for the steps charged a toll for using them, and conceivably made as much money that way as from doing anything else in the North.

Overdressed and out-of-shape Klondikers agonized going up this grade, some collapsing in tears. Julius Price, who tackled Chilkoot Pass in June 1898, recalled, "It is about as fatiguing a climb as could well be imagined. . . . By dint of stolid plodding, with an occasional pause to take breath, we reached the summit." Even then, of course, the hikers couldn't celebrate, for they knew that they had to turn around and do it all over again, retrieving yet another packload of their provisions and paying yet another toll. "It took the average man three months or more to shuttle his ton of goods across the pass," explains Canadian Pierre Berton in *The Klondike Fever.*

Is it any wonder that these gum-boot miners breathed a great sigh of relief when they finally reached Lake Lindeman or Lake Bennett? Yes, they still faced five hundred miles by boat, through fierce winds and tumultuous rapids. But they knew they were on the last leg of their pilgrimage. Once they made it over the lakes and onto the broad, strangely shallow Yukon River—either by handbuilt raft, as many of the first stampeders did, or aboard a small sternwheeler—the figuring was they would be home-free. Next stop: Dawson City and riches beyond imagining.

In his 1900 book, *The Klondike Stampede,* Tappan Adney described the crowds that reached Dawson at the height of the gold rush:

> It is a motley throng—every degree of person gathered from every corner of the earth, from every State of the Union, and from every city—weatherbeaten, sunburned, with snow glasses over their hats, just as they came from the passes. Australians with upturned sleeves and a swagger; young Englishmen in golf stockings and tweeds; would-be miners in mackinaws and rubber boots, or heavy, high-laced shoes; Japanese, Negroes—and women, too, everywhere.

These people had come following the fantasy of easy riches, the conceit that they would be tycoons. But newspaper accounts had led them on, implying that wealth awaited anyone who could reach the

Dawson gold fields. Paul T. Mizony, a seventeen-year-old from San Diego, who landed at Dawson in 1898, noted that "hundreds . . . expected all they would have to do was to pick the nuggets above the ground and some even thought they grew on bushes." Only when the gold-drunk prospectors finished their trip did they understand how hard mining truly was—and that the best claims on Bonanza and Eldorado creeks had already been staked back in 1896, almost a full year *before* the rush started!

ALL THAT GLITTERS . . .

B Y ONE RECKONING, only about four thousand people actually found gold during the epic Klondike Stampede. Most, including veterans of other mineral pursuits, didn't recoup so much as their travel costs.

"This is a country of contradictions," Jonas Houck wrote in the summer of 1898. "It puzzles old miners to know anything about where to dig for gold. They will come here and dig where they think gold should be if it is anywhere in the country and not find anything and give it up in disgust; and some 'greenhorn' will dig where a person who knows anything about mining in other places would never think of looking and strike it rich."

Like Houck, many of the disillusioned no sooner reached Dawson than they left again. Others went to work for the "Klondike Kings," who had found gold and stayed to bleed their claims dry. Some, their passions satisfied by having made the mere chase after chimerical fortune, struck off for the next great adventure at Nome, an outpost on Alaska's cold Bering Sea coast, where gold had been discovered in 1898. Or they joined the Spanish-American War, which erupted in that same year.

George Carmack and his wife, Kate, tried to ride their celebrity beyond the north country. They traveled to Seattle, but the press there treated them as curious savages, remarked on their disorientation among the city's tall buildings, and reported at length on Kate's disorderly conduct under the influence of alcohol. Readers of the *Seattle Times*, for instance, found the following item in their paper on July 27, 1899:

> Mrs. George W. Carmack, the Indian wife of the discoverer of the
> Klondike, and who is probably the richest Indian woman in the
> world, was fined $3.60 by Judge Cann this morning for drunken-
> ness. Mrs. Carmack loaded up on champagne last night, and in
> company with some Indian friends, made Rome howl in the Seattle
> Hotel. Officer Grant gathered her in, and prosecuted her this
> morning. She refused to tell who furnished her the champagne.

Carmack eventually disowned Kate and parted ways with Skookum
Jim and Tagish Charley, never returning to the Yukon after 1900.

Thomas Lippy, the YMCA instructor and the star of the *Excelsior*
landing, took some $2 million out of his claim on lower Eldorado
Creek before selling it in 1903. He used the money to erect a grand
home in Seattle and contribute to various philanthropic enterprises.
But he died bankrupt after a series of bad investments.

Seattle fared considerably better. In 1898, Congress awarded it a
government assay office, ensuring that a large measure of the $174
million in Klondike gold that flowed into the city between 1898 and
1902 would remain there. In fact, many of the people who chose to
stay on Elliott Bay and supply the Klondike prospectors made out better financially than the miners themselves.

By the first decade of the twentieth century, Seattle was expanding, flattening its hilly topography to make streetcar travel easier, and
improving its waterfront services. Many of the people who had once
passed through Seattle on their way to the gold fields returned to live
in the city, driving its population precipitously upward—from 42,000
in the mid-1890s to more than 245,000 in 1910. There was the sense
that the city had shed its frontier vestiges and gained not only fame
but stature through its participation in the Klondike insanity. To celebrate, in 1909 Seattle mounted something of a coming-out party: the
elaborate Alaska-Yukon-Pacific Exposition. While previous American
fairs had commemorated the anniversaries of exploration or settlement,
this one, as historian Norman H. Clark contended, celebrated only the
fact that "in the story of civilization there is probably no record of more
astonishing growth than occurred in the region around Puget Sound."

The Gold Rush Trail Today

Travelers looking to follow the path of the Klondike Stampede a century ago can head out from Seattle, Washington, sail up the Inside Passage to Skagway, Alaska, and then make their way into the Yukon Territory.

SEATTLE

Washington's largest city has grown substantially since the Klondike gold rush overwhelmed its docks with frenzied men and filled its civic coffers with cash. Yet much of what Klondikers saw there in the late 1890s remains intact.

Pioneer Square, Seattle's original center, is now a historic district at the south end of downtown. The square reflects the aesthetics of the Gilded Age, especially in the brick-and-terra cotta structures that crowd around cobblestoned **Pioneer Place Park,** at the intersection of First Avenue and Yesler Way. Be sure not to miss designer Elmer H. Fisher's **Pioneer Building** (606 First Avenue), which the American Institute of Architects applauded in 1892 as "the finest building west of Chicago." Pioneer Place Park is also where you can join one of the irreverent tours of **Underground Seattle,** a buried maze of corridors that were once the sidewalks and first floors of Pioneer Square. Not far away, the **Klondike Gold Rush National Historic Park** (117 South Main Street) offers fine displays of mining equipment and old newspapers from gold-rush days, plus informative videos that recall the rigors of hiking the Chilkoot and White Pass trails. Long gone is Schwabacher's Wharf (near today's Pier 57), where the steamer *Portland* landed in 1897, bearing news of the Klondike strike. But a plaque at **Waterfront Park,** on Alaskan Way, marks the event.

SKAGWAY

Although it fell on hard times after the end of the gold rush, this southeast Alaskan town has since been vastly restored by the U.S. National Park Service. It now appears much as it did in 1898—com-

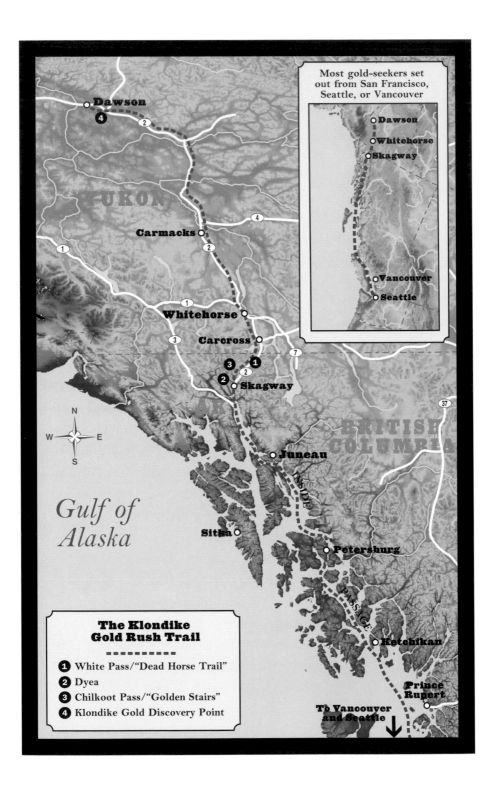

Most gold-seekers set
out from San Francisco,
Seattle, or Vancouver

Dawson

Whitehorse

Skagway

Vancouver

Seattle

Dawson

YUKON

Carmacks

Whitehorse

Carcross

Skagway

Juneau

Gulf of
Alaska

Sitka

BRITISH
COLUMBIA

Petersburg

INSIDE

PASSAGE

Ketchikan

Prince
Rupert

To Vancouver
and Seattle

**The Klondike
Gold Rush Trail**

- - - - - - - - - - -

❶ White Pass/"Dead Horse Trail"

❷ Dyea

❸ Chilkoot Pass/"Golden Stairs"

❹ Klondike Gold Discovery Point

plete with wooden sidewalks. Most of its businesses and historic sites crowd around Broadway, the short main thoroughfare. Start your tour at the Visitors Information Center, housed in the quirky but beautiful **Arctic Brotherhood Hall** (Broadway, between Second and Third Avenues), a rare example of turn-of-the-century drift-wood stick architecture—and the most photographed building in the state. Around the corner is **Soapy Smith's Parlor** (on Second Avenue, between Broadway and State Street), headquarters for the nefarious con man, whose story lives on at several locations. The **Trail of '98 Museum,** on the second floor of city hall (Seventh Avenue and Spring Street), displays Soapy Smith paraphernalia, including his blood-stained tie. Smith himself was laid to rest in the **Gold Rush Cemetery,** not far from the grave of city surveyor Frank Reid, whose bullet ended the crook's reign in 1898. Soapy and the gold rush are recalled in the lively **Days of '98** show, held nightly during the summer at the Eagles Dance Hall.

The treacherous White Pass Trail, which once took prospectors north from Skagway, has pretty much gone to seed since 1900, when it was replaced by the narrow-gauge **White Pass & Yukon Railroad.** A portion of the WP&YR still operates as a tourist attraction, taking passengers on a breathtaking day trip over the summit of White Pass. Hikers might prefer to tackle the well-main-tained **Chilkoot Pass Trail,** a strenuous thirty-three-mile trek that starts at what was once the village of Dyea (accessible by road, nine miles north of Skagway) and concludes at the Yukon's magnificent Lake Bennett.

DAWSON CITY

Walking tours of this historic boomtown begin at the **Visitor Reception Centre** (at Front and King Streets) and offer an excel-lent introduction to the characters and characteristics of Dawson a century ago. The **Dawson City Museum** (on Fifth Avenue, between Mission and Turner Streets) tells the story of the region long before the gold rush, when woolly mammoths trod the Yukon and the Han Indians flourished at the mouth of the Klondike River. Visitors are invited to take in **Fort Herchemer,** the Mounties' command post during the Klondike madness, and to study the pillared

Commissioner's Residence, built in 1900 as a home for the Yukon territorial administrator. Literature lovers might head for the **Robert Service Cabin,** where the poet lived from 1909 to 1912 (and where actor Tom Byrne now gives dramatic daily readings of Service's verse), or wander down to the **Jack London Interpretive Center,** which combines a museum dedicated to the author of *White Fang* and *The Call of the Wild* with a reproduction of the log cabin in which London lived on a nearby stream during the gold rush.

About ten miles southeast of town, along Bonanza Creek Road, a monument marks **Discovery Point,** the place where George Carmack, Skookum Jim, and Tagish Charley first found gold in 1896. To better realize what developed from that find, stop in at **Gold Dredge No. 4,** the largest wooden-hulled gold dredge in North America, which closed in 1966 after thirty-four years of service.

The Klondike Stampede drove most local natives away, but a **Moosehide Indian Village,** abandoned in 1957, remains just to the north of Dawson, its log cabins, schoolhouses, churches, and cemetery a haunting reminder of the lost past. For an overview of Dawson, climb or drive to the top of **Midnight Dome,** two and one-half miles north of town. The panoramic view of the area may make you realize why many miners stayed here even after gold became harder to find.

The Klondike Centennial Society (403-993-1997) has a schedule of gold rush commemorations planned clear through the year 2000. For still more information, contact the Yukon Territorial Department of Tourism, 403-667-5340; the Alaska Division of Tourism, 907-465-5474; and the Skagway Visitors Information Center, 907-983-2854. —*Ellen L. Boyer*

Selected Events
For Travelers

The following lists just a few of the numerous heritage festivals and commemorations that occur each year along America's historic trails:

El Camino Real

First Thanksgiving. This reenactment commemorates the meeting of Juan de Oñate's 1598 expedition and local Native Americans, and the feast they shared on the banks of the Rio Grande. **When/where:** The last weekend in April, at Chamizal National Memorial, in El Paso, Texas. **Contact:** Mission Trail Association of El Paso, 915-534-0630.

Artist and Craftsman Show. Begun in 1972, this is now the nation's biggest offering of Native American arts and crafts, involving eight northern New Mexican pueblos. The show rotates location, so call in advance for directions. **When/where:** The third weekend in July, at various New Mexican pueblos. **Contact:** Eight Northern Indian Pueblo Council, 505-852-4265.

Santa Fe Fiesta. First staged in 1712, this is the oldest festival in the United States. Folk dancing, religious pageantry, and fireworks are featured. **When/where:** The weekend following Labor Day, in Santa Fe, New Mexico. **Contact:** Santa Fe Convention and Visitors Bureau, 800-777-2489.

The Boston Post Road

Barnum Festival. Showman Phineas T. Barnum died in 1891, but the town he once served as mayor continues to glorify his memory each year with street fairs, concerts, and a parade. **When/where:** The weekend closest to July 4, in Bridgeport, Connecticut. **Contact:** Bridgeport Chamber of Commerce, 203-335-3800.

Oyster Festival. Boat races and crafts shows, as well as nautical displays at the Maritime Center (10 North Water Street) honor Norwalk's oystering heritage. **When/where:** The weekend after Labor Day, in Norwalk, Connecticut. **Contact:** Norwalk Chamber of Commerce, 203-866-2521.

Boston Tea Party Reenactment. Men dressed as Mohawk Indians recreate the famous 1773 demonstration of defiance against the British. **When/where:** December 15, on Congress Street at the Harbor Walk, in Boston, Massachusetts. **Contact:** Greater Boston Convention and Visitors Bureau, 617-536-4100.

The Great Wagon Road

Battle of Germantown Reenactment. Significant portions of that 1777 engagement, which resulted in the defeat of General George Washington's army, are staged by men in costume. Once a separate village, Germantown is now part of northwestern Philadelphia. **When/where:** The first Saturday in October, in Philadelphia, Pennsylvania. **Contact:** Cliveden, 215-848-1777.

Election Day, 1860. Amid music and street entertainment, spokesmen for three presidential candidates (Lincoln was not on the ballot in the South) relive the campaign of 1860—a crucial time in determining whether there would be a Civil War. **When/where:** The second weekend in October, in Harpers Ferry, West Virginia. **Contact:** Harpers Ferry National Historical Park, 304-535-6223.

The Wilderness Road

Kentucky Derby Festival. In addition to the thoroughbred race at Churchill Downs, this festival includes an Ohio River steamboat race, a parade, and a huge fireworks show. **When/where:** The two weeks preceding the first Saturday in May, in Louisville, Kentucky. **Contact:** Kentucky Derby Festival, 800-928-3378.

National Storytelling Festival. History, folklore, and fairy tales are in the spotlight at this renowned event. **When/where:** The first full weekend in October, in Jonesborough, Tennessee. **Contact:** National Storytelling Association, 800-525-4514.

Daniel Boone Festival. A pioneer village re-creation, long-rifle shootouts, and square dancing all figure in this salute to the quintessential American pioneer. **When/where:** The second week in October, Barbourville, Kentucky. **Contact:** Barbourville Chamber of Commerce, 606-546-4300.

The River Road

Battle of New Orleans Celebration. Andrew Jackson's 1815 victory over British invaders is reenacted at the Chalmette Battlefield, east of downtown. **When/where:** The weekend closest to January 8, in New Orleans, Louisiana. **Contact:** Chalmette Battlefield, 504-589-4430.

New Orleans Jazz & Heritage Festival. Nightclubs and auditoriums all over town roll to the rhythms of jazz, zydeco, gospel, and blues. The New Orleans Fair Grounds (on Gentilly Boulevard) adds to the mix with an extravaganza of regional dishes. **When/where:** The last weekend in April through the first weekend in May, in New Orleans. **Contact:** Jazz Festival Office, 504-522-4786.

The Natchez Trace

Pilgrimage. The antebellum South rises again, as Natchez opens its historic homes and gardens for touring. **When/where:** The first weekend in March through the first weekend in April, in Natchez, Mississippi. **Contact:** Natchez Pilgrimage, 800-647-6742.

Natchez Trace Festival. Highlights of this salute to the Trace include a fiddlers' jamboree, arts and crafts booths, an antique-car show, and walking tours of historical structures. **When/where:** The last week in April, in Kosciusko, Mississippi. **Contact:** Kosciusko Chamber of Commerce, 601-289-2981.

The Mormon Trail

Oregon Trail Days. In 1830, the first wagon train of pioneers went west along the Platte River (later also paralleled by Mormons), camping in mid-July near present-day Gering. That event is now commemorated with parades, cooking contests, and an Indian gathering. **When/where:** The weekend closest to July 15, in Gering, Nebraska. **Contact:** Gering Civic Center, 308-436-6886.

Pioneer Company Arrival Commemoration. Brigham Young's entry into the valley of the Great Salt Lake is remembered in 1850s style, with brass bands, parades, and old-fashioned speeches. **When/where:** The week of July 24, at This Is the Place State Park, east of Salt Lake City, Utah. **Contact:** This Is the Place State Park Visitors Center, 801-584-8391.

City of Joseph. Held at the Mormon-operated Nauvoo Reservation, this free outdoor performance recalls the seven years (1839–1846) during which Joseph Smith's Latter-day Saints occupied Nauvoo. **When/where:** The first weekend in August, in Nauvoo, Illinois. **Contact:** Nauvoo Visitors Center, 217-453-2237.

THE CALIFORNIA TRAIL

Pony Express Days. A tribute to the short-lived Pony Express, complete with horse races, a parade, and sales of pioneer foods and crafts. **When/where:** The last two weekends in August, in Ely, Nevada. **Contact:** White Pine Chamber of Commerce, 702-289-8877.

Santa-Cali-Gon Days. Independence recalls its days as the starting point for the Santa Fe, Oregon, and California Trails. The celebration includes pioneer wagons, a carnival, and lots of western-style grub. **When/where:** Labor Day weekend, in Independence, Missouri. **Contact:** Independence Chamber of Commerce, 816-252-4745.

U.S. National Gold Panning Championship. California's 1849 gold rush is remembered with a panning competition and historic building tours. Events occur at Marshall Gold Discovery State Historical Park. **When/where:** The first weekend of October, in Coloma, California. **Contact:** Gold Discovery Park Association, 916-622-6198.

CALIFORNIA'S MISSION TRAIL

Swallows Day. Crowds gather to see the birds wing back from their winter homes in Argentina and nest about the gardens of Mission San Juan Capistrano. **When/where:** March 19, in San Juan Capistrano, California. **Contact:** San Juan Capistrano Chamber of Commerce, 714-493-4700.

Old Spanish Days. Spanish and Mexican marketplaces, a carnival and parade, and dancing all figure into this city's largest annual event. **When/where:** The first week in August, in Santa Barbara, California. **Contact:** Old Spanish Days, 805-962-8101.

THE KLONDIKE GOLD RUSH TRAIL

Fire Festival. Fire-fighting equipment parades through Pioneer Square (at the south end of downtown), commemorating Seattle's Great Fire of 1889. **When/where:** Early June, in Seattle, Washington. **Contact:** Pioneer Square Community Council, 206-623-1162.

Dawson City Discovery Days. Music, barbecues, and gold-panning competitions at a variety of venues highlight the anniversary of George Carmack's world-changing 1896 find on Bonanza Creek. **When/where:** Mid-August, in Dawson City, Yukon Territory, Canada. **Contact:** Klondike Visitors Association, 403-993-5575.

A Select Bibliography

Adney, Tappan. *The Klondike Stampede*. New York: Harper & Brothers, 1900. A remarkable first-person insight into the 1897 rush for northern riches.

Ambrose, Stephen E. *Undaunted Courage: Meriwether Lewis, Thomas Jefferson, and the Opening of the American West*. New York: Simon & Schuster, 1996.

Asbury, Herbert. *The French Quarter: An Informal History of the New Orleans Underworld*. New York: Alfred A. Knopf, 1936. An excellent take on the Crescent City's raucous heritage.

Berger, John A. *The Franciscan Missions of California*. New York: G. P. Putnam's Sons, 1941.

Berton, Pierre. *The Klondike Fever: The Life and Death of the Last Great Gold Rush*. New York: Knopf, 1975. Easily the best history of the Klondike Stampede in print.

———. *My Country: The Remarkable Past*. Toronto: McClelland Stewart, 1976.

Boller, Paul F. *Presidential Anecdotes*. New York: Penguin, 1982.

———. *Presidential Campaigns*. New York: Oxford University Press, 1985.

Bridenbaugh, Carl. *Myths and Realities: Societies of the Colonial South*. Baton Rouge: Louisiana State University Press, 1952.

Brown, Dee. *Wondrous Times on the Frontier*. Little Rock: August House, 1991.

———. "Intrigue on the Natchez Trace." *Southern Magazine*, November 1986, 43.

Bultman, Bethany Ewald. *New Orleans*. Oakland: Compass American Guides, 1994.

Coates, Robert M. *The Outlaw Years: The History of the Land Pirates of the Natchez Trace*. New York: Macaulay, 1930.

Cosner, Shaaron. *The Underground Railroad*. New York: Franklin Watts, 1991.

Crutchfield, James A. *The Natchez Trace: A Pictorial History*. Nashville: Rutledge Hill Press, 1985.

Daniels, Jonathan. *The Devil's Backbone: The Story of the Natchez Trace*. New York: McGraw-Hill, 1962.

Dary, David. *Seeking Pleasure in the Old West*. New York: Alfred A. Knopf, 1995.

Donald, David Herbert. *Lincoln*. New York: Simon & Schuster, 1995.

Dorpat, Paul. *Seattle Now and Then*. Vol. 1. Seattle: Tartu Publications, 1984.

Dufour, Charles L. *Ten Flags in the Wind: The Story of Louisiana*. New York: Harper & Row, 1967.

Faragher, John Mack. *Daniel Boone: The Life and Legend of an American Pioneer*. New York: Henry Holt, 1992. A fond and thorough recollection of the eighteenth century's quintessential backwoodsman.

———, ed. *The Encyclopedia of Colonial and Revolutionary America*. 1st Da Capo Press ed. New York: Da Capo Press, 1996.

Faust, Patricia F., ed. *Historical Times Illustrated Encyclopedia of the Civil War.* New York: HarperPerennial, 1991. A convenient resource for anyone who wants to know the basic facts surrounding Civil War battles and personalities.

Forbes, Esther. *Paul Revere and the World He Lived In.* Boston: Houghton Mifflin, 1942.

Gregg, Josiah. *Commerce of the Prairies.* 1844. Reprint, Norman: University of Oklahoma Press, 1954.

Gregg, Kate L., ed. *The Road to Santa Fe: The Journal and Diaries of George Champlin Sibley.* . . . Albuquerque: University of New Mexico Press, 1952.

Harbert, Nancy. *New Mexico.* Oakland: Compass American Guides, 1996.

Holbrook, Stewart H. *The Old Post Road: The Story of the Boston Post Road.* New York· McGraw-Hill, 1962.

Holliday, J. S. *The World Rushed In: The California Gold Rush Experience.* New York: Simon & Schuster, 1981.

Jenkins, Stephen. *The Old Boston Post Road.* New York: G. P. Putnam's Sons, 1914.

Josephy, Alvin M., Jr. *The Indian Heritage of America.* Boston: American Heritage Library/Houghton Mifflin, 1991.

Kimball, Stanley B., and Violet T. Kimball. *Mormon Trail: Voyage of Discovery—The Story Behind the Scenery.* Las Vegas: KC Publications, 1995.

Kincaid, Robert L. *The Wilderness Road.* New York: Bobbs-Merrill, 1947.

Krell, Dorothy, ed. *The California Missions: A Pictorial History.* Menlo Park, Calif· Lane Publishing, 1979.

Lancaster, Bruce. *The American Revolution.* Garden City, N.Y.: Doubleday, 1957

Langguth, A. J. *Patriots: The Men Who Started the American Revolution.* New York: Simon & Schuster, 1988.

Latrobe, Benjamin Henry Boneval. *Impressions Respecting New Orleans: Diary and Sketches, 1818–1820.* New York. Columbia University Press, 1951.

Lavender, David. *The Great West.* New York: American Heritage, 1985. A terrific overview of how and why the West developed as it did.

Lockwood, Charles. *Manhattan Moves Uptown: An Illustrated History.* Boston: Houghton Mifflin, 1976.

Marcy, Randolph B. *The Prairie Traveler.* 1859. Reprint, New York: Perigee/Berkley, 1994. Lots of fun for people wanting to know more about life on the westward trails.

Moorhead, Max L. *New Mexico's Royal Road: Trade and Travel on the Chihuahua Trail.* Norman: University of Oklahoma Press, 1958.

Morgan, Murray. *Skid Road: An Informal Portrait of Seattle.* Rev. ed. New York: Viking Press, 1971.

Nelson, Truman. *The Old Man: John Brown at Harper's Ferry.* New York: Holt, Rinehart & Winston, 1973.

Nies, Judith. *Native American History: A Chronology of the Vast Achievements of a Culture and Their Links to World Events.* New York: Ballantine, 1996.

Pattie, James Ohio. *The Personal Narrative of James O. Pattie.* 1831. Reprint, Philadelphia: J. B. Lippincott, 1962.

Pierce, J. Kingston. *San Francisco, You're History!* Seattle: Sasquatch Books, 1995.

Rouse, Parke, Jr. *The Great Wagon Road: From Philadelphia to the South.* New York: McGraw-Hill, 1973.

Sherman, John. *Santa Fe: A Pictorial History.* Norfolk, Va.: Donning Company, 1983.

Stegner, Wallace. *The Gathering of Zion: The Story of the Mormon Trail.* New York: McGraw-Hill, 1964. Educational, but also great reading for anyone interested in the cross-country migrations.

Sternberg, Mary Ann. *Along the River Road: Past and Present on Louisiana's Historic Byway.* Baton Rouge: Louisiana State University Press, 1996.

Stern, Robert A. M. *Pride of Place: Building the American Dream.* Boston: Houghton Mifflin, 1986.

Stewart, George R. *The California Trail: An Epic with Many Heroes.* New York: McGraw-Hill, 1962.

———. *Ordeal by Hunger: The Story of the Donner Party.* 1936. Reprint, New York: Pocket Books, 1971.

Tac, Pablo. *Indian Life and Customs at Mission San Luis Rey.* San Luis Rey, Calif.: Old Mission, 1958.

Turner, Frederick Jackson. *The Significance of the Frontier in American History.* Madison: State Historical Society of Wisconsin, 1894.

Ward, Geoffrey C. *The Civil War.* New York: Vintage, 1994.

———. *The West: An Illustrated History.* New York: Little, Brown, 1996. A broad and insightful overview of America's westward movement.

Weber, Msgr. Francis J. *Prominent Visitors to the California Missions (1786–1842).* Los Angeles: Dawson's Book Shop, 1991.

Wise, Winifred E. *Fray Junípero Serra and the California Conquest.* New York: Charles Scribner's Sons, 1967.

Wolf, Edwin II. *Philadelphia: Portrait of an American City.* New and enl. ed. with an additional chapter by Kenneth Finkel. Philadelphia: Camino Books, 1990.

Producers'
Acknowledgments

We knew that the rise or fall of a television series on America's historic trails would depend on the tenacity, talent, and chemistry of the *Trails* team. After the producers, Patricia Larson, Sandra Nisbet, and Patty Conroy, found key stories on the routes, surveyed sites, and wrote scripts, they began the shoots—thousands of driving miles with tireless crews and series host Tom Bodett. Several months later, when the last edit was made, our talented host and the production team had made a very good thing.

Tom Bodett was a great fit, a talent suggested by American Program Service vice president Niki Vettel. Tom is unusual in a media world packed with personalities vying for just one more on-camera moment. To our delight, putting people at ease comes naturally to him; he paid close attention to each park ranger, tour guide, and storyteller we talked to along the trails.

There were visual challenges. How do you make six hundred miles of Nebraska plains come alive? And the Shenandoah Valley on a very long drive on a very quiet Sunday? Those puzzles often lay in the hands of another Tom—Tom Speer of KCTS. He and Valerie Vozza and Karel Bauer were the photographers. They shot desert, rivers, mountains, and glaciers along endless miles of roads. On-line editor Cleven Ticeson and editor David Ris added their patience and magic. The original music of Denny Gore helped define each trail's personality and unique story. Doug DePriest, Patricia Newi, and Gayla Jamison of The Travel Channel provided creative response all along the way.

The financial backing and encouragement of American Program Service president John Porter and APS vice president Bill Dale allowed us the freedom to focus on the wonderful stories and incredible scenery that remain vital to our country—from sweeping prairie vistas to Cajun swamps and pulsating cities—each part of *America's Historic Trails.*

—Nelsa Gidney and John Givens
Executive Producers, *America's Historic Trails*

Permissions & Credits

Reprinted Material
We gratefully acknowledge the kind permission of the publishers to reprint the following:
Page 21: excerpted from *New Mexico's Royal Road: Trade and Travel on the Chihuahua Trail*, by Max L. Moorhead, University of Oklahoma Press, 1958.
Page 65, bottom: excerpted from *The Great Wagon Road: From Philadelphia to the South*, by Parke Rouse Jr., McGraw-Hill, 1973.
Page 90 and page 92, bottom: excerpted from *Daniel Boone: The Life and Legend of an American Pioneer*, by John Mack Faragher, Henry Holt, 1992.
Page 113, bottom: excerpted from *Lincoln*, by David Herbert Donald, Simon & Schuster, 1995.
Page 128, bottom: excerpted from *The Natchez Trace: A Pictorial History*, by James A. Crutchfield, Rutledge Hill Press, Nashville, 1985.
Page 142, bottom: excerpted from *The Devil's Backbone: The Story of the Natchez Trace*, by Jonathan Daniels, McGraw-Hill, 1962.
Page 185, bottom: excerpted from *The California Trail: An Epic with Many Heroes*, by George Stewart, McGraw-Hill, 1962.
Page 190, bottom: excerpted from *The West: An Illustrated History*, by Geoffrey C. Ward, Little, Brown and Company, Inc., 1996.

Photographs and Illustrations
Maps on pages vi-vii, 28, 50, 76, 102, 122, 144, 168, 192, 216, and 244, by Alex Lyon.
Chapter opening maps and map on page 154, by Lisa Moore/KCTS.
Photographs and illustrations are reproduced courtesy of the following:

El Camino Real
Page 7: Corbis-Bettmann.
Page 12, top: Michael D. Kimak.
Page 12, bottom: Ritch, 1882-3.
Page 17, top: Pat Kimak.
Page 17, bottom: Ritch, 1882-3.
Page 23, top: Davis, 1857.
Page 23, bottom: Marion Smith/Small World Productions, Inc.
Page 24, top: Corbis-Bettmann.
Page 24, bottom: Ladd, 1891.

The Boston Post Road
Page 33, top: Greater Boston Convention & Visitors Bureau, Inc.
Page 33, bottom: Corbis-Bettmann.
Page 39, top: John Givens/Small World Productions, Inc.
Page 39, bottom: Corbis-Bettmann. Color engraving of Boston Harbor with British ships, 1768, by Paul Revere.
Page 43, top: Greater Boston Convention & Visitors Bureau, Inc.
Page 43, bottom: Corbis-Bettmann.
Page 47, top and bottom: Corbis-Bettmann.

The Great Wagon Road
Page 57: The Library Company of Philadelphia.
Page 61, top and bottom: Corbis-Bettmann.
Page 67, top and bottom: Corbis-Bettmann.
Page 73, top: Corbis-Bettmann. Painting by Balling.
Page 73, bottom: Corbis-Bettmann.

The Wilderness Road
Page 81, top: Corbis-Bettmann. Engraving of painting by W. Ranney.
Page 81, bottom: John Givens/Small World Productions, Inc.
Page 85, top: Corbis-Bettmann.
Page 85, bottom: Virginia Tourism Corporation.
Page 93: Corbis-Bettmann.
Page 99, top: Corbis-Bettmann.
Page 99, bottom: Corbis-Bettmann. Drawing by J. W. Hill; engraving by Wellstood & Peters.

The River Road
Page 107: Corbis-Bettmann. *The Jolly Flat Boat Men*, engraving by T. Daving from a painting by George C. Bingham, 1847.

Page 110, top left and right: Corbis-Bettmann.

Page 110, bottom: New Orleans Convention & Tourist Bureau.

Page 116, top and bottom: Corbis-Bettmann.

Page 121, top: Corbis-Bettmann.

Page 121, bottom: John Givens/Small World Productions, Inc.

The Natchez Trace

Page 127, top: Historic New Orleans Collection, 1974.25.30151.

Page 127, bottom: Corbis-Bettmann.

Page 132, top: *A Cahokia Market*, by Michael Hampshire/Cahokia Mounds State Historic Site.

Page 132, middle: John Givens/Small World Productions, Inc.

Page 135, top: Historic New Orleans Collection, 1984.34 PC 30-13-A.

Page 135, bottom: John Givens/Small World Productions, Inc.

Page 141: David Wright/Nashville Convention & Visitors Bureau.

The Mormon Trail

Page 149, top: Corbis-Bettmann. Painting by A. Lamb.

Page 149, bottom: Corbis-Bettmann.

Page 154, middle: Painting by William Henry Jackson/Scotts Bluff National Monument.

Page 154, bottom: California Historical Society, San Francisco FN-30595.

Page 159, top: Corbis-Bettmann.

Page 159, bottom: Painting by William Henry Jackson/Scotts Bluff National Monument.

Page 165, top: Corbis-Bettmann. Color engraving by Savage & Ottinger.

Page 165, middle and bottom: Corbis-Bettmann.

The California Trail

Page 173: Corbis-Bettmann.

Page 179, top: Corbis-Bettmann. Lantern slide.

Page 179, bottom: Corbis-Bettmann. Engraving by Darley and Hall, 1869.

Page 183: Corbis-Bettmann.

Page 187, top: Corbis-Bettmann.

Page 187, middle: *Washing Gold in Creek, California*, by Tom Duncan, from his sketchbook, 1851. California Historical Society, San Francisco, acc. no. 63-5-3-2. Gift of Carl I. Wheat. Photo: M. Lee Fatherree.

Page 187, bottom: *The Prairie Schooner*, California Historical Society, San Francisco. FN-30597.

California's Mission Trail

Page 197: California Historical Society, San Francisco. Photo by Norman T. Van Pelt. FN-30602.

Page 200, top: *Father Serra Celebrates Mass at Monterey*, by Leon Trousset, ca. 1870. California Historical Society, San Francisco, acc. no. 68 56 1 2.

Page 200, bottom: California Historical Society, San Francisco. Photo by Elite Photo Service. De Young Collection 39476. FN 21509.

Page 206, top: "100 Young are Taught the Religion, 1862, Mission San Juan, Monterey County, Cal." California Historical Society, San Francisco. Copy photo print by Martin Behrman. FN-04466.

Page 206, middle: Mission San Francisco de Asís, by Oriana Day, Fine Arts Museums of San Francisco, 37571. Gift of Eleanor Martin.

Page 206, bottom: Mission San Francisco Solano de Sonoma, by Oriana Day, Fine Arts Museums of San Francisco, 37573. Gift of Eleanor Martin.

Page 209: California Historical Society, San Francisco FN-30591.

The Klondike Gold Rush Trail

Page 221, top: Museum of History & Industry, Puget Sound Maritime Historical Society, neg. no. 88.33.116.

Page 221, bottom: Seattle-King County News Bureau.

Page 226, top: Special Collections, University of Washington Libraries, Hegg photo, neg. no. 687.

Page 226, middle: Museum of History & Industry, Puget Sound Maritime Historical Society, neg. no. 11811.

Page 226, bottom: Special Collections, University of Washington Libraries, Hegg photo, neg. no. 1174.

Page 233, top: Special Collections, University of Washington Libraries, Hegg photo, neg. no. 97.

Page 233, bottom left: Special Collections, University of Washington Libraries, Hegg photo, neg. no. 247.

Page 233, bottom right: Harry M. Walker/Alaska Stock.

Page 235, top: The Clara Rust Photo Collection, acc. no. 67-110-270N. Archives, Alaska and Polar Regions Department, University of Alaska, Fairbanks.

Page 235, bottom: Special Collections, University of Washington Libraries, Hegg photo, neg. no. 3059.

Index

Retrace these fascinating trails with Tom Bodett and the America's Historic Trails crew.

You can visit the historic sites and enjoy the contemporary scenes again and again by ordering the *America's Historic Trails* videos. These hour-long videos each contain two full shows from the popular series.

 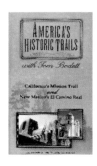 

1. THE OLD POST ROAD, BOSTON TO NEW YORK

2. THE RIVER ROAD AND THE NATCHEZ TRACE

3. THE GREAT WAGON ROAD AND THE WILDERNESS ROAD

4. THE MORMON TRAIL AND THE CALIFORNIA TRAIL

5. EL CAMINO REAL TO SANTA FE, AND CALIFORNIA'S MISSION TRAIL

6. THE YUKON GOLD RUSH TRAIL

Each only $24.95 plus shipping. Or order all six for just $124.95 plus shipping—a full 20% savings.

Call 1-800-319-9909